Automotive
BODYWORK AND
RUST REPAIR

Matt Joseph

WABASH CARNEGIE P LIB

1230 9100 227 394 9

629.2602 Jos
Automotive bodywork and rust
repair
Joseph, Matt, 1944-

WITHDRAWN

S-A DESIGN

CarTech®

WABASH CARNEGIE PUBLIC LIBRARY
WABASH, INDIANA

CarTech®

CarTech®, Inc.
39966 Grand Avenue
North Branch, MN 55056
Phone: 651-277-1200 or 800-551-4754
Fax: 651-277-1203
www.cartechbooks.com

© 2009 by Matt Joseph

All rights reserved. No part of this publication may be reproduced or utilized in any form or by any means, electronic or mechanical, including photocopying, recording, or by any information storage and retrieval system, without prior permission from the Publisher. All text, photographs, and artwork are the property of the Author unless otherwise noted or credited.

The information in this work is true and complete to the best of our knowledge. However, all information is presented without any guarantee on the part of the Author or Publisher, who also disclaim any liability incurred in connection with the use of the information and any implied warranties of merchantability or fitness for a particular purpose. Readers are responsible for taking suitable and appropriate safety measures when performing any of the operations or activities described in this work.

All trademarks, trade names, model names and numbers, and other product designations referred to herein are the property of their respective owners and are used solely for identification purposes. This work is a publication of CarTech, Inc., and has not been licensed, approved, sponsored, or endorsed by any other person or entity. The Publisher is not associated with any product, service, or vendor mentioned in this book, and does not endorse the products or services of any vendor mentioned in this book.

Edit by Bob Wilson and Scott Parkhurst
Layout by Chris Fayers

ISBN 978-1-932494-97-6
Item No. SA166

Library of Congress Cataloging-in-Publication Data

Joseph, Matt
  Automotive bodywork and rust repair / by Matt Joseph.
    p. cm.
  ISBN 978-1-932494-97-6
  1. Automobiles—Bodies—Maintenance and repair. 2. Automobiles—Conservation and restoration. I. Title.

  TL255.J67 2009
  629.2'60288—dc22

                                2009016169

Written, edited, and designed in the U.S.A.
Printed in China
10 9 8 7 6

Dedication

To the legions of craftsmen who, over the centuries, managed to forget about the rigidity of sheet steel and treated it as if it were plastic in order to form it into a myriad of useful and beautiful shapes and structures.

Front Cover:
Being adept at bodywork not only helps in restoration, but modification as well. Here, a transmission tunnel is being altered to accommodate an aftermarket transmission. (Robert Genet photo)

Title Page:
One of the more common areas of rust is the lower corner of doors. Material is being removed to facilitate a repair.

Back Cover Photos

Top Left:
The sound that you hear when you hit metal on an anvil brims with useful information. A good anvil rings on impact. An inferior anvil thuds.

Top Right:
Plastic filler is filed in much the same way as lead filler. The same body files used for lead can be used with plastic fillers.

Middle Left:
High-speed abrasive disks are great for cutting into contoured panels, but are pretty much limited to cutting straight lines.

Middle Right:
It is best to cut a temporary line into either the old or the new panel, for a trial fitting.

Bottom Left:
Hammering off-dolly is a precision operation that is used to shape metal without stretching it.

Bottom Right:
Fabricating a splash shield involves rolling the first of three lengthwise beads into it with a hand-operated bead roller.

PGUK
63 Hatton Garden
London EC1N 8LE, England
Phone: 020 7061 1980 • Fax: 020 7242 3725
www.pguk.co.uk

Renniks Publications Ltd.
3/37-39 Green Street
Banksmeadow, NSW 2109, Australia
Phone: 2 9695 7055 • Fax: 2 9695 7355
www.renniks.com

CONTENTS

ACKNOWLEDGMENTS

As the author, one of the greatest rewards for writing this book has been all I have learned while doing it. Part of this is because an author has to clarify his or her own thinking about the specific subjects of the work. When you are explaining something, there is no room for cobwebs and ambiguities in your own mind.

A larger benefit is that doing research for and writing this book has given me the wonderful opportunity to meet some incredible people—people who are among the best practitioners of metal crafts in the world. You will meet many of them as you read these pages.

Herb Statz, from Waunakee, Wisconsin, has worked tirelessly with me. He modeled the skills, techniques, and processes shown in many of the photographs in this book. You can't miss him. He and his skilled hands are in more than half of the photos. Beyond providing hands, Herb provided the enormous benefit of his knowledge and wisdom, gained from his varied careers as a mechanic, body shop metal man, draftsman, aviator, airplane builder, and farmer. Herb brings to any work that he does the knowledge from his varied background, a great sense of humor, and a practical and genuine wisdom. I simply could not have written this book without his help.

Muscle Car Restorations, Inc., in Chippewa Falls, Wisconsin, generously opened its metal shop to me. I spent several days there studying and photographing many projects in progress. It was a great and enlightening experience. I learned much about how quality work can be done on a production-like basis. Watching the skilled metal men at MCR, Inc., complete complex and difficult projects—certainly and quickly—inspired me with some of the confidence needed to do my own sheetmetal work in a more planned and efficient manner. I doubt if any other shop surpasses MCR's ability to produce consistently great restoration results, on time and on budget, with the muscle cars on which they work.

L'Cars, in Cameron, Wisconsin, and its genial proprietor, Bob Lorkowski, embody the essence of a craft guild approach to automotive restoration. This is a full service restoration shop that can perform almost every restoration task, from engine machine work to autobody metal work, upholstery, and refinishing. Their teams do all of this work so well, and on such an incredible variety of automobiles, that I once designated L'Cars as "the best restoration facility in the world." Everything I saw there, in two trips to talk to and photograph their metal men, has only strengthened that opinion, even though I have seen several other top-ranked restoration shops since I first wrote those words.

The atmosphere in the L'Cars metal shop is so relaxed and amiable that you sometimes have to pinch yourself to remember how incredibly challenging and difficult some of the work being done there is, and how superb the results of that work are. L'Cars has some of the best equipment that I have ever seen. More important, it has workers like Blaine, Wayne, and Matt, who know how to use that equipment to full advantage. These men also know how to use the simple, traditional tools of body work—hammers, dollies, and the like—as well as I have ever seen it done. And they do it with good humor, learning and sharing knowledge with each other as they go along. The results are spectacular, embodying the highest quality that I have ever seen in this work. These men make the most difficult tasks almost seem like routine chores, and bring what seems impossible to within reach.

Sam Fiorani of the Eastwood Company helped me out with some great photographs from Eastwood's files. Several of them appear in this book, to the book's great advantage.

To the individuals and organizations noted above, I offer my sincere and grateful thanks for kindly contributing their access, time, and knowledge to this book. And special thanks for generously teaching me a great deal that I did not know about sheetmetal work, just when I was beginning to have the dangerous thought that I already knew everything.

INTRODUCTION

It's fun to daydream about owning some of the great collectible cars out there, and restoring their body metal. Or how about constructing warm and hot rods from the remains of those cars, or from scratch? With good metal working skills, some experience, and some equipment, those daydreams can become realities that will swell your chest with pride in what you have created.

With enough money, anyone can buy a great restored or modified car, or commission the restoration or modification of one. With enough skill, some people can do the work that creates these treasures, rather than pay someone.

The purpose of this book is to present known and sound practices for working with automotive sheet steel—practices and skills that give consistently good results. This is a huge topic, one that has consumed the lifeworks of many craftsmen. That is because these craftsmen's skills, and the results that they have achieved, have been, and are, practiced on lifelong learning curves. This book is intended to communicate many of the basic approaches and skills in the automotive steel metal craft. Work with aluminum panels is not covered because, while it is similar in many ways to steel panel work, it is still a specialty topic that is outside of the mainstream of automotive panel work.

This book is aimed at beginners in this field, and at those who have some sheetmetal skills but want to improve them. It is simply a source of the information that enables you to begin in this work, or to advance your skills in it for improved results.

This book covers basic processes and skills. It is not an advanced text on this topic. Don't expect to hammer perfect tulip petals out of 22-gauge metal stock when you finish it. The basic skills and procedures covered here are the necessary background for advancing in this work. Equipped with them, you should be able to perform most of the tasks that you need to do autobody panel work, from removing simple dents to fabricating sections of panels and even whole panels.

For almost any autobody project or task, there are many different ways to achieve desired results. Some are better, and/or more efficient, than others. Some are substandard. My purpose in writing this book is to describe many of the main and proven approaches to doing very good automotive sheetmetal work. If you master these, you are well placed on that learning curve that I mentioned. You may advance on your own or with the help of written works by Ron Fournier, Fay Butler, and some of the other legendary practitioners in automotive metal work.

When I was much younger, I met a gentleman who had been a panel beater in the early twentieth century. He was a robust man for his advanced age, and spoke in a booming voice. He had worked in an itinerant crew of six metal men who had traveled an annual circuit, from one luxury-car-builder's factory to the next. Their job was to hand hammer sheet steel, or aluminum stock, into the rear body surround sections for the large luxury cars of that period.

In those days, the factories involved in the limited production of expensive cars did not have big enough dies and presses to stamp out the huge rear body sections for their cars. They had to be formed by hand.

The elderly panel beater whom I met in the mid 1950s described the work that he and his crew had performed. They had wooden "bucks" on which they hammer-formed the metal, and could produce one surround section in less than a day.

He told me that when a section was finished, they would stop hammering, look at each other, and nod assent to indicate that each craftsman was satisfied with the work. Then they would move the completed section off the last wooden buck, and place a new piece of flat stock onto the first buck.

At that point in his description of this work, he asked me, "Do you know why we shook our heads to agree that a panel was finished?"

I answered, "Yes, because you were all pretty deaf."

"Right," he said, "But how did you know that? Most people never get it."

"Well," I replied, "You are less than 3 feet away from me and you are yelling at me. I imagine that six men hammering on a sheet of metal would make you deaf in short order."

Fortunately, vehicle factories now have easier and more humane ways to form large panels. However, the proposition for repairing damage and custom-forming new panels, and panel parts, is still much like the craft exercised by that panel beater, so many years ago. There are some exotic tools and devices that can do it faster but they are expensive, and it takes a practiced skill to use them properly. The basics of the sheetmetal craft have remained pretty constant over the years. Learn them, and you should be able to accomplish great things in this work.

As you read this book you may note that some of the material is repeated in different contexts. That is because many procedures are used in different contexts, and it is easier to learn them and to realize their full potentials if you see them in those different settings. If, as you read this book, you have the vague feeling that you have read something in it previously, you are probably right. It is organized that way for a reason.

This book may differ from other books that cover, or include, this topic in two major ways. First, I do not try to communicate to you everything that I know, but mostly what you need to know to do this work. Second, I always try to do more than just explain how to perform a particular task or procedure. I try to state the reasons for doing it that way. When you understand those reasons, you will have the knowledge base that is necessary for you to continue to improve and innovate, on your own, in this field. After you gain good grounding in metal working basics, you may surprise yourself with what you can accomplish.

While various machines can speed autobody metal repair and forming operations, the good old hammer and dolly are still the basis for much of this work. Learn to use them properly, and you will have two great friends for life.

WHAT YOU SHOULD KNOW
BEFORE YOU START

Pounding and forcing thin metal sections into shapes that humans want and need has a long history. While there is disagreement about exactly when and where people began to work with metals, it was certainly in prehistoric times and began with soft metals like gold and copper.

The discovery of how to control fire made extracting metals from mined ores more efficient than had been finding nuggets of almost pure metal. It also led to the ability to create alloys of various metals, by melting them. In many civilizations Copper Age developments were succeeded by Bronze Age advances, bronze being an alloy of copper and tin. Longer-surviving civilizations usually progressed from copper and bronze to iron and steel.

The qualities of metal, in particular its plasticity and strength, made it ideal for uses as varied as making ornaments, cookware, and weapons. In these and other uses, it had many great advantages over other materials like wood, bone, and ceramics. Various processes were applied to early metals: annealing, tempering, bending, stamping, rolling, casting, forging, cutting, soldering,

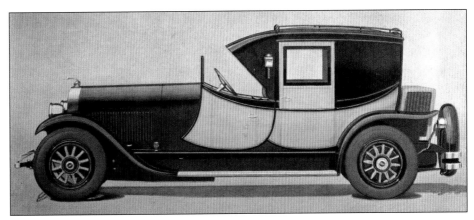

Styling can be unique and/or spectacular. This artist's conception of the 1926 Judkins Coaching Brougham body on a Lincoln chassis illustrates those potentials. While this body's sheetmetal is relatively simple, it was all hand hammered from flat stock. Note: The hood and fenders were supplied by Lincoln.

welding, and many others. These were the precursors of many modern metal working processes still in use today.

The earliest metal forming techniques involved beating pure metals and alloys into small, flat formats. Then those sheet stocks were formed into useful or ornamental items like knives and pendants. We know that such ancient civilizations as the Hittites, Mesopotamians, and Babylonians were well along in using variants of some of those processes, thousands of years BCE.

Think about that the next time that you are at a car show, and admire some difficult-to-form body feature of a hot rod or custom car. The ability to produce it began thousands of years ago, with anonymous, ancient metal workers, beating copper into crude and unlovely bracelets or kitchen pots. The latest die stamping and rolling processes that produce modern automobiles are basically developments on those ancient metal arts. It's kind of humbling, isn't it?

These late-nineteenth-century tools—a tinner's hammer and blacksmith's mushroom anvil—are not very different from some tools that we still use today. While new power tools have come into use since then, we continue to use some of the old tools in sheetmetal repair and fabrication.

The rear quarter of this 2009 Mercedes-Benz SLK350 exhibits almost every type of crown that there is: high, medium, low, and reverse. Only no-crown is missing. Each type of crown in this panel works into another type. It is truly a showcase of the metal-stamping art.

The iconic 2005 Scion xB exhibits very little crown in any of its panels, all are very low-crown. It figures that this anti-car would employ anti-crown stampings.

In the modern sheetmetal fabrication and repair field, we use highly evolved versions of much of the knowledge, and many of the tools and techniques, employed by those ancient metal formers. But we have advanced greatly from where they left off. Every tool, device, and process that we use today is better than what they had. Our raw material, the sheetmetal itself, is pure and consistent beyond anything that they could imagine. Our knowledge is greater, and our results are often more daring and always more uniform and durable than their best efforts. For all that, we still beat metal with hammers, roll it through wheels, and weld it with heat. Some general aspects and principles of metal work have changed little over time.

Panel Types, Configurations and Reinforcements

Ancient metal workers may not have had a word for "crown," but they certainly understood its significance. You need to understand this basic concept to work with sheetmetal. All formed metal shapes have some characteristic of crown—no or low crown, medium crown, high crown, reverse crown, or combination crown.

Flat metal has no crown. It may be bent, or formed into a simple arc, but it has no crown. Metal acquires crown when it is shaped in ways that cause it to fall away from a point, any point, in every direction. That is the essence of crown. The significance of crown is that it stiffens panels, and areas of panels, where it exists. This is because the stamping or rolling processes that are used to create crown in panels tend to harden them, and because an arched, three-dimensional structure is inherently stronger than a flat one. The more crown a panel has, the tougher it is likely to be in resisting the impact of a collision, or the hammer blows that a metal worker strikes to repair it. High-crown panels have more crown than low-crown panels. You can often move the metal in no-crown and low-crown areas of panels with your fingertips. This is not possible in highly crowned areas of panels.

Reverse crown is simply crown that faces away from the outside of a car. "Concave crown" would also describe this configuration. Combination-crown panels have different kinds of crown that work into each other, such as low into high crowns, or high or low crowns that work into reverse-crown areas.

All of this is important because crown imparts strength to panels, and therefore is more resistant to force applied to repair damaged areas where it exists. It is also important because crown is forgiving, up to a point, when you repair areas that have it. This is because stretched metal can be hidden in crowned areas. Since these areas are, by their nature, bulged shapes, a small additional bulge often fits undiscernibly into them. Very-low-crown and no-crown metal cannot hide stretches. They show as unsightly bulges and/or ripple distortions.

I am not exactly advocating autobody dishonesty here. However, this work involves reaching goals that are mostly judged on their

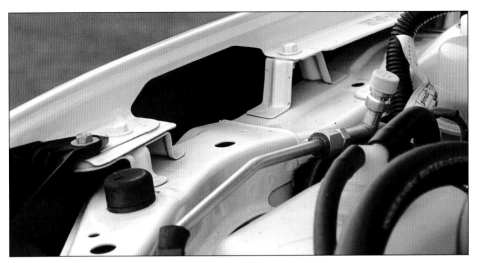

How panels are supported makes a tremendous difference in how you approach their repair. This 2008 Mitsubishi Galant's upper fender attachments are very unusual. Short strut pieces attach the fender tops to the car's inner fenders. Anyone who repairs these fenders has to take this into account.

content than iron, the even dispersal of what carbon it does have makes it strong and somewhat plastic, or deformable, unlike various irons. Mild sheet steel, the stuff of autobodies, is roughly .25-percent carbon. Above that concentration of carbon, steels begin to fit into the medium steel classification. Between .6-percent and 1-percent carbon, steels are considered hard or high-carbon. Ultra hard steels, like tool steels, may contain between 1-percent and 2-percent carbon.

The softness of panel steel allows it to undergo the highly organized brutality of stamping it into complex three-dimensional shapes like doors, hoods, roofs, and fenders. Using heat and enormous pressure, automotive body steel is stamped into final sheet format. While it is primarily an alloy of iron and carbon, several other elements—which, in some cases, have names that are hard to remember and

visual merits. At times, and in some situations, a good practitioner uses characteristics of panel configuration to slightly trick the eye. (There will be more on this topic, later.)

Along with crown, how a panel is supported and attached to a vehicle is critical in understanding how it performs under impact, and how best to remove impact damage from it. Many panels have strengthening structures welded or bolted under them. Panels that are attached to vehicles by welding them to substructure perform differently from those that are bolted to substructure. Unless you deal with them, bent or damaged substructure reinforcements and fastening points that impart strength to panels, cause panels to resist restoration to their original formats. Always consider this factor when you plan panel repair or restoration work.

truly amazing material. It is a complex alloy of iron, carbon, and other elements. It has been heat treated in its manufacture to disperse the carbon evenly into the steel's granular structure. While steel has less carbon

Autobody Steel

The steel sheet stock that is formed into automobile panels is a

Throughout most of automotive history, all panels were stamped out in presses, like the ones shown here in a General Motors stamping room in the mid 1970s. More recently, some very large stampings are rolled into panels by dies that move in two dimensions. **(Photo supplied by General Motors Corp.)**

difficult to pronounce—are routinely added to it to give it the special characteristics that are needed to form it into automotive panels.

New car panels are presently in the range of 22-gauge to 23-gauge; that is, .0299 and .0269 inch. Note that as the gauge number increases, the thickness of steel sheet stock gets thinner. The way that this works involves an arcane formula that takes into account the weight of a cubic foot of the material involved. To make things thoroughly confusing, basing gauge on weight means that the same gauge number applied to different metals gives different thicknesses. For example, while 22-gauge sheet steel is .0299 inch thick, 22-gauge galvanized steel is .031 inch thick, 22-gauge aluminum sheet stock is .025 inch thick, and 22-gauge stainless steel is .031 inch thick.

The important things to remember are that as gauge numbers increase, thickness decreases, and that the same gauge numbers for different metals may translate into slightly different thicknesses.

Finally, there is a misconception that gauge designations involve the number of sheets of a particular gauge that can be fit into 1 inch. This, simply, is not true. Common gauge numbers for automotive outer-body steels are:

- 18-gauge .0478 inch
- 19-gauge .0418 inch
- 20-gauge .0359 inch
- 21-gauge .0329 inch
- 22-gauge .0299 inch
- 23-gauge .0269 inch
- 24-gauge .0239 inch

Thickness is important because, in part, it determines how difficult it will be to repair damaged body pan-

Thin panels are hard, presenting several problems in repair. It is easy to cut through, when welding them. Their hardness and thinness make them difficult to file because files skitter over them, rather than cut in. Worse, very little metal can be removed before they become dangerously thin.

els. In most cases, the thinner that body metal is the more problems it tends to present in repair. That is because the thinner body metal is, the more difficult it is to form and to weld. The alloys used in thinner panel sections tend to be harder than the older, thicker panels, because they contain more carbon. That makes them more difficult to deform with body tools, without taking them beyond their yield points (fracturing them). Their hardness also makes them very difficult to surface file for the purpose of leveling them. Welding thinner metal is always more challenging, due to the tendency of thinner sections to melt and "drop out" at welding temperatures. That outcome also can be very hard on a metal worker's shoes.

Plasticity and Elasticity

When I speak of the hardness of metal, I am generally describing several significant characteristics, two of which are particularly important to anyone working in panel fabrication

and repair: plasticity and elasticity. Plasticity is the ability of metal to deform without fracturing. The point of fracture is called the "yield" point. Automotive panels are stamped at the factory from flat stock into complex, three-dimensional shapes. The fact that this can be done is proof of their plasticity. When a body repair technician works on them with hammers, dollies, and other tools, they are again deformed, courtesy of their plasticity.

Plasticity under tension is called ductility, and produces stretching when it occurs. Think of the bumper over-rider on a truck smashing into the door of your vehicle. It deforms it—plasticity—and it probably will put the metal under tension and stretch it—ductility. When plasticity occurs under compression, as opposed to tension, it is called malleability, and produces the opposite of stretching by compacting or "upsetting." In upsetting, metal is piled into itself.

Let's go back to that unfortunate damage to your vehicle's door that occurred when a truck hit it. After the accident, a technician removed the inner panel from the door. Then, the technician began to fix the damage by hammering the ridge near the center of the dent down and out against a dolly, centered under it on the outside of the door. If the technician had read this book, he or she would probably have had a better first move. The accident probably stretched the metal in the door's skin because it was deformed while being held rigidly at both ends by the door's substructure. The attempt to hammer it out put the area near the hammering under compression because the dolly was supporting the undeformed metal on either side of

Upsetting can be useful. Here, it is used to shrink a stretched area. The metal is heated until it bulges, and then hammered down. The hot metal piles into itself because it is bounded by unyielding cold metal. The resulting upset makes the heated area thicker and laterally smaller.

the ridge. The result of hammering down on the obvious ridge, with a dolly under it, was to compress the metal there latterly, or to upset it.

This is a critically important distinction in autobody work. When you stretch metal you are effectively exchanging some of its thickness for increased lateral dimension. When you upset metal, you are exchanging some of its lateral dimension for increased thickness. At various points in working with body metal, you need to create upsets, and even stretches, on purpose. At other times, you will need to avoid these dimensional transformations, or have to correct them. It is critical that you understand exactly what stretches and upsets are, and why and how they occur. Later, I will discuss how to purposely create them, and what situations call for creating them.

Elasticity in metal is its ability to flex to a limit—its elastic limit—and still return to its original shape, on its own. Some call this characteristic memory, or spring back. You might have encountered this when you slammed the hatch on a minivan or

SUV, and had the queasy sensation of feeling your hand deform the hatch metal where you were pushing against it. But then, as you released the panel, you felt the metal under your hand return to its rightful shape. You can thank elasticity for that good outcome. If the metal didn't spring back, it was because you exceeded its elastic limit.

Elasticity is critical because damaged panels usually contain a small minority of surface area that has been pushed, or deformed, beyond its elastic limit. Most of what may look like damaged metal—because it is out of position—has not been deformed beyond this limit, and will return to its pre-accident shape when you release the small areas of badly deformed metal that are holding it out of place in the damage. I don't want to sound excessively rosy about these matters but, to the untrained eye, panel damage almost always looks worse than it is.

Work Hardening: The Metal Remembers

The great elephant hiding discreetly in this sheetmetal living room is called work hardening. This is the tendency of metals, like mild sheet steel, to become progressively harder as they are deformed beyond their elastic limits.

Doubtless you have already performed experiments involving this factor, although you may not realize it. If you, like most people, ever tried to straighten out a paper clip with your fingers, you encountered work hardening. What you discovered was that it is all but impossible to get the three bends out of a paper clip with your bare hands. What happened when you tried to do this—probably

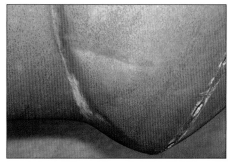

Good news! This dent looks worse than it is. Most of the displaced metal is being held out of place by the ridge in its middle. Once that ridge is unlocked, most of the damaged area will spring back into its proper place, on its own.

under the cover of a pile of books or a knapsack, so that your teacher would not see you performing this metallurgical experiment—was that before any of the three bends in the paper clip could be straightened, the metal stopped moving in the bends and bent on either side of them, leaving shapes like saddles between two opposite-facing humps, in kind of a camelback configuration. The saddles were what was left of the original bends. The humps were new bends, in the opposite direction, that occurred when the metal in the original bends stiffened as you bent it, and approached its elastic limit. Then, the opposite-facing humps were made as you continued to apply pressure.

That poor paper clip began its life as a straight piece of wire. Forming it into a paper clip work hardened the metal in its bends. When you tried to straighten it, you made some progress, but work hardening made complete straightening impossible, so the metal bent on either side of the work-hardened area. This is not trivial. Work hardening is terrifically important in body work. You must learn to identify it, predict it,

An Example of Work Hardening

Here is a simple but dramatic example of the work-hardening effect.

Herb clasps a strip of 22-gauge mild steel in a pair of sheetmetal pliers and bends its middle to as close to a right angle as the jaws of the pliers allow. Then, he closes the bend as far as he can in the pliers' jaws.

After removing the strip from the pliers, Herb attempts to straighten the bend with his fingers. But the bend has work hardened and the metal wants to bend everywhere else, in the non-work-hardened metal, and not in the first bend that he made. Frustrated, Herb tries to straighten the bend by holding the metal in the pliers and forcing it, but that doesn't work. Then, he tries to straighten it with his hands against a wood table top, but the first work-hardened bend stubbornly refuses to budge.

Finally, Herb is able to hammer the original bend and the side bends flat on an anvil. However, evidence of all three bends remains visible on the flattened piece.

This sequence is a testimonial to the persistence of work-hardened metal.

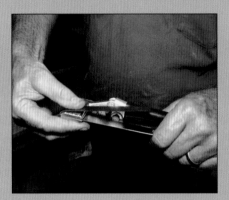
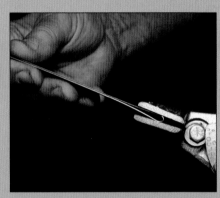
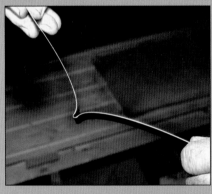

Annealing Effects

One way to mitigate work-hardening effects is to anneal metal. In this process, metal is heated to its critical temperature, roughly 1,600 degrees F in the case of mild sheet steel, and allowed to cool slowly in air. The effect is to relieve the metal's stiffness and reverse the work-hardening effect.

In this demonstration, a strip of sheetmetal is bent as close to a right angle as it is possible to do with bare hands. Then, unlike the demonstration of work hardening, it is heated with an oxy-acetylene torch to roughly 1,600 degrees F and allowed to cool.

Now, it is easy to straighten the bend with bare hands. The two strips were bent almost identically. Both were straightened by hand, one with annealing and the other without it. It's pretty easy to tell which is which.

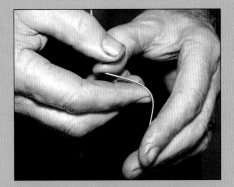

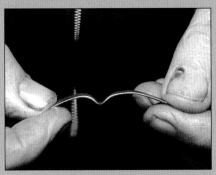

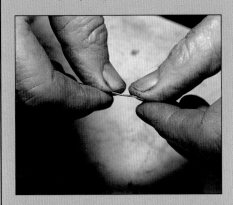
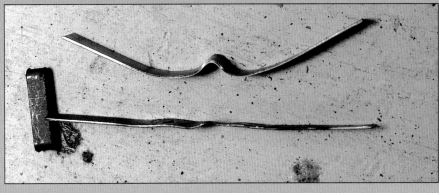

and deal with it, because it tends to be a factor in almost all of your collision damage and fabrication efforts.

For the record, work hardening occurs because steel has a granular structure. Bending it rearranges and distorts its grains. Beyond a certain point, this becomes difficult, and somewhere beyond that, the steel will fracture; that is, it will reach and exceed its plastic limit. Maybe

in your frustration, when you couldn't straighten that paper clip, you bent it back and forth until it broke. Do you remember that it felt warm at the place where you were bending it, before it broke? That heat was generated by the friction of the grains in its structure deforming and riding against each other as you bent the paper clip back and forth.

Heat also has the ability to rearrange those grains for important purposes. Beyond certain temperatures—different ones for different metals and alloys of metals—the grain structures of metals rearrange themselves and eliminate work-hardening effects. This process is called annealing, and only works if sheetmetal air cools slowly, after being heated to its critical temperature. In the case of autobody steel, that temperature is roughly 1,600 degrees F, which appears as a color between bright red (1,550 degrees F) and salmon (1,650 degrees F). How steel cools, after it has been heated, determines many of the characteristics of the hardness that it exhibits. For example, quenching it (cooling it rapidly with air, water, or oil) after it has been heated to its critical temperature, tends to rearrange its grains in ways that harden it.

There is more discussion of the effects of heat on sheet steel in later chapters, with particular regard to using annealing and quenching to solve problems caused by work hardening from moving cold metal, and hardening softened areas near welds.

At the Factory and Afterward

Autobody panels begin their lives in near-ideal conditions. Clean, uniform sheet stock was stamped or rolled into shape. Huge machines accomplished this work by exerting many tons of pressure on flat sheet stock that was inserted between the drawing and rolling dies of stamping devices. In such operations, flat metal is deformed by enormous force that stretches and shapes it. The metal is clamped at its edges by "binder rings," and then acted on by dies that force it into desired shapes. Later, it is trimmed and pierced at attachment points.

For the metal worker, the important thing about these processes is that the stretching and forming of sheetmetal between dies work hardens it. That is one of the reasons for stamping it; to make it stronger. The other reason, of course, is styling. If cars were fabricated from unstamped sheetmetal, their panels would liter-

After a panel is stamped, it may still need detail work. Employees in this 1975 GM plant are shown performing some of that work. **(Photo supplied by General Motors Corp.)**

ally flutter in the wind, and from road vibrations. Stamping imparts strength, and helps to eliminate most flutter. Besides, no one would want to drive a car that looked like a steel box.

When you repair damaged sheetmetal, you must deal with the work hardening that occurred in the original stamping or rolling process that turned flat stock into finished panels, and with the additional deformations that occurred when it was damaged. There is also the factor of road vibration, which, over long periods, hardens panels as they travel down the road. It is important to keep all of this in mind when you find a panel resisting your best efforts to change its shape and restore it to its original configuration.

One of the worst forms of damage that you will ever encounter is bad repair work. A range of people, from the truly clueless to the dedicat-

This twice-mangled fender suffered two kinds of damage: first a collision, then someone made it worse by trying to repair it. After hammering on it with no good result, he or she decided to cut out some of the damage, then gave up.

edly inept, may have tried to repair the damage before you. Their misguided efforts, often with very large hammers and other destructive devices, may have made things worse or much worse than they were. Collisions deform and work harden metal.

They also may stretch or upset it. Bad body work, the kind that roughs out damage and then gobs filler over crude work, tends to make these problems more severe. These situations will tax the full range of your abilities, talents, and patience.

Impact is not sheetmetal's only enemy as it ages. The other major problems gather under the brown banner of corrosion, a.k.a. rust. Rust is birthed by a chemical reaction between water and metal. Road salt, an electrolyte in dirty water, enhances the speed of this reaction. Rust occurs when moisture gets through or around paint and other anti-corrosion surface treatments. Since water is very adept at infiltrating small spaces (through capillary action) and at penetrating coatings, it is a cinch to attack vulnerable areas like door seams and panel attachment points. A great deal of body work on cars involves repairing the ravages of rust. Sometimes, small areas of perforation damage can be welded shut. More often, panels require the excision of diseased areas, and replacement with sound metal.

Necessary Tools and Equipment

Somewhere between having the basic tools for autobody work, and having the latest, most exotic, and most advanced metal-forming devices ever made, there is a happy medium of being reasonably well equipped for most of what you encounter. An el cheapo starter body tool kit, with three unbalanced body hammers and a crudely cast dolly, probably won't take you very far in this work. On the other hand, roaring out and acquiring the likes of a good English wheel, a Pull-

This one is as bad as it looks. Even though the destroyed panel is flat and relatively easy to form, economics dictate installing a replacement fender panel, assuming that sound metal can be found for its attachment.

Massive, power forming machines, like this Pullmax, come in many brands and configurations. They can be fitted with a variety of specialized tooling or with general tooling like these Steck power-shrinking heads. They can form metal quickly, but really are beyond the needs of most shops.

max power forming machine, and a high-quality TIG welder is almost certainly way beyond the needs of novice- or intermediate-level autobody metal work.

The best approach is to acquire tools and equipment as you find the

One of these air disc sander/grinders is an expensive professional model. The other is a low-end, almost-generic knockoff that is very inexpensive. They are almost identical in performance, and probably in durability. The inexpensive one can be replaced more than three times for what the expensive one costs.

need for them, not just because they are there. When that need arises, it is a good idea, in most cases, to stick to top-quality tools—ones that come from reputable vendors and that will last for the rest of your working life. There are exceptions to this. Some air tools, like the die grinders and air disc sanders that are so useful in autobody work, largely have become disposable tools. Buying good ones with name brands probably is a waste of money. Most people I know buy cheap ones and replace them as needed. Since the prestige versions of these tools cost between three and five times more than the throw-aways, and the repair (tune-up) kits for them cost as much as the generic versions of these tools, this makes great sense.

However, items like cheap body hammers or tin shears tend to create bad results and should be avoided. My general rule is: If something makes direct contact with metal, like a file, hammer, or dolly, it should be

Tools tend to multiply, as if by magic. Most of my hammers, dollies, picks, pries, files, and other bodywork hand tools, are mounted on this wall. My wife thinks it's excessive and, truth be told, I could get by with about 20 percent of them.

Many small and relatively inexpensive tools, like these body files, sheet-metal pliers, and 4½-inch electric grinder, are endlessly handy for autobody metal work.

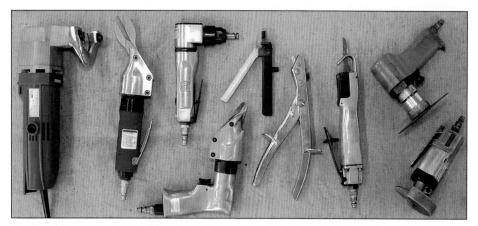

Each of these metal-cutting tools is very useful. From left to right: electric power shear, air power shear, air nibbler, air power shear, hand nibbler, hand shear, air hack saw, and two air disc grinders in different disc sizes and configurations.

top quality. Otherwise, evaluate the economics of replacement strategies for tools that don't contact the metal.

To get started in autobody work, you need some basic hand tools for shaping metal. I recommend an assortment of hammers and a few dollies. The hammers should have faces of various crowns, sizes, and shapes. A set of soft hammers, say plastic and/or rawhide mallets, is a great addition. A shot bag is a good item to have to back up hammering various shapes, and a good anvil is essential.

Small items, like sheetmetal pliers and an assortment of hand shears, are essential when you start this work. A few good body files of differing tooth count and some rigid and flexible holders for them are necessary for many jobs.

A good electric disc sander is a must for doing this work; 7 or 9 inches will do. A small electric or air hand grinder, 4 or 4½ inches, will be endlessly useful. Some way of cutting metal with rotary abrasive wheels is very desirable. A 3-inch air muffler cutter can be bought for less than $10, and fitted with more-useful 4-inch cutting wheels. Air nibblers, shears, and small reciprocating saws have become very inexpensive in recent years, and are extremely useful in this work.

A good MIG welder and an oxy-acetylene torch are highly desirable for performing many bodywork tasks. Likewise, a good plasma arc cutter is a great asset. You might want to put these items on your wish list, if you do not already own them.

As you do more fabrication work, you will want a metal shear, a slip

As you advance in this work, you find that you need a good oxy-acetylene torch setup. No other source of high heat, like propane or oxy-propane, has the versatility of oxy-acetylene. While you can weld panel metal with oxy-acetylene, there are better ways to do it.

When it comes to welding sheetmetal, a MIG welder is the best all-around bet. The TIG welder does finer work with less distortion, but the equipment is expensive and the skill level needed is higher.

This old, air-percussion fender-smoothing hammer is very useful for rough-forming metal. Modern versions of it start at $50 and escalate to more than $1,000. In any price range, it is well worth having. The modern name for this tool is planishing hammer.

This device combines the features of a slip-roll (top), a finger brake (mid-section), and a shear (bottom). It performs all three functions reasonably well, but not as well as the individual, dedicated tools. Still, for a few hundred bucks, you get great capability.

This kind of heavy-metal-forming equipment, power hammers and large English wheels, is great for professional use. For big restoration shops, prototype shops, and pattern shops that do forming work in high volume, this equipment earns its keep. For most small shops, it's overkill.

roll, and a metal brake. These devices vary in quality from expensive to very expensive. There is even a common unit that embodies all three functions in one tool and, while it is a bit clumsy, it provides an economical approach to doing reasonably good work.

There are hundreds, maybe thousands, more tools and devices that may be helpful in pursuing metal work. The key to your tool and equipment program is to figure out what you may need regularly, versus what you will probably use no more than once a year. Purchasing the latter class of tools can be put off for a long time. Hey—if you only need to use something once a year, you might consider borrowing it.

The main point in acquiring tools is to avoid the extremes of

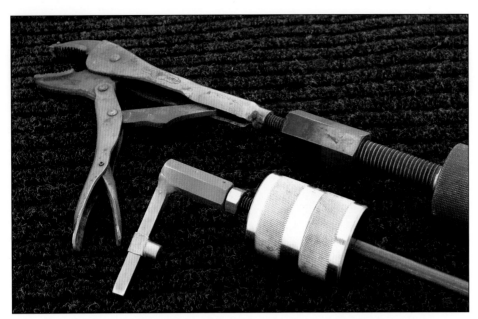

It is often helpful to make special tools for jobs like holding work pieces. These two homemade tools are based on commercial slide hammers. One uses a pair of locking pliers for pulling out things. The other is for bumping metal toward you through access holes.

A good anvil, like the one shown here, provides information when you hammer against it. The sound that you hear when you hit metal on it brims with useful information. A good anvil rings on impact. An inferior anvil thuds.

under equipping and over equipping. If you only have three chipped hammers in your repertoire, and one of them is a carpenter's hammer, your metal work will show it. At the reasonable middle ground, a quality planishing hammer is a very good investment for a wide range of projects. At the extreme, an old Yoder or Pettengell power hammer, hulking in the corner of your workplace, taking up the space of a BMW Mini, gathering dust, and sagging the floor under its enormous weight, will do you little good if, through ignorance or lack of opportunity, you never use it. In fact, it will do you no good at all.

In some cases you will fabricate special tools for special tasks as you go along. This is particularly true where the right tool does not exist, or is too expensive. Always keep your mind open to making tools when you need them, particularly in areas like fixturing. Devices to hold your

work can often be easily fabricated from scrap metal.

Tools and equipment tend to be as good and useful as the person using them. Don't waste time spooning after expensive and exotic stuff. Great equipment hardly ever makes it possible to do a job. Usually and at best, it increases the efficiency of doing it. Keep that in mind when you peruse tool catalogs. Many great sheetmetal fabrications were completed with very simple tools, in very simple settings, with planning, skill, and patience.

Find a happy medium. If you realize that you badly need something to work more efficiently and to get better results, lay your plans to acquire it. But, if you find that you have tools and equipment that you never use—that's why there are garage sales, classified columns, Craig's List, and eBay.

General Considerations

As you pursue autobody metal work, you can often find comfort zones in many of the varied tasks that you perform. That is, you find specific ways of doing things that "just feel right," and that feel better than other ways of performing the same tasks. Never undervalue that sense of something feeling right, it is not absolutely infallible, but it is usually important.

Beyond that, each metal worker brings to this work his or her own personality, character, and experience. Attributes like keen observation, sensitivity, logic, and the ability to plan are all helpful. If you do it right, this work will concentrate these traits, as well as your attained skills.

Traditionally, humans are considered to have five senses. You will

This fender was damaged by collision and by crude attempts to hammer out its damage. Now, there is a range of approaches to repairing it, from dealing with its stretched and deformed metal to removing the worst of it and sectioning in new metal.

do. Practice hammering out dents on junk fenders, before you try it on a repairable or restorable fender. Practice welding on metal that is similar to the metal you want to weld, and get your materials and settings right, before you ruin a good panel. Try out new tools or processes on scrap, before you try them out on something important. You get the idea.

Some of the tools, equipment, and processes that you will use in this work are inherently dangerous. There are sharp edges, caustic chemicals, flying abrasive grits, electric shocks, and many other hazards to consider.

Always consider safety first. No sheetmetal creation is worth the loss or impairment of sight or hearing, or worse. Read manufacturers' warnings about their tools and supplies, and take them to heart. Some hazards, like those posed by sheetmetal brakes and welding torches, are pretty obvious. Other hazards, like those posed by lead filings and airborne zinc fumes, are less obvious but just as serious. If you have any questions about safety, ask them. It will be worth your effort.

I try to note some of the safety hazards in this work as I go along, but I do not know and am not able to mention all of them. As I said, if you have any doubts about the safety of some tool, procedure, or process, ask questions about it. Don't become a victim of something that could have been avoided. You are responsible for your own safety. While I try to inform you about relevant safety hazards as you read this book, the author, editors, publisher, and agents of this book cannot ensure your safety in this work. Only you can do that.

need to use four of them, and to effectively interpret what they tell you, to do good work in this field. Hmm, let's see—sight, sound, touch, smell, and taste. Sight and touch are obvious. They directly inform you regarding the contours, dimensions, and surface characteristics of the metal on which you work. Sound is critical in things like how a hammer sounds hitting metal, or how a panel resounds when you tap on it. Smell is useful when you heat metal. It helps to inform you regarding its temperature. Okay, I don't have any use for the sense of taste in metal work. I'm still working on that one.

Each of the four senses noted above can provide you with useful information, if you interpret what it tells you in the sheetmetal way. For example, your sense of feel means

different things in sheetmetal work than it does in refinishing. To be good at this work, you need to train your senses to comprehend things in ways that are appropriate to and useful in this work.

Most sheetmetal tasks can be performed in many ways. Some give better results, or are more efficient, than others. A few of them are just plain wrong, and fewer are indisputably the only way to do something. As you pursue this work, you will learn which ways give you the best results.

The best way to learn what works best for you is practice. Experience is more valuable when it is attained without ruining valuable metal. Before you strike with any hammer or other device, always try to practice what you are planning to

LIMITS OF MATERIALS, EQUIPMENT AND SKILLS

As with any other work, many factors limit the autobody metal repair and fabrication projects that you attempt—and your results. These include your skills and organizing abilities, and the limits of the materials and processes that you employ. Just because you want to repair something or wish to fabricate some shape, does not mean that it can be done or, more important, that you can do it. These are limits that you have to discover.

A good first step in organizing any project is to visualize how you and your resources best plug into it. Anything can seem difficult and intimidating the first time that you do it. You may worry over all of the various things that can go wrong. Later, after you have successfully done it, you will have the confidence to know that you can overcome whatever problems it presented. As you go further in autobody metal work, your confidence level will increase, and so will the difficulty of the jobs that you are comfortable attempting.

After you master several different aspects of this work, you will realize that many complex jobs that

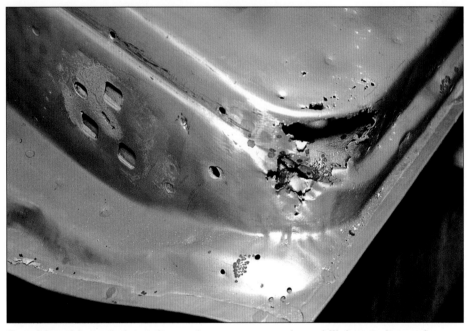

Repairing this rusted-out, lower door corner requires skill, ingenuity, and imagination. True, the surface is not an accurate one, but just preserving its authentic roughness poses problems. There are many ways to approach this job that will work: All require some planning.

at first seemed between difficult and impossible become possible when you break them down into specific tasks that you are pretty sure you can successfully complete.

Before you get to that point of knowing that your knowledge, skills, and judgment are up to a job, you

have to be certain that your materials, processes, and procedures also are up to it.

The limits of inferior and/or inappropriate materials can haunt and destroy your best intentions and most ambitious jobs. Take sheetmetal, for example; it is available in

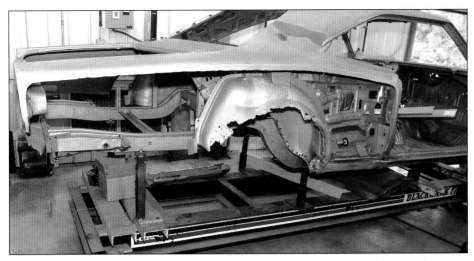

The metal restoration of this Dodge Super Bee takes high confidence, because it is a very challenging job. The plan for this restoration is necessarily complex, and the skills and judgment required to do it are definitely advanced.

When you make new metal for a panel like this E-Type Jaguar cowl section, there are plenty of things to worry about without having to wonder if the metal is high-quality material.

many places and for many prices. If you want to buy a large amount inexpensively, just go someplace where someone is removing an old tin roof. You can buy the rusty, dented old roofing for the proverbial song.

But there are problems with using roofing tin in autobody pro-

jects. It is too thin for most fabrication and repair jobs and its carbon content is higher than is desirable for automotive work, making it harder than hammered owl poop. And that is when it is new. If you try to make a fender patch out of a salvaged bit of this stuff, you can add the problems of rust, denting, nail holes, and work hardening to the list of problems.

"Ah-hah," you might say, "But my local plumbing supply store sells 26-gauge double-galvanized HVAC duct tin in 4 x 8- and 4 x 10-foot sheets, and it's pretty cheap, figured by the square foot." Sorry, but you knew that I was going to rain on that parade. HVAC duct tin tends to be too soft for autobody repair or fabrication work, and 26-gauge is decidedly too thin for it.

There is also sheet steel sold in various thicknesses at hardware stores and lumber yards. It isn't inexpensive, but it comes in different sized sheets, and says "weldable sheetmetal" or something like that on the sticker that states it size, gauge, and universal price code. In fact, this is definitely closer to metal

that you might be able to use for autobody work. At least it comes in reasonable gauges for that use, and may have characteristics that are fairly close to those that are desirable for autobody panel work. The problem is that it is specified for a wide range of hobby and homeowner projects, and probably lacks the very specific and necessary characteristics for first-class automotive work.

The best way to acquire good sheetmetal for autobody metal projects is to look for it in places that specialize in supplying the autobody trades. Body shop supply outfits usually have a line of sheetmetal, in a few different gauges and specifications. At least this metal is intended for the purpose for which you are going to use it. And, consider this: These suppliers rely on repeat business from body shops for their livelihoods. If they supply products that are bad for the purposes for which their clients buy them, they tend to lose customers and

A good stock of sheetmetal, in varied gauges and sizes, is a great asset. This material comes protected by preservative oil to keep it corrosion free. Still, it is best to keep your stock of metal fresh and to store it well so it doesn't corrode.

cease to exist. There are also mail-order companies that supply panel steel to the autobody and panel-fabrication trades. It is usually pretty good metal for those purposes.

Another intriguing source of panel steel for some projects is automotive salvage yards. If you need a particular crown or configuration for part of a fabrication, or for a repair patch, you often can find something close to the shape that you need, incorporated in the decklid, door, or fender of some unrelated salvage panel. If that panel isn't too rusty or damaged for your use, you can buy it and cut out what you need. You never find the perfect item for what you need, but it is often much easier to modify an already stamped section of a panel to exactly what you do need than it is to start from scratch with virgin flat stock. I know many metal workers who keep a supply of salvage panels around, just in case.

In general, the same rules that apply to acquiring good-quality panel steel apply to most other supplies that you will use in this work. Things like welding supplies, filling supplies, and fasteners should be high-grade items that are intended for automotive work. Using the cheapest versions of these things that are sold to the general public does not result in top-quality automotive work. Off-brand soldering supplies, or welding rod and wire, may be perfectly okay or they may be junk. The small amounts of money that you save by buying this stuff are not worth the risk of messing up a project by using it. There are enough inherent problems in this work that are difficult to predict, without taking chances on the materials and supplies that you use.

Even when you buy what are supposed to be top-quality materials

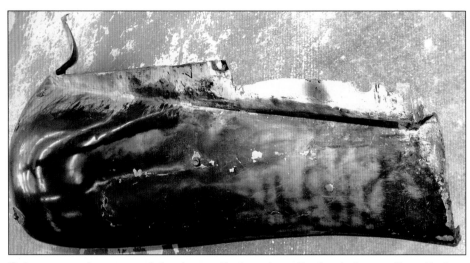

Salvage panels may contain shapes that work as the basis for sections that you need to fabricate. Many metal workers have a stock of donor panels for just that purpose. This fender has many such possibilities.

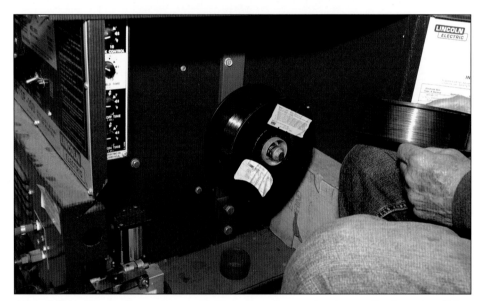

All welding wire looks pretty much the same but varies in quality from terrible to terrific. Different wires work better in specific applications. It is a good idea to try several of them to find out what works best for the jobs that you do.

and supplies from reputable vendors, it is always a good idea to test them, to see how they perform when you use them in an application. If something is not going to work well for you, it is best to know that before you commit to using it.

If you find a new source of sheetmetal, welding wire, or rod, try it out, experiment with it.

Pound the metal into various shapes to see how it reacts to various processes, like hammering, power hammering, and wheeling. With welding supplies, make trial welds. See if you get good bead formation and penetration. In the end, you will benefit from using only those materials with which you are comfortable.

You should remember that no single material or supply is likely to be ideal for everything that you do with that class of material or supply. Sheetmetal of different specifications, and from different sources, works best in some specific applications, and not as well in others. Some welding supplies are fine for one type of job, but less desirable in other applications. When you evaluate new materials and processes, you should keep this in mind and remember what works best in which circumstances, and for what purposes.

Considerations similar to those governing the limits of materials, supplies, and procedures apply to your own skills and to your equipment. In some cases these will be adequate for particular projects and in other cases, without upgrading them, they will not. Fortunately, in autobody metal work, most people engage in the continuous improvement of their skills, tools, and equipment.

One great resource that can be yours without any investment in tools and equipment is planning your jobs. This sounds simple, and for the most part it is. However anyone can let a job progress with little or no advance planning, and end up with uncertain results. Take two separate examples: repairing a rust-out and repairing a dent. You can plan these jobs minutely, probing the extent of the rust-out and analyzing the nature of the dent. Then, you can formulate the best and most efficient ways of dealing with these jobs.

In the case of the rust-out, this involves welding in enough new metal to do the job completely, and so that it will be durable, while avoiding excessive heat buildup and resulting distortion in the panel. In this case, that means keeping the

The best way to evaluate a new material is to work with it to see how it performs in your applications. For example, testing how a sheetmetal forms is a good idea, before you commit to using it for a job.

All gas welding rod is not created equal. If someone tells you that a wire coat hanger will do, don't believe them. Good welding rod has a flow and penetration that inferior rod cannot provide.

repair area to the minimum necessary size to get it done with a good result. In the case of the dent, accurate analysis allows you to move the least amount of metal that completely unlocks the undamaged metal configured into the dent. This results in the least possible collateral damage to adjacent metal from stretching and deforming areas that do not really need to be worked.

The alternative to this kind of planning is to throw yourself, willy-nilly, into a job and let one move dictate the next, with little or no planning at all. Sometimes, this happens when a job seems so simple that it doesn't require any planning. Often, this approach results in letting one mistake or miscalculation dictate the next, as the job careens toward disaster. It sounds pretty dumb, but we have all been there, in one way or another, and I claim no exception to that dubious distinction.

Of course, it is possible to over-analyze or over-plan your work, to the point that these approaches become paralytic. Then, all that you can see are cascades of hypothetical problems, leading to catastrophe. Good planning in body metal work stops short of that kind micro planning, but goes deep enough to avoid most foreseeable problems.

Inherent Advantages

There are certain propositions in bodywork that amount to inherent advantages in the nature of this work that you can leverage for your benefit. Here are two simple ones: Automobiles are mostly bilateral, and you can only see one side of a vehicle at a time.

That means that their left and right sides are, or should be, mirror images of each other. And that can be a huge advantage when you have to repair or fabricate a shape for which

This fender skirt illustrates the bilateralism of auto bodies. The one on the other side of this Packard is a mirror image of this one, and can be used to pattern it. In this case, absolute bilateralism is not necessary because you can never see both fender skirts at once.

you have no pattern. With a panel like a badly damaged hood or roof, you still can determine its proper final shape because you have the other side for a model. Of course, you have to translate the measurements of the good side into its mirror image, but this is not always difficult. For example, if 5 inches back from its front, the outer edge of a hood falls 1$\frac{3}{16}$ inches from the high point at its center, it should do this on both its right and left sides. When you are removing a dent from it or sectioning in a rust repair, this kind of information is priceless. Of course, you usually have to plot many points this way for this trick to be useful.

When you inspect your progress restoring that hood, you can use that measurement, and numerous similar measurements, to know how to proceed in the job, and to confirm when you have it right. The bilateralism and symmetry of the hood informs your eye when the panel is right, but the use of bilateral measurements helps you to get there. In some cases,

translating bilateral measurements enables you to build models of shapes that you need to fabricate from scratch.

The inherent advantage of vehicle bilateralism does not end with symmetry, but couples with another inherent advantage of vehicle configuration that may make your work easier. You cannot see both sides of a vehicle at the same time, unless, of course, it is parked alongside a mirror, or some other perfectly accurate reflecting surface, which is extremely unlikely.

The fact that you can only see one side of a car at a time can be an enormous advantage if you have to fabricate, or massively repair, an item like a fender or fender skirt. You can use the fender skirt from the other side to translate and create a pattern for the one that you fabricate. In this case, the final fit of the fender skirt has to be to the metal on the side where it belongs. But patterning from the other side will get you started on the shape. After you have made the actual piece, and blended it to the

metal on the side where it will be used, it may not exactly match the one on the other side from which the pattern was created. That is not a problem because, after they are mounted, you never see or compare the two fender skirts at once.

This brings up another point about human perception. People often tend to see what they expect to see. About 90 percent of all lightning strikes originate from the ground upward. But we tend to see it as striking down. Why? Because we expect to see fast-moving things fall out of the sky, not rush up into it. The same rule of perception applies to bodywork. People expect to see most panels formed into smooth arcs and contours, with sharper arcs, creases, or angles at their ends, and in some other areas. If you are able to make metal work into those arcs and creases with reasonable but not necessarily perfect accuracy, your work will pass visual inspection.

Put bluntly, some of the best bodywork that you are likely to see would never pass a close dimensional inspection with calipers, dial indicators, or laser scanning. Fortunately, that is not a problem because, after it leaves the factory, it doesn't have to pass that kind of rigorous dimensional inspection.

This is not an invitation to do sloppy work that meets the low standard of close enough. It is simply recognition of the reality that the human eye does not see things with perfect dimensional perception of accuracy.

Divide and Conquer

Most bodywork jobs can be divided into tasks and subtasks. In many cases, these can become routine. What looks like an incredibly

Forming the new metal to section in rust repairs for this fender is a complex job, but it can be broken down into multiple simple tasks. Always consider approaching complex jobs as several simple tasks.

Always record the exact construction of panel areas that you need to replicate. Written notes and photographs may help enormously, after you have cut out and destroyed original sections of these panels. Without good records, what seemed easy to remember may become difficult as time passes.

difficult repair, or a massively challenging fabrication, often can be approached this way, as a series of simpler tasks. For example, faced with having to create a complex fender patch to repair a rusted or hopelessly damaged area, the job can look impossible at your skill and equipment levels. But when the piece that you need to fabricate is analyzed for its exact content, you may discover that simpler tasks that you have mastered will add up to its completion.

Let's say that this section of an old fender has some crown, a dropped edge with a narrow bead, and a wire folded under the edge of the bead. That looks intimidating.

But by using body hammers and mallets, you can form the body of the repair area on a shot bag, or on a wooden form that you create for that purpose. You can model and cut metal into the shape of the edge and you can wrap it around the edge wire. Then, you can align and weld the folded bead area to the larger piece that you have made. Sure, it's simpler in the telling than it is in the doing. But the fact remains, this seemingly complex job can be divided into areas and tasks that are relatively simple, and then assembled into a finished piece that is complex.

Would it be better to make the section described above in one piece? Probably it would. And someday you may have the experience, skill, and equipment to do that. But before that day arrives, it is good to know that you can build complex shapes out of simpler ones that are already within your competence. Later, when you achieve great expertise and proficiency in this work, it will be fun to remember the cumbersome approaches that you once had to take to do jobs that you can now do much more simply and much better.

TYPES OF JOBS

This chapter looks at the core tasks used in damage and rust repair jobs, and at some of the most basic strategies and skills needed to master them. What you need to know starts here.

Damage Repair

The analysis of crash damage is the first and often most critical step in repairing it. Before the 1930s, there was little or no literature available to indicate standard operating procedures for this crucial first step in repair. While some practitioners—body and fender men—may have had fairly modern approaches to repairing deformed metal, most of them did not. They simply hit metal with hammers against dolly blocks and hoped for the best, and that everything would come out right. If metal was high, they hit it down. If it was low, they hit it up. In this process, they often inflicted terrible additional damage to metal, like stretching it and cracking it, but they managed to hide this damage under the filler material of that period, lead.

All of that changed in the early 1930s, when the Fairmont Forge tool

This reprinted version of the 1953 edition of The Key to Metal Bumping *is still available today. Its advice regarding the basics of analyzing collision damage and moving metal remains clear, to the point, and useful.*

company issued catalogs that contained the first easily accessible scientific information on sheetmetal repair. This methodical approach to repairing damaged autobody panels revolutionized the craft and trade of autobody repair. After a revision in

the mid 1930s, this information was issued as a booklet of a little more than 100 pages, titled *The Key to Metal Bumping*, by Frank T. Sargent. In various formats, this book has been more or less continuously in print since then, with reprints of the 1953 edition still available.

That book revolutionized autobody repair by putting theory under it, and by specifying a series of standard procedures to guide it. It is, simply, the Holy Grail of sheet steel repair practice. While much about the autobody crafts has changed in the more than 75 years since *The Key to Metal Bumping* was first published, everything in it is still accurate, relevant, and useful. Anyone seriously pursuing the sheetmetal craft should examine a copy of this trove of body panel wisdom.

The nugget of *The Key to Metal Bumping* is that body damage consists of direct and indirect components. The first is deformed metal that is displaced beyond the elastic limit of the panel material, and that is holding the indirectly damaged metal out-of-place. Relieve the direct damage, the book advises, and the indirect damage will mostly spring back into its proper place. This is exciting because the area of indirect damage usually greatly exceeds the area of directly damaged metal. Unlocking the directly damaged metal is the key that enables you to solve the repair puzzle, usually with a great deal less intervention than might first seem necessary.

The Key to Metal Bumping divides direct damage into ridges, or outward bends and V-channels, which are concave, or reverse, ridges. Buckles and rolled buckles (added later to the damage vocabulary) involve metal that has been forced out of place, by surrounding metal as damage occurs. The book suggests that all direct damage can be described in the categories and characteristics of V-channels and ridges. As with all great theories, author Frank Sargent proposes a concept that is relatively simple but that explains much. He suggests that if you look at what appears to be complex panel damage, you can reduce it to combinations of the items noted above, ridges and V-channels. With the addition of buckles and rolled buckles, this theory becomes comprehensive.

Sargent proposes a method of working out damage that employs the least use of force, a novel concept at the time. Taking account of work-hardening factors, he advises working out the ridges and V-channels (mostly off-dolly) that represent direct and, to a lesser degree, indirect damage. When this is done, most of the rest of the indirect damage will be released. The panel will then return to its original, undamaged format, or close to it. And yes, it is as simple as that.

Of course, a complex deformation or a series of deformations in a panel look anything but simple.

This damage is somewhat complex, and noodling the sequence of the event(s) that caused it is of medium difficulty. Still, the time taken to work out a theory of that sequence is well spent when you have to remove damage like this.

Here, *The Key to Metal Bumping* offers a tremendously useful and (for the time) revolutionary concept of how to look at collision damage. It advises examining complex damage, and figuring out the order in which the metal was deformed; that is, the sequence of events in the collision that deformed it. Where was the panel first struck? Where did the striking force go next? What effect did the deforming metal have on adjacent metal, and how did that interact with the deforming force as it continued to deform the panel? This is, in its essence, a cause-and-effect theory.

While this kind of investigation may sound complex and difficult, it really isn't. There are only so many possibilities for a sequence of events that produces collision damage. Items like paint scrapes and pressure embosses on metal provide excellent clues to the order in which damage occurred. With some experience, it becomes relatively easy to formulate a plausible theory regarding what deformed a panel, and in what sequence. Please note that such theories do not have to be perfect, but merely plausible and possible, to provide the basis for corrective action.

Once a body practitioner has such a theory of damage in mind, *The Key to Metal Bumping* advises removing the damage in the reverse order of how it was created. In other words, you correct the last event in the damage sequence first, and work back to the first damage caused by the initial impact.

The reason for this approach is that, when it is followed, the best possible effort produces the best possible result. Taking damage out in the reverse order from how it was inflicted causes indirect damage to spring back, mostly without applying unnecessary and possibly damaging force to it. And, as they say on TV, "It really, really works!"

An Example of Simple Damage Repair

You can reduce complex damage, that is, damage that may involve multiple events and interrelated deformations of metal, to its simple components by using the type of analysis noted above. To make this work, you need to know how to correct simple damage. Let's illustrate this process with a straightforward dent.

The dent in our example was made by a single impact against the hood. It cannot be determined exactly how the damage occurred. It may have resulted from an object like a tree branch falling onto the hood, or by the car being driven into a low-hanging object. It clearly occurred in one incident that resulted in a mostly straight dent, with a lateral crease at its center. This is among the simplest of all dents, and one of the easiest to remove.

The first step in correcting this damage was to determine its extent and boundaries. This was accomplished by outlining the obvious damage area with chalk lines, followed by lightly board sanding the damaged area, to more exactly define those boundaries.

Then, it was possible to see exactly where deformed metal existed, and to outline the damage with precision. While the preceding steps may seem a bit fussy, note that they yielded some very useful information: The damage area was actually larger than the first chalk line estimate indicated.

The best approach to removing this damage was to work out the crease in its center, the V-channel represented by line A-B, which was locking most of the metal in the dent out of place. Note that this was the first damage that occurred as the

dent was created. Removing this crease had to be done in a way that did not upset or stretch the metal on either side of the crease, indicated by lines C and D, which was bounded by undamaged metal.

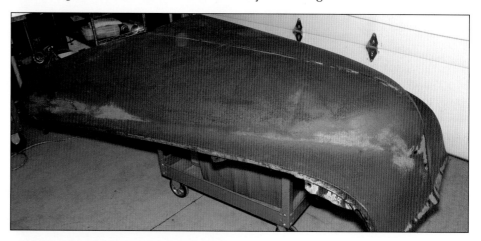

1 This simple dent in the hood of a late 1940s Chrysler is about as basic as sheetmetal damage gets. It happened in a single incident. Other than pulling surrounding metal from the hood into the dent's crease, there was little secondary damage. Relieving the center crease, without causing further deformation beyond the damage boundaries, is the challenge here. As the crease is worked up, caution is needed to not upset the indirectly damaged metal.

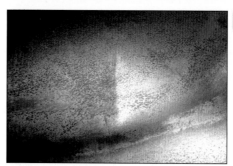

2 Analysis of this damage is simple. An object impacted the hood along line A-B, creasing it and pulling metal in from as far away as lines C and D. Returning the metal in the crease A-B to its original position will release most of the indirect damage between C and D.

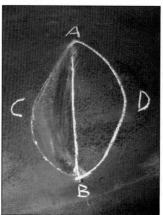

3 Some board sanding revealed the exact limits of the out-of-place metal. The damage area was larger than the first chalk estimate indicated. Note that this is very heavy sheetmetal, between 20- and 21-gauge.

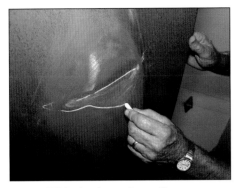

4 With the board sanding completed, the size and shape of the damage area was confirmed. This had already been determined by feeling the metal but, in the planning stages of a repair, an accurate visual representation of damage is a more useful than a tactile one.

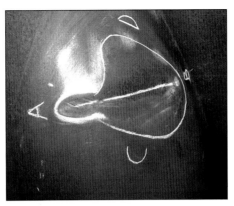

5 The limits of the damage area were now redrawn in chalk. It was important to stabilize the metal along lines C and D, as repair force was applied to crease A-B. This prevented spreading the damage into new areas beyond C and D.

6 The underside of the damaged area looked like this. Crease A-B is evident, and you can see a hint of line D, near A. Knowing where things are on the back side of this panel was critical, because this was where most of the force to repair it was applied.

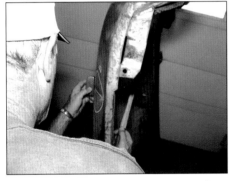

7 The deepest damage, near A, was worked up with a hammer-off-dolly technique. The dolly was alternated between supporting the metal along lines C and D, as the crease was worked up by hammering it on the underside of the panel.

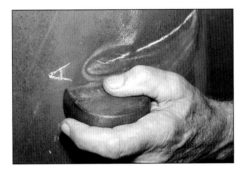

8 Here is a typical dolly position on line C, near A, for hammering up crease A-B. The dolly was used to prevent metal beyond line C from bulging out, as A-B was hammered up. It was critical to avoid upsetting the metal between A-B and C as this was done.

9 From the back side, the hammering along A-B looked like this. Note the upright positioning of the hood to provide good ergonomics for working on this damage. There was plenty of room to swing the hammer and hold the dolly, and the access and position were comfortable for the metal man.

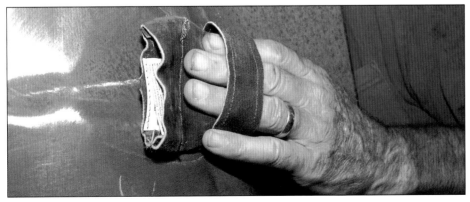

10 After the worst of the damage had been hammered up, it remained to level the metal in the damage area. A light shot bag was used to support the metal, as hammering continued. The shot bag reduced the chance that an accidental on-dolly hammer blow might stretch the metal.

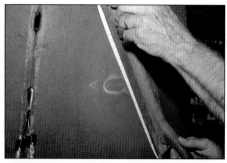

11 At this point, the damage area was again board sanded to indicate progress, and to see what remained to be done. This inspection indicated that while much progress had been made raising the crease, more metal in the crease area needed to be worked up.

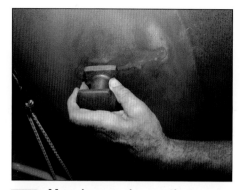

12 More hammering on the crease A-B was done, with the area immediately adjacent to the crease supported off-dolly. Note that much of the indirect damage had come up to level, and that the damage area had been greatly reduced.

13 The underside of the damage area was beginning to look much better. Very little of crease A-B or damage boundaries C and D remained visible. However, parts of crease A-B stubbornly remained.

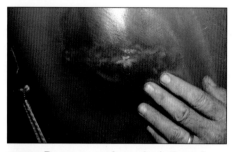

14 By now, surface deviations in the damage area had been reduced to no more than a few thousandths of an inch in depth. At this point, feeling the damage was as useful as, or better than, seeing it.

15 The weapon of choice for raising the remaining low spots was a pick hammer. It can precisely move small areas of metal in very small increments, if you use it with concentration and patience.

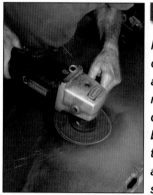

16 With pick hammering completed and its results confirmed by feeling the surface, a disc sander was applied to the formerly damaged area to level it and to indicate any low spots that may remain.

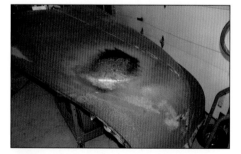

17 After a little contouring with a flexible body file and some more disc sanding, the repair area looked like this. The hood could now be stripped, primed, and painted. No filler was needed in the repair area, because the metal was now level.

To accomplish this, a mildly crowned hammer was used to strike the back of the V-channel with a slapping motion, while a flat dolly block was held loosely against the metal under the hammer. The dolly was offset to a location against the damage boundary, alternating between the sides of the dent, along lines C and D. The dolly block prevented the hammering force from inflicting further deformation beyond lines C and D.

After the major damage was hammered out, the dolly block was replaced with a small, handheld shot bag, to back up the area where lighter hammering was done.

At this point, most of the damage has been removed, and a great majority of the metal between lines C and D has sprung back into place, as ridge A-B was driven up. Some more hammer-off-dolly work, followed by board sanding, revealed the progress that had been made. Some depressed areas in the original crease remained to be worked out.

These low areas were raised with a pick hammer. This procedure involves lightly tapping them up, raising the depressed metal a few thousandths of an inch. Never get wild with a pick hammer because that will make a terrible, pocked mess of your work. Feel depressed areas with your fingertips, and raise them with a gentle touch with your pick hammer. The repair area was then disc sanded to indicate remaining low spots, and filed to level it.

Several of the previous steps (hammering-off-dolly, pick hammering, and filing) were repeated until the panel was level. The job took about 40 minutes, and resulted in a surface that required no application of filler material before it was painted.

This example of the removal of a simple dent illustrates the main features of this work. The damage was analyzed to determine how it had occurred, and removed in the reverse order of its occurrence. Care was taken to use as little force as possible during the repair. Removal of the main V-channel was accomplished in ways that minimized any possible stretching or upsetting of the metal, and that stabilized the edges of the damage area to avoid causing additional injury beyond them.

Of course all of this takes practice, and requires a feel for the metal and for what it is doing as you work on it. These processes are the basic ones used to remove dents. The principles behind them apply to all sheetmetal operations, including fabrications.

Small Rust Repairs

Repairing small rust-outs is one of the most common jobs in autobody metal work. The first step is to determine the extent of the damage. This requires judgment: You do not want to remove serviceable metal

Probing with an awl is a good diagnostic technique. Delicate abrasive blasting also helps to reveal weak and potentially perforated metal. Areas like this wire-edged hood section are vulnerable to rust because they can trap moisture.

You can abrasively blast sheetmetal without damaging it, if you use combinations of low blast pressures, shallow nozzle angles, long nozzle-to-work distances, and abrasive-rich air/abrasive mixtures. Without taking these precautions, you can badly warp sheetmetal.

from an original panel, but you also do not want to fail to go far enough to remove all of the diseased metal from a repair area.

Cleaning and probing a suspected rust area with a pick should reveal its extent. Abrasive blasting helps to expose the extent of damage, but runs the risk of warping the panel. While it is possible to clean metal for inspection with blast media like silica sand,

silicon carbide, and aluminum oxide, it takes a very light application of these blasting media to avoid deforming and damaging a panel. That kind of restraint involves exercising terrific skill and judgment, but abrasive blasting can provide excellent cleaning. Glass bead blasting media should never be used on body panels because this stretches the side of the panel to

Don't attempt to weld shut porosities and small holes on visible outer body metal. This approach is shown here, on a floor pan. It works because there are few holes, and the metal can be protected from further attack by corrosion.

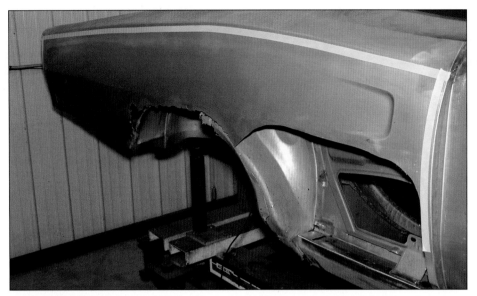

There is no option here. The large area of this panel, outlined in tape, has to be replaced with new metal. Trying to repair it would be a violation of the law of diminishing returns.

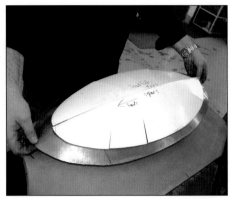

This paper pattern was used to check a complex shape: the top of a 1941 Willys fender that required sectioning. By cutting flaps into the paper, a three-dimensional pattern of the fender top was formed.

which it is applied, and causes warping. Blast processes that use media like soda and plastic bead—known as soda blasting and PMB, respectively—clean metal without warping it, but not as thoroughly as harder blast media. Other processes that can accomplish good cleaning are dip stripping in heated chemical baths that employ electrolysis, and the application of various abrasive wheels.

Once the extent of rust damage is revealed, a repair strategy and repair material can be selected. In some cases, welding shut small defects (like pinholes) suffices, particularly if they are not in highly visible areas of panels, and if there are not too many of them. In other cases, replacement of large sections of panels may be required. These are judgment calls that depend largely on your skills and resources, and on what level of results you are seeking.

If you opt to replace part of a panel, known as sectioning, there are several possibilities for securing the metal that you need. You may be able to buy a panel containing the section that you need from an original equipment manufacturer (OEM), or from an aftermarket supplier. You may have to find it as a salvage panel. Failing that, you may have to modify a similar panel, or fabricate one from scratch. In that case, you should choose sheetmetal stock that is similar to the material that you are repairing in type and thickness. It should also be material that you can form easily, but that holds its shape after it is formed.

If you have to form the section that you need from sheet stock, or to modify it from an existing formed piece, you need some method of patterning the original area, so that your section or patch conforms to it. There are many methods of patterning sheetmetal in three dimensions; some are very elaborate, while others are quite simple. Different situations may mandate using specific patterning techniques. In general, the simplest techniques are often the best.

A contour template was created for the fender top. It was drawn on paper, using a set of standard body curves (the blue plastic pieces). Then, a paper template was transferred to cardboard. The cardboard template was used to check progress, as the fender top was being formed.

There are many methods of cutting out metal that will be replaced. (The use of these tools, and forming patch panels, are discussed later.)

Patterning and Forming a Small Rust Repair Patch

These photos illustrate a very simple method of patterning a small rust patch for a decklid. It was damaged by rust that formed in an area between the metal skin and the supporting structure behind it. The rust area was outlined, and a slightly larger area was marked for the patch.

A patch pattern template was formed from a soldered grid of number-12 copper electrical wire. This wire is easy to hand bend, and holds its shape well, when used as a pattern to check the progress of the sheetmetal patch panel formed from it. The first step was to bend it by hand, to bring the pattern grid to the shape of the metal that the patch panel would replace. The pattern grid was repeatedly checked against the original panel as it was formed to it.

In the final stages of the patterning operation, the pattern was held to the panel on one side with a magnet, while fine adjustments were made to the pattern grid.

A wooden stick was used to help form the copper-wire grid against the decklid surface, until it conformed perfectly to that surface, giving a faithful impression of the metal under it.

1 The red felt-tip-marker line indicates the metal that had to be cut out to make this rust repair. Access problems with supporting structure made cutting out the area bounded by the white lines a better strategy than just cutting out the weak metal.

2 The patterning technique used to model the metal that was removed started by soldering number-12 copper electrical wire into a grid, roughly the size of the metal to be cut out. The grid was then formed by hand to conform to the panel.

3 After each modification to the pattern grid, it was checked against the metal that it was being formed to model. This process took several repeated steps, but each one brought the pattern grid closer to the panel's contours.

4 As the grid became closer to the panel's shape, a strong magnet was used to hold one of its edges against the panel, so that both hands could be used to refine its shape, and to reveal areas that needed further forming.

5 One corner of the grid that resisted forming was bent with the handle of a wire brush. More pressure could be exerted with the wooden handle than would be possible with bare hands.

6 After a few minutes, the wire-pattern grid exactly modeled the surface. It was now a nearly perfect template for checking the new metal that would be formed.

This scissors-like pair of pneumatic metal shears is one of the more unusual devices that can be used to cut sheetmetal. It works surprisingly well, if you can get the access room to maneuver it.

This is the panel patch that that was modeled earlier. Modern planishing hammers had origin in old, light-duty body shop power hammers used to smooth large panels. They are useful for stretching and forming metal.

A leather bag filled with lead or steel shot and a plastic mallet can do wonders forming contours in sheetmetal. Smaller shot bags are shown to the left of the one that is being used here.

This blacksmith's mushroom anvil, used with a medium-crown body hammer, allows very controlled forming of metal by stretching and shaping it.

This old tire-patching support device makes an excellent anvil for the shape that is being formed on it. Sometimes you can innovate with the tools that you use to form body metal.

The forming technique chosen to make a repair patch depends on the type of surface configuration that is required. Many fabrications for rust-repair patches employ relatively simple methods.

Small Patch Piece Welding Methods

There are three common methods for welding in small panel patches: oxy-acetylene, MIG welding, and TIG welding.

Oxy-acetylene, or torch welding, was once the dominant method for performing this work. It produced good results, but required considerable skill, and produced enough heat around the welds made with this method to badly distort the surrounding metal. Correcting this distortion took considerable time and effort. The same was true of arc welding, a process that also was once used on sheetmetal, but that had tremendous drawbacks in terms of the skill required to perform it and the distortion that it inflicted on panels.

In the 1970s, metal inert gas (MIG) welding began to replace torch welding in body shops. MIG is a form

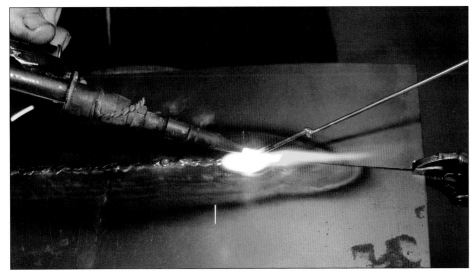

Oxy-acetylene torch welding was the original method of joining sheetmetal panels. It produces satisfactory welds, but requires a high level of skill. Note that the welding rod is used to shield the weld puddle from the torch's most intense heat.

TIG welding requires expensive equipment and can be difficult to learn, but it creates terrifically strong joints with minimal heat distortion. When quality is paramount, TIG is the way to join sheetmetal panels or pieces.

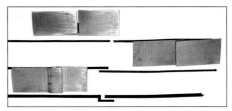

From top to bottom are a butt seam, lap seam, and offset lap seam. If properly made, butt seams are best for appearance and durability. It takes some practice to make this joint but once you master it, you will be glad that you did.

This MIG welding unit is typical of the high-quality modern welders that make it easy to do excellent panel attachment work, with very little heat distortion compared older techniques like oxy-acetylene torch and stick arc welding.

of electric, or arc, welding. It requires less skill than torch welding, and produces far less panel distortion. It has become the standard method of welding autobody sheet steel in repair shops. Basically, this method feeds a continuous electrode, or wire, into the weld puddle, while shielding the weld area from high temperature oxidation with a neutral gas that flows through the welding handle nozzle, blanketing the weld area until it can cool a bit.

When the electrode wire strikes the welding target, it creates a short circuit that heats and melts the wire into the base metal. This creates and sustains a weld puddle. The heat melts off the end of the wire and breaks the short circuit, but the wire re-feeds into the weld, recreating the short circuit, and repeating the cycle. Another name for this phase of the MIG welding process is short arc welding, a term that describes the actual cycle of the process.

Today, MIG welders are compact, relatively inexpensive, and highly perfected. That is why MIG is by far the most popular method of panel welding in use today. However, tungsten inert gas (TIG) welding also has a distinct place in this work. On the upside, TIG welding produces the best welds and the least distortion of any welding method. Its advantages of quality are beyond dispute. However, it requires considerable skill to perform, and TIG equipment is very expensive. It is also a slow welding process, as such things go, but TIG should be considered if ultimate welding quality is your goal.

In addition to choosing a welding process, it is necessary to decide what type of panel joint to use. Panel joints fall into three types: butt, lap, and offset lap. Butt welded joints are by far the best. Lap welded and offset lap welded joints may seem easier to make, but are really more difficult. A

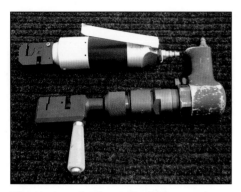

These panel-edge offsetters create offsets in the edges of sheetmetal for lap welding. The one on top is air-over-hydraulic; the one on the bottom runs off an air-driven zip gun.

properly fitted butt joint has a finished look on both sides; something that is critical when the underside of a repair patch may be visible. Also it doesn't reveal its attachment point as it ages and is subjected to flexing and vibration. Lap welded and offset lap welded joints have a tendency to reappear in sheetmetal surfaces as they age, because the metal in them is double thickness and behaves differently than a consistent butt welded area.

Large section patches, like the rusted-out bottoms of doors, present the same problems as small patches, except that they have to integrate and look good in longer runs of metal and, therefore, must fit into larger curves and sweeps. This means that they can be more difficult to get right than small patches, even though the considerations in fitting them are similar to those for small area patches.

Patterning and forming small patch pieces is covered in more detail in Chapters 5 and 12. Similar techniques are used to form large patch panels. Many different approaches to patterning yield good results. You should choose a patterning technique that captures an appropriate

level of detail, and that has sufficient accuracy for what you are fabricating. It should also be a technique with which you are comfortable, and in which you have confidence.

Materials used to make patch pieces should be similar to the metal that will surround them. This is absolutely necessary in the case of large patch pieces or panels. If a piece that is being cut out and replaced is 20-gauge metal, the replacement piece should match it in thickness. Sheetmetal described as 1018 and 1020 cold roll is about right for most forming operations used to create small patches and larger panel sections. These steels are also very suitable for welding.

Patch pieces and panels can be positioned for welding in many ways. Locking pliers, magnets, sheet-

Holding patch pieces temporarily in place with magnets for tack welding works very well for most shapes and configurations. This piece had a tendency to tilt out of position, so several magnets were used to secure it.

metal clips, and Clecos are among the most favored devices used to hold these panels in place prior to tack welding, and for welding them into final position.

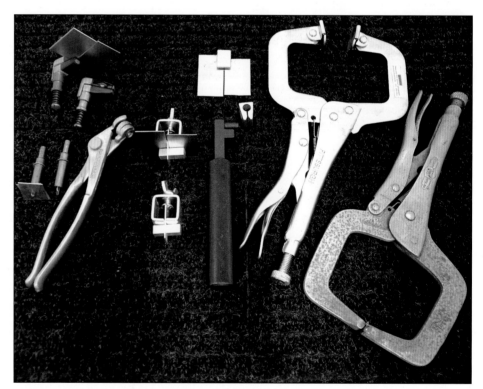

Here are several devices and their installation tools for holding sheetmetal pieces in place for tack welding. On the left: Clecos and Cleco edge holders. To their right: wing nut clips; compression edge clips; and on the far right, locking pliers. The top set has self-aligning swivel ends, a handy feature.

CLEANING, MODELING AND CUTTING

This chapter discusses the best ways to clean, model, and cut sheetmetal. These tasks are basic to all panel sectioning jobs, and to many fabrication projects. They are crucial to everything that follows.

Preparing and Cleaning Sheetmetal

Whether panel steel is old or new, it is important to clean it to bare metal at a fairly early stage of working with it. You can begin working with dirty steel; and sometimes it's advantageous to start work with steel panels that still have old paint and/or rust on them. Filing and sanding these things off can help to indicate surface deformations and damage. In a sense, these defects can become a kind of guide coat as work progresses.

However, by the time you get to hammer forming or welding panel materials, you should be thinking about cleaning them. This is also true of new metal that is used in repair and for fabrication projects. While new steel-panel material looks clean, it is usually coated with preservative oil before it is shipped. This oil

Cleaning metal can be one of the most important and time-consuming preparations in metal work. If it is done properly, it should reveal the true condition of the sheetmetal, and indicate repair measures that may need to be pursued.

should be removed with an appropriate solvent before new metal is welded or passed on for painting.

There are many ways to clean sheetmetal. Body shop practice was once to treat it with muriatic acid (hydrochloric acid/HCL), or to use a blow torch to burn off old paint.

Neither of these practices is recommended or even acceptable today.

Paint can be removed with any of several solvents designed for that purpose. These vary in speed and thoroughness. If you have to strip paint from a large panel, like a door or hood, general-purpose paint

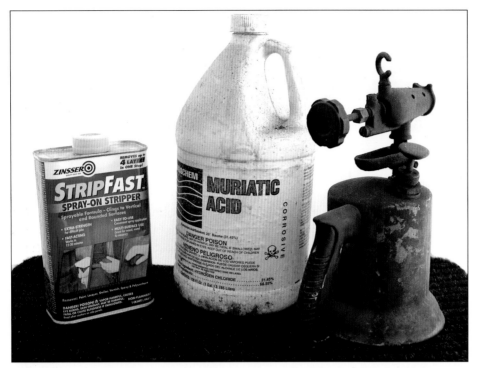

Chemical paint stripper is one way to remove old paint. This is a general-purpose product. Aircraft stripper is a better bet for autobody panels. Muriatic acid and blow torches (on the right) were once used for paint removal. These were dangerous practices, and are now obsolete.

Twisted wire cup brushes, like this one, are good for digging into rust pits in sheetmetal. It is important to change them often because their wires bend and their ends dull quickly.

Disc sanding works well to remove paint and rust from body panels. You have to be careful with this technique not to overheat metal and warp it. Done properly, disc sanding is a slow metal-cleaning method.

strippers will work, and aircraft-type paint remover is a particularly good way to do this job.

Disc sanding with abrasive paper mounted on a 7- or 9-inch electric sander is also an acceptable but slow way to remove paint. It has an advantage over chemical means of paint removal: It also removes surface rust. Old body shop practice was to use 36-grit, and even extremely coarse 24-grit, abrasive papers for this purpose. Open-coat abrasive papers in the 60- to 80-grit range are best for this purpose, and leave panel surfaces that do not require as much cleaning up to remove abrasive gouges.

There are many other varieties of spinning devices—abrasive paper flap, wire, and mesh-pad-type wheels, for example—that will clean metal. Some of these can work on 4½-inch grinders, and produce very good results. Some of the plastic mesh discs sold for this purpose work surprisingly well for paint and surface rust removal. One great advantage that abrasive papers mounted on larger disc sanders (say,

7- and 9-inch devices) have is that they indicate surface defects and features, while removing paint and rust. Wire cup wheels are very good for digging into rust pits but tend to dull and bend quickly, losing much of their effectiveness.

If you are working with larger panels, like whole bodies, hoods, decklids, or doors, you should consider dip stripping as a method of paint and rust removal. At one time there were many dip-strip tanks in the United States. Unfortunately, some of the operators of these facilities disposed of their spent chemicals in irresponsible ways, like dumping them into city sewer systems. Since much of the paint dissolved in these effluents contained lead, many of these facilities ran into regulatory problems, and were forced out of business. There are still some dip strippers left, and, depending on your distance from one of them, this technique may be a good way for you to cleanse bodies and panels to bare metal.

My experience with dip stripping tells me that this service can vary greatly in quality and effectiveness between vendors. Some systems use heated chemicals. Many of them use electrolytic action to enhance cleaning. Some operators of these services are more careful about the chemistry in their tanks than others. In sum, if there is a reputable dip stripper relatively close to you, you should consider this method of cleaning your metal panels. In most cases, stripping a single door or decklid does not justify driving any great distance to a dip-strip tank. On the other hand, if you have a complete car to strip, or if you live near a dip tank, this method may be a valid approach.

Abrasive blasting, sometimes called sandblasting, is another major category of metal-cleaning technology. Blasting is a terrific method for cleaning metal if it is performed by a skilled professional. In addition to getting metal metallurgically clean (as the abrasive blasting industry claims for some blast media), this approach leaves an excellent tooth on finished metal. This means that the surface will have nooks, crags, and crannies that will help paint to mechanically adhere to it.

There are two downsides to abrasive blasting to clean autobody panel metal. The first is that blasting tends to expand surfaces to which it is applied. Media, like glass bead, do this in the extreme. When you expand one side of a surface, but not the other, the metal tends to bend around the unexpanded side. Put simply, it will warp. And, no, you cannot blast the other side to bring it back into proper shape. I wish that it was that easy.

I have seen fenders and doors ruined beyond the possibility of

With considerable patience, abrasive blasting works well to clean sheet metal thoroughly. You have to be careful to work slowly, or you will warp the metal. Media-rich air/abrasive mixtures, low numerical blast angles, low blast pressures, and long nozzle-to-target distances help to prevent distortion.

repair by what someone thought was safe blasting. The only way to safely blast sheetmetal is to do it very slowly. Soft or small blast media, like soda and polystyrene beads, are very slow ways to clean metal. They do not remove deep, pitted rust very well, if at all, but they do avoid the warping hazard. Harder media, like silica sand, tungsten carbide, aluminum oxide, and cold chilled copper slag, will produce very clean

metal. But they must be used slowly, due to their potential to warp metal. This means a combination of a numerically low nozzle-to-target angle, low blast pressures, media-rich mixtures with air, and/or long nozzle-to-target distances.

Any of these approaches, or combinations of them, makes the blast removal of paint and rust from sheetmetal very slow. However, if you are willing to exercise the restraint to do this, which is often very difficult, you can blast sheetmetal clean with good results.

The second downside of blast-cleaning metal is that it leaves it so clean that any moisture in the air tends to rust it almost immediately. In dry environments this is a smaller problem than in wet ones. In all situations, blasted parts should be worked on quickly, re-cleaned, and then painted or treated with a preservative immediately.

Cutting Panel Materials

There is no perfect, or best, way to cut sheetmetal materials. Different

If you are lucky enough to have a good jump shear like this one, you can make straight, clean cuts in sheetmetal almost effortlessly. Hand-cutting techniques for this kind of job are never quite as good.

Band sawing is a great way to make accurate, smooth-cut lines in flat sheetmetal. Unfortunately, a good, metal-cutting band saw is an expensive piece of equipment.

A stationary hand shear, like this Beverly shear, is a great way to cut very accurate shapes into flat sheetmetal. This type of shear is throatless, so there is no limit to the depth of cut that you can make with it into panel steel.

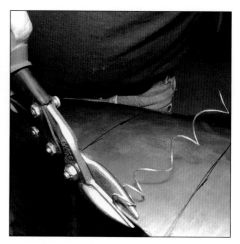

Aircraft snips are great for making accurate cuts in flat sheetmetal, and work well on mildly curved surfaces. They cut reasonably quickly and are relatively inexpensive.

methods of cutting metal work best in different situations.

If a straight line is required, it is best to shear flat metal in a metal shear. A stationary or hand shear is a very good approach to delicate detail work. Another possibility is using pneumatic and electric shears of various types. Tin snips and aircraft-type snips are good for small shearing jobs in flat and curved metal. Band sawing is a very good way to cut flat metal stock very accurately and quickly. Unfortunately, good metal band saws are quite expensive.

Reciprocating pneumatic saws offer a very effective and inexpensive way to cut detailed lines in panels, and are particularly useful for cutting bad metal out of large, contoured panels. High-speed abrasive discs mounted in air grinders are another way of making accurate cuts. This method is favored by many body shops and custom

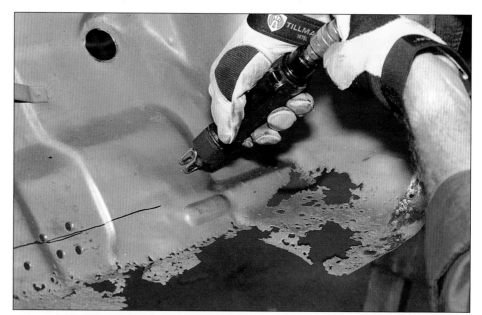

Air-driven saber saws are cheap and are capable of making accurate cuts in contoured sheetmetal. They are the body shop standby for excising diseased areas in panels.

builders. Electric hand shears are also very accurate and fast for making simple cuts.

Nibblers, both air and electric, have some application to cutting autobody metal, particularly when there is no direct entry to begin a cut. Unfortunately, they are messy to use because they spew crescent-shaped metal fragments from their cut paths, all over creation. Find some use for those fragments, and you may become wealthy and appreciated by many. Hole saws and punches are also options for opening up areas, so that you can use other

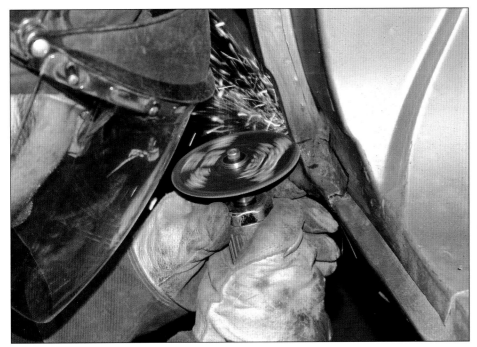

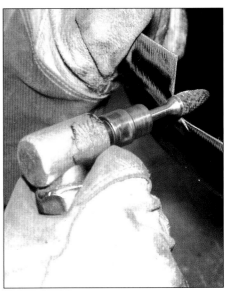

High-speed abrasive disks, mounted in air die grinders or muffler cutters, are great for cutting into contoured panels, but are pretty much limited to cutting straight lines.

Carbide burrs mounted in air die grinders, like the angle grinder shown here, are a terrific way to fine tune metal edges for fit-up to other edges. These tools are surprisingly inexpensive.

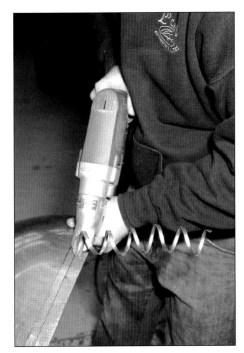

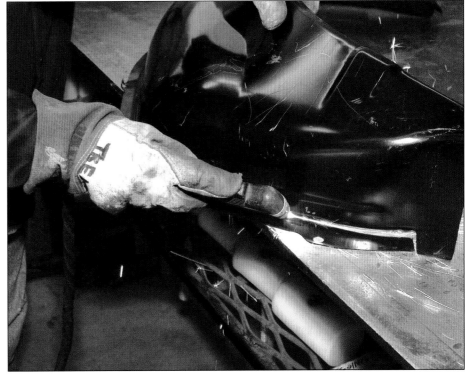

This type of electrically driven hand shear cuts metal quickly and accurately, and is not limited to flat surfaces. Air-driven versions of this tool lack sufficient torque, and do not work as well as electrically driven versions.

Plasma arc cutters cut very quickly, but lack the accuracy of mechanical methods of cutting metal. They work well on curved surfaces, and leave weldable edges. Despite the intense heat that they generate, they cause little distortion in metal because their cutting heat is contained very locally.

cutting methods when interior cuts in metal panels are required.

Plasma arc cutting is a high-tech method of severing sheetmetal. It is very fast, and leaves edges that are still weldable, unlike cutting with an oxy-acetylene torch. However, the lack of fine control of plasma-arc cut lines restricts the use of this method to situations where fine accuracy along cut lines is not required.

Fine adjustments to metal edges are often made with die grinders and files. This is particularly true when parts are being fine-tuned for tack welding and welding. High-speed electric and pneumatic die grinders are also very useful for making these kinds of fine adjustments.

Getting Shapes and Contours Right

There are many ways to create three-dimensional models and forms for sheetmetal objects. These may vary from those that just indicate dimensions to be followed, to those that can be used, almost like dies, in

These wire patterns almost look like art, but are really forms that are incredibly useful for checking metal as it is formed into faithful replicas of original parts. They are also quite durable.

the actual forming process. In either case, these models and forms serve as standards against which to check the fidelity of the metal that you are forming. Sometimes, the metal is intended to replicate some original part, section, or feature of a vehicle. Other times, it is designed to guide the construction of a custom part or panel for an entirely new fabrication.

Very advanced prototype shops have computer-driven systems and hardware that can sense existing or conceptual shapes, turn them into numerical coordinates, and automatically form them in various plastic materials or shave them out of blocks of clay. This kind of capability is wonderful to behold, but presently it is way beyond the scope or needs of most sheetmetal projects that don't involve automobile prototyping and manufacturing.

My favorite method of transferring most simple contours and dimensions from existing shapes to models is to use number-12 copper electrical wire, or grids made from this wire. Examples of this technique are shown in Chapter 3 and Chapter 12. Every shop has its own favored methods of modeling shapes. Wire forms are a favorite with many. Oth-

Paper templates can be made as drawings or as three-dimensional representations of original metal. This paper model is a combination of drawing and contouring to capture the shape of a part that will be formed in metal.

ers have developed various modeling methods in paper, both with flat drawings and by forming the paper into three dimensions. Clay and wooden-buck modeling are steps beyond that.

When I want to model all of a shape in three dimensions, I usually use the old egg crate modeling construction. It is relatively quick, easy to do, accurate, and inexpensive in material costs.

Good, old metal files are great for straightening cut lines in metal edges, and for removing burrs and other imperfections. They can be used in combination with handheld edge deburrers to produce very clean edges.

Making an Egg Crate Pattern/Model

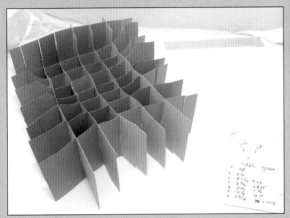

We created this egg-crate pattern to physically represent the dimensions of the hood scoop shown in the next photograph. It is useful for guiding metal forming to the correct dimensions. The footprint diagram of the part and its recorded measurements are to the right of the model.

The actual shape that will be transferred to, and cut out of, each rib is captured with a plastic profile gauge, for transfer to each rib. This technique results in a very accurate pattern.

Poster board is an adequate material for making this kind of model. It has the advantage of being very easy to cut accurately. Some plastic materials are a little stronger, and metal is even more durable.

The strange-looking items in the photo are patterns for the hood scoop on a 1953 Aston-Martin DB2. This technique of creating a three-dimensional model provides a pattern that is useful as a guide and check for fabricating this shape. As the shape is formed in metal, the pattern can be laid over it to check fit, and to indicate changes that need to be made. This type of pattern also can be made in a convex format, in contrast to the concave format shown. The

The hood scoop was measured longitudinally and laterally to create its footprint diagram. The tape grid was drawn on to, and then cut into, the egg-crate model's ribs. Indexing numbers and letters identify each rib. Guide marks on the tape strips identify which of their edges are pertinent.

choice between the two is a matter of personal preference.

In making this form, the first step was to lay out strips of ¼-inch tape in a grid along the hood scoop. Note that the tape positions were identified by letters and numbers to keep confusion to a minimum when the contours that they represented were transferred to cardboard and assembled as an egg crate. The marked edges of the tape (forward or rear edge, and left or right edge) were marked to indicate which edge was used, and became the indexing points for the parts of the egg crate model. Dimensions of the footprint of the scoop were taken and transferred to a sheet of paper.

A profile gauge was applied to the contours of the scoop, and the profiles transferred to the egg crate cardboard in pencil. Then, the profiles marked on the cardboard were cut out, and the slots of the egg crate were fitted together.

The assembled model yielded a usefully faithful three-dimensional facsimile of the hood scoop.

There were some other steps and nuances that are not shown in the accompanying photographs. For example, each long cardboard piece (yellow) was indexed against the front of the hood scoop to confirm its exact height as compared to the profile gauge reading. And some diagonal profiles were indicated as a check of overall accuracy.

This type of model can be made out of many materials, like plastic or metal, depending on the situation's requirements. When metal egg crate models are made, they can be soldered or welded together, and will retain their accuracy permanently. This is a great advantage when a part has to be formed several times.

FORMING, FITTING AND SMOOTHING

This chapter covers shaping, fitting, and smoothing sheetmetal with hand tools and power forming equipment. These are the operations that turn flat stock into the finished shapes that you need and want.

Simple Tools and Equipment

Most autobody metal work is performed with relatively simple and traditional tools like body hammers and dollies. Add a few really straightforward but clever tools that speed work and enhance capabilities, and you have the basis for tackling most projects in this field.

Beyond that, there are several expensive, specialty tools and machines that greatly increase the speed of working with sheetmetal, and add capabilities that are beyond what is possible with simple tools. For example, the use of expensive tensioning machinery to pull out and to straighten large panels, like the sides of vehicles, can produce results that are either impossible or prohibitively time consuming if you try to achieve them with simple tools.

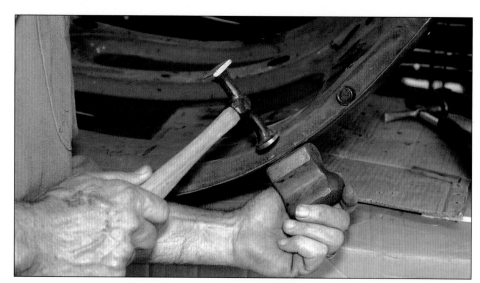

While various machines can speed autobody metal repair and forming operations, the good old hammer and dolly are still the basis for much of this work. Learn to use them properly, and you will have two great friends for life.

While the old masters of the metal crafts were able to hand hammer some very complex panels, or at least parts of them, and join those parts together with welds, this kind of work is so skill intensive and time consuming that there are only a handful of shops left on our planet with those capabilities. Advanced, modern metal-forming equipment has made it possible to accomplish what those old masters did in a fraction of the time that they required, and with no loss in quality. But that kind of equipment is exotic and very expensive, and it only applies to advanced projects.

Machines like Pullmax formers, fitted with Steck and Eckold shrinking/forming heads, cost many tens of thousands of dollars. They can accomplish truly wonderful things with incredible speed, compared to simple tools. They also require

This Pullmax power former is one of the most sought after and versatile machines in the custom metal-forming universe. It operates quietly and allows for many types of operations that move metal with great precision.

Here is a Pullmax power former, fitted with Steck shrinking/forming heads. The backs of the forming dies deform metal in a V-configuration. Then, the fronts of the dies (not visible here) flatten the V-formed metal. This causes local upsets that quickly and radically shrink and form sheetmetal.

The Eckold shrinking/forming heads mechanically gather metal as they press against and grip it. This upsets and smoothes it, which allows the machine operator to form it. The process works when the heads close on the metal, gripping it, and mechanically move laterally toward each other.

tremendous skill to operate. Sure, anyone can shove sheetmetal into one of these devices. But to know when and where to use them, at what settings and with what material movements, and for how many cycles, are issues that require a great deal of experience to get right.

While there are limits to what can be done with the simple tools I mentioned, those limits are often beyond what many metal workers assume. It is hard to communicate these limits in specific terms because they vary with individual skills and aptitudes, but I'll take a stab at it: Generally, if you have to make something like a complete fender, or most of one, for a 1930s automobile, or the nose section for an AC or Ford Cobra, that work is best left to people with advanced skills and equipment. However, if you need to form one side of a cowl for that 1930s automobile, it should be possible with fairly basic tools and devices.

In general, remember that there are limitations to what can be done without highly advanced skills and

equipment, but that those limitations are pretty far out on the scale of projects that people working with autobody metal usually encounter. Before you pine for some expensive metal working machine for a specific job or task, consider if it can be done acceptably with the tools that you already have, or can access.

Applying Plasticity/Elasticity, Work Hardening and Annealing

The characteristics of plasticity, elasticity, and work hardening were discussed, in detail, in Chapter 1. Here, we will see how they apply to actual metal work.

Plasticity is the characteristic of sheetmetal that allows it to be deformed without breaking. This characteristic comes into play whenever its shape is changed. If metal's plasticity is exercised under tension, such as die stamping it into a panel, it will be stretched. This is normal. However, if metal is deformed in a collision, or if it is stretched beyond

its plastic limit in the process of fabricating it, this must be counteracted. That is, the metal must be shrunk. This is done by upsetting it, literally compacting it into itself, so that some of its lateral dimension can be exchanged for increased thickness.

The opposite is also true. If metal is shrunk in a collision or in fabrication, by being deformed while it is under compression, then upsetting occurs. This amounts to shrinking. Areas affected by this kind of shrinking must be stretched back to the point where they can assume their correct shapes.

Elasticity is the ability of metal to bend, up to a point, and then return to its original format by simply releasing it from the force(s) that bent it, or that are holding it in its modified shape. This ability of metal to remember its last stable configuration is an important ally for anyone working with sheetmetal. It is often referred to as memory.

Work hardening is the characteristic of metal that causes it to become progressively harder to deform in

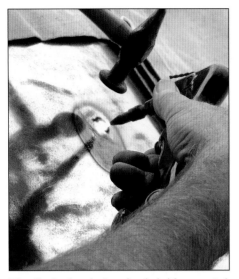

The first step in torch-shrinking metal is to heat a small spot to bright red. This causes it to pop out as the hot metal expands. But it cannot spread beyond the heated spot, laterally, because it is bounded by unheated and unyielding metal.

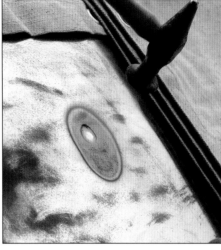

The second step in torch shrinking is to lightly hammer down the heated, bulged spot, with a dolly behind it. This piles the metal into itself, causing an upset that shrinks it. As the metal cools, it can be quenched with a damp sponge or rag to moderate the shrinking.

those area(s) where its elastic limit is exceeded as its shape is changed.

The applications of the rules of plasticity, elasticity, and work hardening are critical in any but the simplest work with body metal. Each of these factors would become an insurmountable obstacle if it could not be counteracted relatively easily—fortunately, it can be.

Stretching is the most common problem in autobody work. Correcting it requires shrinking the metal in the affected area. There are various approaches to doing this. The traditional method is to heat a small area of the stretched metal—an area roughly between dime and nickel size—with an oxyacetylene torch to red hot. It is heated until a combination of its expansion, and its being bounded by the unheated and unyielding metal that surrounds it, causes it bulge up. The bulged area is then quickly hammered down with a

body hammer, while it is supported by a dolly that is held behind the un-bulged metal surrounding the heated spot. The bulged spot is hammered back to level with the panel, but no further, as this would cause the metal

to be hit directly against the dolly, which would re-stretch it. In the traditional torch-shrinking method, a damp sponge may be applied to the shrink spot to quench it. That stops the shrinking, and controls the result of the operation. When using this shrinking technique, it is common to use a pattern that groups five spots (four of them around one in the center).

This method takes some practice, but works well. Other methods of shrinking include serrated spinning discs mounted in body sanders or grinders. The disc's serrations impact and heat metal at high spots. These combined actions, heating and impact, tend to upset and shrink these high spots—but not necessarily stretched spots. There are also numerous shrinking attachments for MIG and resistance (spot) welders that work with varying effectiveness to shrink metal. For mild shrinking, there are hammers and dollies that are patterned, or that actually move parts of their surfaces, to pull metal together as it is hit and to upset it.

The serrated hammers (left) and the dolly (front) cause minor shrinking when they impact metal. The disc (center) causes heating and impact when it is rotated at high speed against metal, shrinking it. The hammer (right) employs a central face to hold metal and a rotating rim that gathers it.

This old planishing hammer can form metal quickly, but with limited accuracy. Think of it as a massive stretching machine that thins the material that it impacts, causing it to stretch and contour.

Bending the two corner areas of this fabrication requires moving the metal beyond its plastic limit. The solution is to bend it part way and then to anneal it with a torch. After that, it can be hammered down to where it belongs.

to use it. When you have done this, you will find that annealing will join shrinking and stretching as one of your best allies in metal work.

Hammering Techniques that Work

Hammers and dollies are the basic tools of sheetmetal work. Hammers vary in size and configuration. They range from configurations that are flat, to those that are highly crowned, and from square faces to round faces. There are also pick hammers, designed to raise small areas of metal in very small increments, and specialty hammers for accessing hard-to-reach areas, or for performing special jobs like door skinning.

Hammers should have smooth, clean striking surfaces, to avoid scarring what they hit. Good hammers

The hardest things about shrinking are to know where to shrink, and how much to shrink. Unfortunately, something called false stretch compounds this difficulty. Basically, where you see a bulge or wave in metal may not be the origin point of an apparent stretch. What appears to be a stretched area in a panel may be set up by an actual stretch that is many inches away from an apparent deformation. Your experience will help you to learn to deal with this issue. For now, be aware that it exists.

In metal work, shrunk or upset metal probably is not as common as stretched metal, but it can cause similar havoc in the shape of a panel. Shrunk metal is often a result of the upsetting of an area(s) of a panel in the course of dinging dents out of it. Removing upsets of this sort is refreshingly simple, again involving an exchange of lateral dimension for thickness. And, again, knowing where to stretch metal is more difficult than stretching it because stretching metal only involves mak-

ing it thinner and, thereby, laterally broader. You can do this by hitting it between a body hammer and a dolly, or with a planishing hammer, or other type of power hammer.

Work hardening may progress to the point that metal becomes so hard and resistant to further movement that it fractures rather than yield to your attempts to change its shape with tools like hammers. When this happens, the solution is to anneal it. This reforms its crystalline structure to make it soft and workable again. It is done with steel panels by heating the metal with an oxy-acetylene torch to a temperature between 1,550 and 1,600 degrees F (between bright red and salmon red), and allowing it to air cool. Sometimes, depending on the metal and the situation, it may be advantageous to apply a damp sponge to the annealed surface, after it has cooled substantially, to slightly enhance its stiffness, and to give it structural strength.

You will need to experiment with annealing to master when and how

The first four tools (from the bottom up) are general-purpose combination body hammers, in various crowns. The fifth is a door-skinning hammer. The sixth is a low-crown hammer, with both round and square faces (the latter is for working up to flat edges). The seventh tool is a hammer for fender dinging.

The two rawhide mallets (lower left) provide soft, yielding surfaces for moving metal. The lower one is shot-filled, giving it a dead-blow feature. The plastic poly mallets (top) offer resilient, shaped impacting surfaces that are great for forming shapes in metal without marring it.

have a feel and balance that makes them natural and comfortable to swing. They are best swung with the arm, from the elbow, with a slight flexing or unwinding of the wrist. The motion against the metal for most procedures should be a slapping action that allows rebound, sometimes with a little bit of sliding thrown in. This is not like driving nails.

Hammers should be held somewhat loosely, and with a limber wrist behind them, to allow them to rebound. You should pay attention to that rebound because it contains information about what is happening to the metal that you are hammering. The sound that a hammer makes also communicates information about what its impacts are doing to the metal. Most beginners, and a few professionals, tend to hit too hard with body hammers, expecting one or a few master blows to move the metal. In most situations, it is far preferable to use several lighter blows. Good metal workers develop distinctive rhythms and timbres to their hammer blows.

Some jobs are best performed with specialty hammers like those with rubber, rawhide, or plastic heads. Choosing the right hammer for a task involves both experience and personal preference.

Dollies are used to support metal that is being hammered. In some cases, such as in tight-access situations against the backs of fenders, they are also used as hammers. Most dollies are made of cast iron, and present several different and useful contours for working surfaces. When hammering metal that is supported by a dolly, there is the critically important distinction between on-dolly and off-dolly techniques. Work on-dolly means that the dolly directly supports the metal that you are hammering and is placed exactly under and in contact with the area that is being hammered. This means that you are hitting the metal between the hammer and the dolly. The inevitable

Hammering off-dolly is a precision operation that is used to shape metal without stretching it. The work shown here is a fine-tuning operation, in the final stages of forming and flattening a surface.

result is to stretch that metal. Sometimes this might be your object, or part of it, but sometimes it produces the unwanted result of stretching.

Hammering off-dolly is much more common, and usually more useful. In this technique, the dolly is

Dollies like these offer many useful surfaces for backing up hammer work. The three on the left are for working very small areas. The two larger dollies, with handles, can be mounted in vises and used in fabricating. The front dolly is rubber clad, and provides a somewhat resilient surface.

This photo shows hammering on-dolly, but in this case the dolly is rubber clad. This allows for fine shaping, without much danger of stretching the metal. Hammering on-dolly with an iron dolly can cause excessive stretching, even if you are careful to control this tendency.

Shot bags come in many sizes and shapes, and can be filled with many materials. The large, square bag (center) contains lead shot, and is useful for forming fairly large items. The smaller bags (right) are hand held, for backing up stationary items. The round bag (left) works both ways.

not held directly under the metal that is hammered, but offset from it. An example would be holding a dolly under one or the other side of a ridge that is being hammered down. The result is to level the ridge to the panel. There may be some unwanted upsetting of the metal that is hammered this way but this can be corrected easily, later.

Hammering off-dolly makes good use of the rebounding action of the dolly, after it is impacted by the metal that is being struck against it with a hammer. After the hammer blow is struck, the dolly rebounds against the metal and acts to push it out, toward the hammering force. For this to work, the dolly must be pressed against the back of what you are hammering. You can easily imagine that driving a configuration like a ridge down at its center, while holding a dolly, alternately, under each side of the ridge, tends to level the panel, and remove the ridge. As the ridge goes down, the metal bordering it is kept level by the dolly's

rebound action. Various specialty dollies are available in many different shapes and, in some cases, are clad in relatively soft materials, like rubber, to give them resilience, or dampening.

Shot and sand bags are very useful for hammer forming three-dimensional shapes. These bags can be filled with steel or lead shot, as well as sand or other materials. They are used to back up metal in a somewhat yielding manner. As you hammer metal on a shot bag, it dishes out. This provides relatively smooth forming and controlled stretching in the same operation. Shaped plastic mallets, used with shot-bag backing, is a particularly effective hand-forming combination.

Every autobody practitioner has some favorite backing surface for hammering metal. These can range from anvils to blocks of various woods, and even plastic materials. One of my favorite backup surfaces is between one and three thicknesses (layers) of heavy, corrugated cardboard.

Bending, Beading and Prying

The fastest way to move a lot of sheetmetal in a broad area is with devices that bend and bead it. Bending and beading apply more to fabrication than to repair. Prying, another form of mechanical bending, is used mostly in repair work. The mainstays of equipment for bending body metal are brakes and slip rolls. Brakes are used to make straight-line bends, in sheet stock, to very precise angles. They also can be used to radius flat material by applying numerous, successive, small bends to it. Finger brakes, or box and pan brakes, are useful for making bends in local areas, with standing metal on one or both sides of those bends. Slip rolls are used to impart permanent curvature in one plane to panel materials. Bead rollers are specialty tools that are capable of rolling shallow beads or other shapes into flat or slightly curved sheetmetal.

Picks and pries are used locally to move metal, particularly in poor

This 16-foot sheetmetal brake is beyond the needs of most situations. It can be used for making bends in small items, too, and operates with an ease and precision that are wonderful. The counter balances make it very easy to control.

Hand-operated bead rollers, like this one, form beads and ribs into sheetmetal. Numerous forming and folding dies are available for bead rollers. Some of the more interesting combinations use a soft top die and a hard bottom one.

This finger or box-and-pan brake provides for bending around three-dimensional features of metal. It is shown here making a bend that would be impossible with a flat brake.

access areas, where hammers and dollies cannot reach it.

All of the tools that are used for bending, beading, and prying represent non-impact methods of moving and modifying metal.

Power Forming

Eventually someone realized that the action of striking metal with a hammer on a dolly could be mechanized, thereby greatly increasing the amount of force and frequency of its application. This realization led to some pretty violent devices for forming metal. The most famous of the early versions of these were the Pettingell and Yoder power hammers. These were huge, noisy devices that used a wide variety of shaping/stretching dies to greatly speed the process of custom forming metal.

Over the years, power hammers evolved into much more compact, quiet, and effective machines. Foremost in the modern crop of such devices is the Pullmax, a machine used widely in prototype and advanced metal restoration shops.

In contrast to the earliest power hammers, modern machines, like the Pullmax, are as often used with the likes of Eckold shrinking dies and Steck shrinking/shaping dies. These are general-purpose heads that can form and/or shrink metal very locally and with no fuss. They are relatively quiet and easy to use. The

Pries and their close cousins, spoons, are used in many operations. The more robust items shown here, spoons, do prying duty or provide hammering backups. The lighter items are used only for prying. The homemade edge bender (top) is an item I fabricated from an old car spring.

Slip rolls, like this hand-operated machine, provide for uniformly bending metal in one plane. They impart predictable and continuous curves to sheet-metal. Slip rolls can also be set to put several different curvatures in the same panel, and to flatten distorted metal.

tricky part of the proposition is to know when, where, for how long, and at what pressure settings to use them. Before you add a Pullmax or other power hammer to your want list, you should know that these are very expensive machines that are in the province of professional, not amateur, use.

Pulling Approaches to Moving Metal

So far, most of our attention has been directed toward hitting metal down with a hammer, or using a dolly to hit or rebound it out. There are also times when it is desirable to pull metal. These situations are sometimes encountered in repair work. In the most elaborate processes, pulling plates are soldered, brazed, or welded to areas that require massive pulling force to return them to something close to their original positions. Then mechanical or hydraulic force is used to pull them out by the plates. This is very heavy duty repair work that requires considerable equipment.

Smaller scale pulling is commonly performed to remove dents, where most of the displaced metal is locked out of position by a very small area of metal, and where access issues prevent using impact tools to push out that small area. Manual and mechanically activated suction cups can be used for very light duty pulling. Some shops employ the barbaric practice of using a slide-hammer to push or puncture (or shoot) a hardened screw through an area of a panel that is to be pulled. Then, the screw is tightened into the metal by turning it, and the slide-hammer is operated in the other direction to pull the metal out by the screw. Avoid this rough approach.

A more refined version of this practice is to use a stud welder to weld a steel stud to a depressed area of a panel, and then to use a slide-hammer with a special clamp, that holds the stud's head, to pull the metal out. When this operation is finished, the stud can be ground level to the panel.

Smoothing, Stretching, Shrinking and Forming Operations

Two of the simplest machines made for metal working, the English wheel and the planishing hammer, are extremely useful for basic fabricating jobs. These exist in both relatively inexpensive and high-end versions.

English wheels were among the earliest applications of machines to metal forming. While these devices

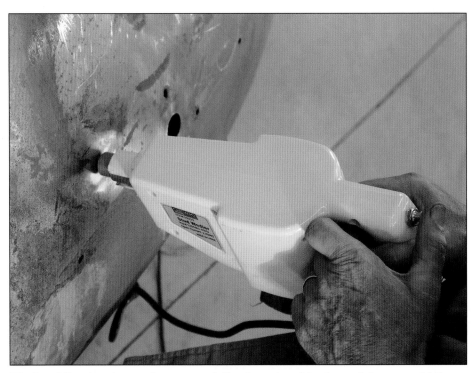

Stud welding involves using a specialized spot welder to resistance weld the head of a stud to part of a panel, for the purpose of pulling its metal out. The welding operation is very fast.

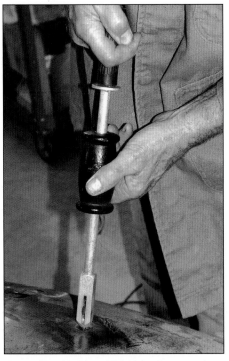

Once the stud is welded to the panel, a specialized slide hammer grips its shank. The stud is then slide hammered away from the panel, pulling out the low metal. The stud is then twisted or cut off, and the area is ground flat.

This stud-welder attachment is great for pulling up small dings. The tool's copper tip is resistance welded to the ding's center, and then pried away from the panel with the tool's levers. When the area is level, the tool is twisted slightly to break the weld, and removed.

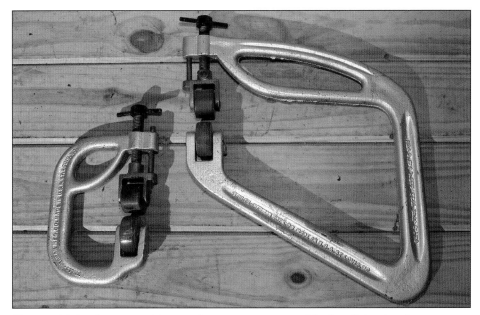

These old fender-smoothing tools amount to portable English wheels. Although they date from the days of the Model T Ford, they are still useful in some situations. They are intended more to smooth than to stretch metal.

through the wheels at different angles makes it possible to form almost any curved or dished shape. It takes considerable practice to know where, with which wheel combinations, with what pressures, and for how many strokes to use an English wheel. When you begin to learn how to determine and combine these variables, it is amazing what you can accomplish with this simple device. Wheeling is often performed after some kind of impact procedure, like hammering metal into a shot bag, has been used to rough out a shape in it. In these cases, wheeling can fine tune the format of the metal, and smooth out the results of the impacts used to form it before it is wheeled.

Unlike the power hammering devices mentioned earlier in this

are only powered by human muscles, knowledge, and imagination, they are almost always larger items than can be hand held, and are incredibly useful for stretching, forming, and smoothing metal for fabrications.

The basic device is a C-clamp-shaped unit with two opposing wheels that can be incrementally tensioned against each other. The wheels usually differ in diameter, while the tension between them is adjustable. The top wheel is generally flat, and much larger than the bottom wheel. The bottom wheel usually has varying degrees of lateral curvature, and is almost always available in different contours.

The principle of the English wheel is that as metal is pushed and pulled between the tensioned wheels, the pressure stretches and forms it. The curvature—and thus the contact patch area and resulting pressure—of the shaped wheel helps to determine the contour that is worked into the wheeled metal. Stroking the metal

This imaginative wheel combination, mounted on an English wheel, uses a creasing lower wheel and a soft upper wheel, literally a caster wheel. The result is to allow forming without excessive stretching.

English wheels come in many formats, constructions, and sizes. This is among the best that I have ever seen. The main issue is stability. A good wheel is firm enough to not get sprung, but resilient enough to apply great torque when it is needed. Note the foot-tensioning adjustment.

chapter, English wheels vary from inexpensive to very expensive. Even if your use for one is only occasional, you still may be able to justify buying a less-expensive version of this very versatile and useful tool. For serious jobs, the larger and more stable English wheels work far better than the cheap ones.

Planishing hammers are relatively inexpensive air-driven power hammers that first appeared on the scene as devices intended for removing dents from fenders and from the turret tops of some automobiles that arrived in the mid 1930s. They are basically C-clamp-shaped frames that hold two opposing working surfaces: a small anvil, and a forming hammer. The hammer is operated as a pneumatic percussion device, with a rapid cycle rate. Put simply, metal hammered between a planishing hammer's members gets pounded, often. The force of that pounding is adjustable by varying either the air pressure supplied to the device, the length of the hammer's stroke, or both.

As autobody tools, the original planishing hammers were pretty poor because they stretched metal badly. However, some genius figured out that if you mount a planishing hammer on a stand, and supply a foot control for its air supply, you have a device that is capable of stretching and forming metal very quickly. Modern planishing hammers vary from being very inexpensive tools that use muffled zip guns to drive their hammers, to being very precise and somewhat expensive tools that are easier to control, and quite predictable. Again, somewhere on that continuum, there may be a planishing hammer that fits your needs. These tools can do forming very quickly and without roughing up a surface too badly.

This high-end planishing hammer offers considerable precision and controllability. It is capable of roughing out and moving much metal very quickly. Unlike mechanical power hammers and English wheels, planishing hammers should not be used for finishing operations.

BUMPING TO MOVE THE METAL THE RIGHT WAY

Bumping is the heavy lifting in most autobody repair work. Its tools and techniques also have application to many fabrication projects. To be sure, bumping is not always the heavy lifting in body work. There are repair jobs that begin on frame machines, or with body-pulling posts—even heavier lifting than bumping—that are then followed by bumping operations. And some body-metal fabrications never employ bumping. Those that do may have their heavy lifting beginnings in sheetmetal brakes, or on slip rolls, before any bumping techniques are applied to them.

The fact remains, bumping describes the group of actions that move metal with the likes of hammers and dollies, to push things pretty much into final shape. This does not mean that bumping operations, by their nature, require heavy hammering or prying with large tools. That may be the case but subtle approaches are also possible.

In this regard, let's consider a large area of damage to a low- to medium-crown panel; say, a single impact at one point that deforms 70 percent of the area of a relatively flat

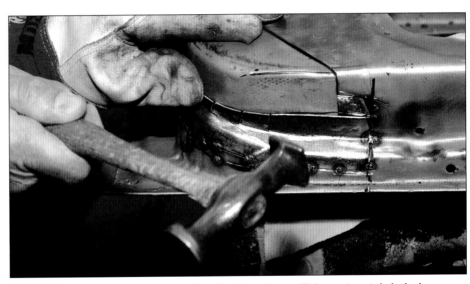

Bumping means to shape metal to final contours. This rust patch is being shaped and bumped into final position so that welding it in can be finished. Note the use of a square-faced hammer to work up against an edge.

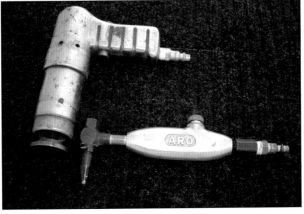

These pneumatic tools illustrate the gap between subtle work and violent assault on sheetmetal. The fender gun (top left) is more likely to do harm than good. The percussion hammer (bottom right) can slowly persuade small areas of metal to move a few thousandths of an inch.

door or quarter panel. It may look terrible because so much metal is displaced. However, to a seasoned metal worker, it may be possible to return 95 percent or more of the damaged area to its original contours with a couple of very undramatic and uncomplicated moves. Sometimes, most of this kind of damage can be pulled out with a suction device, or driven out with one, or a few, well-aimed blows with a rubber mallet.

Unfortunately, it is just as possible that attempting to remove this kind of damage with those approaches will be unsuccessful. It may even inflict further and more serious damage to a panel by creating ridges, V-channels, and minor upsets. The outcome depends on the skill and judgment of the metal worker.

In this case, the original shape, thickness, and hardness of the panel; the depth and configuration of the damage to it; any supporting structure behind it; and the specific nature of the tools and maneuvers employed to remove the damage determine whether the action fails or succeeds. In other words, simple approaches to bumping metal require keen judgments. A rubber hammer, used inappropriately, can cause almost as much damage as a metal hammer.

One scheme for damage removal that never fails is described and illustrated in Chapter 3. It involves analyzing how damage occurred, and removing it in the reverse order of that sequence. What never works is simply banging against what seems to be high metal, and hoping that by doing so, everything will come out alright. That approach will produce additional and severe damage, in the form of additional deformations with upsets and stretches, galore.

At first glance, working with what almost amounts to a blunt pick hammer, over a shot bag, seems to be metal finishing. However, the hammer is being used to change a contour in the metal, not just a surface irregularity. That, by definition, is bumping.

Another bumping secret is to work firmly but gently. Usually, using the least possible force and impact, and applying it incrementally, is the best approach. If you swing a hammer too hard, or pry metal too far, you will be on the road to creating problems that are larger than the ones you started with. Think before you strike. Always consider possible alternatives to what may seem to be the obvious approach to removing damage.

As you fight the tendency to just flail at damaged metal with big, nasty tools, it is often important to remember to back up what you are hitting or prying, whether your tool is a hammer, dolly, or pry. Whatever you are hammering is attached to other metal. As you drive it, you are driving that other metal. This is how bad body workers add unwanted upsets and stretches to initial damage. It is also critical to hit metal at the right angle. A ridge can be hammered or pushed up or down from many angles. When you stop to

think about it, some are much more corrective and less destructive than others. It pays to take the time to think about this before you swing into action.

Backing up metal as you hammer and/or pry on it usually saves you considerable grief. Hammering off-dolly, or with a dolly, or other backing surface supporting the area around where you are hammering, is usually desirable, unless you intend to stretch metal. Using soft backings often works well. These include rubber-clad dollies, dollies temporarily faced with a soft material like corrugated cardboard, hand-held shot bags, and blocks of soft wood.

Using the right impact tools, tools with the right contacting surfaces, is another way to move metal without damaging it. Rubber, plastic, and rawhide hammers have a definite place in metal bumping operations. If a surface will yield to these tools, it is often a good idea to use them. If not, then harder tools are required. When hammering a

This combination, a soft rubber mallet and a corrugated cardboard backing, is about as mild as it gets. You won't knock down any ridges this way, but you may correct a small defect without creating a bigger one.

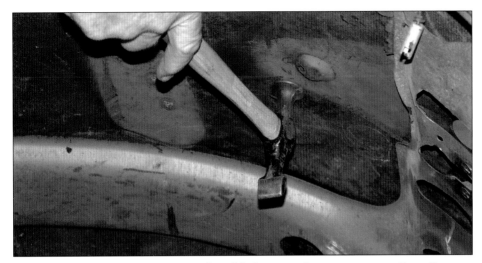

Even from the back, you can see that this hammer has more crown than the reverse crown on the metal that it is hitting. This is necessary, or the hammer face's outer edges would deform the metal while its center would fail to reach it.

Sometimes, you can make special tools that greatly speed work and improve uniformity and quality for specific bumping jobs. This little die is used to back up hammering the end of a rib into a proper and consistent round or spear shape.

crowned surface, a hammer with a fairly low crown probably works best for most purposes because it distributes hammering force over a wide area, and minimizes denting damage. However, dead-flat hammer faces have limited application to this work. Each different situation requires its own, appropriate, hammer crown. There is no single hammer that does it all.

When working on reverse-crown surfaces, a hammer must have more crown than the surface on which it is used, or its edges will imprint the metal, without actually contacting it at the hammer's center. Square-faced hammers are great for working up to edges, but should not be used in other situations because their corners can cause damage to reverse-crown configurations.

When you hammer against a reverse-crown area, both on-dolly and off-dolly, or against any other unyielding backup surface, the crown of the support surface should be greater than that of the metal. If the backing is held against a convex area, its crown should be chosen for the purpose intended. For example, if you want to stretch metal, you select more crown in your backing than if you do not want to stretch metal. In the case of dollies, these tools usually offer many different crowns in a single tool. With about half a dozen different dollies, you should be equipped with just about every crown and configuration that you will ever need. On some occasions, you may want to create a custom shape to hammer against for a particular purpose or situation. Cutting such a shape out of wood, or making it out of metal is often useful.

Hammering against either of these spoons greatly lessens the chance of a stray hammer blow damaging the panel. Placing a spoon or pry between your hammer and the metal spreads its force and averages its blow onto a broader surface area.

The other major category of bumping tools is prying bars and spoons. These helpful devices come in an almost limitless variety of sizes and shapes, and have specific and general uses. Prying can be difficult to control and is used primarily where access problems prevent direct hammering approaches. For example, when metal that you need to work on is directly behind substructure. Some pries are twisted to move metal, while others are levered or hammered.

When you hammer on a broad pry, you are really using it as a body spoon. Spoons, and pries used as spoons, are employed to address areas where access is a problem, or where it is desirable to spread hammering force over a wide area of metal. That last case is very important. In situations that require the minor movement of a broad area of metal, a spoon will distribute a hammer's force to accomplish that kind of application. Hammering on spoons is often overlooked. It is a very clean and effective approach to the problem of moving large amounts of surface over small, incremental distances.

Beyond the rules covering the best ways to move metal (without unacceptably upsetting or stretching it), and the rules of sequence for attacking complex damage, each metal worker finds his or her own comfort level in the choices of procedures and tools to get jobs done. For example, if a situation requires more hammering pressure than can be generated in a small space, it makes perfect sense to use a dolly as your hammer. That might be the case when hammering out the side of a fender from behind, when it has been pushed in, and where there is insufficient room to swing a hammer.

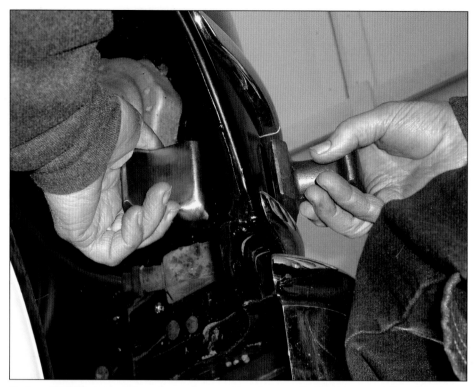

Dolly-off-dolly is one way to make a swing in very limited space. The dimple removal that is the object of this exercise works, because the hitting dolly's face has more crown than the panel's inside.

Let's take that case a bit further. If you are working inside a fender to hammer down a ridge, and using a dolly as your impact tool, you run the enormous risk of missing the exact spot that you are trying to hammer out, or of hitting it hard enough to further damage it. You just don't have the control over a dolly used that way that you would have over a hammer.

Here are two solutions to that problem: One is to position a spoon on the apex of the ridge, and then drive the spoon against it with a dolly. This would allow more accurate positioning of the force than would be possible with a direct dolly hit. It would also spread the force along the ridge, which would improve the odds on a favorable outcome. The second solution, which takes skill and practice, is to use two dollies, and hammer carefully with them on opposite sides of the panel, in opposite directions. Of course, they must be offset from each other for this to work.

In any specific situation, there are almost always numerous ways to approach a bumping task or job. As you gain experience, you learn which ones work best for you, and you will probably create a few new ones, as you go along.

The next step in working metal is metal finishing, the fine adjustment of surfaces to near-dimensional perfection. It is very important that bumping operations return or bring surfaces very close to correct positions before metal finishing measures are applied. Good metal workers know that a little time spent getting bumping right can save significant time in metal finishing.

The Case of Bumping the Run Down Spare Tire Cover

The panel in front was dragged and flattened. The one in the rear is in near perfect shape, and can be used as a model for reshaping the damaged panel. The Door County Civil Defense Auxiliary Police sticker on the good panel is probably unique.

We will never know who ran down this Triumph TR-3 spare tire cover. But my friend, Herb Statz, who worked with me to fix it, had a first-class idea for bumping out most of the damage to it in a few easy moves.

The cover had been dragged and flattened by the time that we received it, and the license plate part of the panel was severely pushed in and leveled. Since the damage was too locked-in to remove with rubber, plastic, or rawhide mallets, I reached for one of our large dollies, to begin bashing out the worst of it.

Herb stopped me before I struck with the dolly, saying, "Hey, let me try something." Then, using some scrap wood and some large C-clamps, he rigged a small metal table as a lever press. In a couple of moves, he had the panel pushed back to its original depth, and pretty well straightened out. He had to tighten the levering clamp a couple of times, and he hit the wooden ram board with a rubber hammer a few times, for added persuasion. As he tightened and hammered, he levered up one edge of the panel with a soft pry. In just a few minutes he had the panel bumped into pretty good shape.

Next, he checked the profile shape of the tire cover against a template that he had made out of cardboard from a good spare tire cover, and found it bent and warped in a couple of places. Since the original accident and our lever press bumping ministrations had not caused any upsets or stretches in the panel, a little careful bumping with a dead-blow plastic mallet returned it to its original format, with no further actions needed.

I suspect that if Herb had not intervened, convincing me to use his lever press method instead of my big-hammer approach, we would have spent a much longer time trying to straighten out that panel.

Using some old wood scraps and a couple of large C-clamps, it took Herb Statz just a few minutes to devise and implement this makeshift lever press. With a little help from a rubber hammer and a plastic pry, he quickly restored the panel's basic shape, with no collateral damage.

With the basic damage repaired, Herb made a cardboard model of both sides of the good panel, to compare shapes. He then corrected the areas of the damaged panel that were warping it.

Some of the straightening work was done with a dead-blow hammer on the panel's back, and more was done to reshape its edges. Herb's technique for removing the worst damage minimized the panel's warping.

METAL FINISHING

In the metal finishing stage of body work, final panel contour adjustments are made and most surface defects are removed. Making a final correction to the contour of a sectioned door is shown here. Note that Blaine is working with his sightline aligned with the panel's surface.

and shaving metal off them, to make small dimensional and curvature changes.

For those reasons, I think that metal finishing is the most critical stage of this work. It may lack the visually dramatic outcomes of bumping, but when it is done well, it is the part of metal work that produces much of the wow factor in great autobody repairs and fabrications.

One copasetic aspect of metal finishing is that the tools used to accomplish it are refreshingly few, simple, and relatively inexpensive. Of course, there is an offsetting downside to that proposition: You have to use those tools correctly to get good results, and that is not always easy. This chapter focuses on the correct use of metal finishing tools—body files, pick hammers, and disc sanders—to achieve great results.

Indicating, Feeling and Other Human Tools to Determine Panel Surfaces

Metal finishing is the critical step in preparing metal for painting. It occurs between the bumping stage, where metal is hammered, pried, pushed, or pulled into shape, and the filling stage, where very small defects in metal-finished surfaces are filled, just before panels are painted. By its nature, metal finishing is finer work than bumping, yet offers more latitude for correction than the filling stage that follows it. In metal finishing, you can still modify surfaces by moving them

If you need to change the contour of a panel, it should be done before

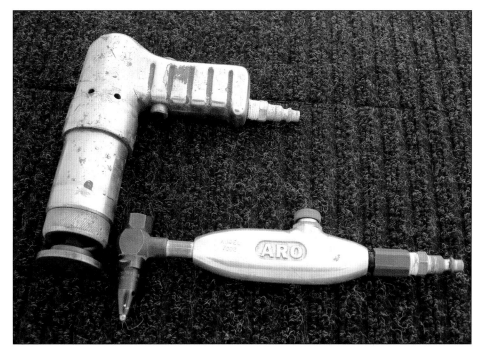

These two tools illustrate the difference between bumping and metal finishing. The pneumatic body hammer (top left) has a 1-inch stroke, for moving metal and removing ridges. The pneumatic percussion hammer (bottom right) can pick light metal a few thousandths of an inch in metal finishing work.

case with character lines of various configurations (for example, 1960s phony louvers in some Chrysler products' rear fender flanks).

It is this feature, the smoothness of crowns and combination crowns, that metal finishing must preserve. It also must level minor surface deviations, in the form of small bumps and depressions. Metal finishing is the last appeal in the matter of panel crown continuity. It is also very close to the last appeal in the matter of panel smoothness.

Unlike bumping, where you can sense surfaces visually, and by feeling them, metal finishing works at a finer level. It works at the edge of the ability of the human sense of touch to sense deviations, and beyond the capabilities of unaided visual inspection of unpainted metal surfaces to define consistency. The solution to

metal finishing operations begin. But if you need to make sure that a contour is perfectly consistent in very small dimensions, and that it is contained in a nearly perfect surface, metal finishing is where you get these results.

Any crown or combination of crowns in a panel must flow smoothly—by itself, or as one crown into another. If the requirements of practical matters, like covering up vehicle mechanisms, or opening doors, requires a panel surface to be discontinuous in crown, well, that is why stylists employ creases, character lines, and the other discontinuous or angular ploys and styling components of their trade. Sometimes, I suppose, they do these things just for fun. What autobody panels do not have is irregular and illogical interruptions to the flow of crowns, unless such features are consistent and repeated, as can be the

Body files come in many sizes, shapes, tooth counts, and configurations. These are unusual, special-purposes files. None of them are currently available, but they do show up at swap meets and auctions. There are situations where they work much better than flat files.

exceeding those human limits is to find deviations with files and disc sanders. Once these are located, metal finishing procedures work to correct them. In the case of low spots, the deviations are raised with hammers, usually pick hammers, and leveled with more filing or disc sanding. If the deviations are bumps (projections), they are filed or sanded to level.

These are very fine adjustments, involving as little as 1 or 2 thousandths of an inch. In a 20-, 21-, or 22-gauge panel, there is not much thickness to file or sand off, without rendering that area of the panel dangerously thin. The point is: You must have a panel correct and level before metal finishing is a reasonable approach to achieving final contours and smoothness.

The first metal finishing tool that you should learn to use is the 14-inch body file. It is a masterpiece of functional tool design, evolved to perfection over many years of development. Used correctly and in moderation, it can do wonderful things for you. Foremost among these things is filing off high spots and revealing low spots in panels. It does this by slightly cutting away surface metal above low spots, and leaving them visually obvious as slight voids in an otherwise continuous, filed, shiny surface.

Once low spots are located, they can be raised with hammers and/or pick hammers, and re-filed. This process is repeated until no low spots are revealed, at which point the panel surface is level. However, it cannot be repeated *ad infinitum*, because each filing cycle removes metal and makes a panel thinner. You need to accomplish leveling in three or fewer filing applications, and that third one should be very light.

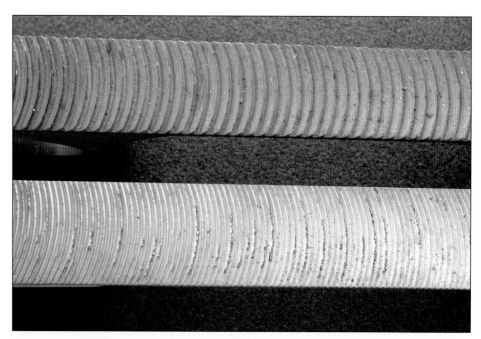

The coarse file (top) has a 6-per-inch tooth count, while the fine file (bottom) sports an amazing 16 teeth per inch. Most body files are in the 8-tooth-per-inch range, ideal for most jobs. Finer files than that are for very fine finishing jobs and for working on aluminum panels.

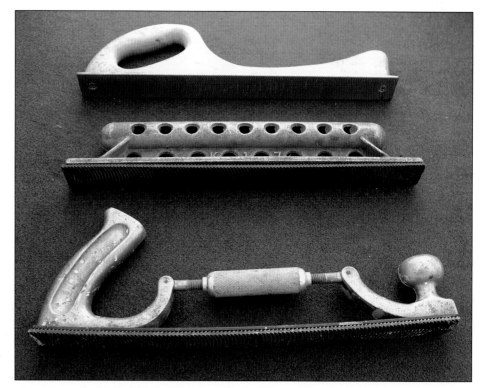

These are the basic file holders that I use. They offer comfortable gripping surfaces and can be rocked, toe to heal, naturally. The flexible holder (bottom) offers adjustable contour, from mild concave to mild convex, and is the most usable holder for general work.

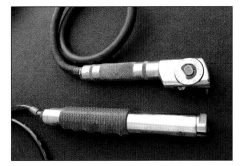

Pick hammering takes skill and practice. Some inventions purport to make it easier. These pneumatic picks are placed against low spots and triggered with foot valves. True, you don't have to hit an invisible spot from afar with them, but they are difficult to locate and hard to control.

Always keep in mind that the object of metal finishing is to achieve correct contours and smooth metal with a minimum of material removal. Beyond that, try to leave as little need for body filler—plastic or metal—as is possible. After metal finishing, it is best to use little or no filler.

Filing Done Right

All 14-inch, flat, body files come in a variety of tooth counts—between 6 and 16 teeth per inch. The finer files tend to cut more smoothly, but to remove less metal in a stroke than the coarser ones, making them somewhat easier to use. They are intended for finishing work. A body file with 8 teeth per inch is good for general metal finishing work.

Although it is possible to sharpen dull files several times, it is difficult to find file sharpening services these days, so it is best to try to keep your files sharp for as long as possible. One trick to accomplish this is to brush their teeth lightly with turpentine, from time to time. This retards rust and lubricates the cutting action. It

The proper motion with a body file is forward, away from you, and slightly sideways. As the file is moved, your down force on it should be shifted from its front to its back. You should always file toward areas of lower crown.

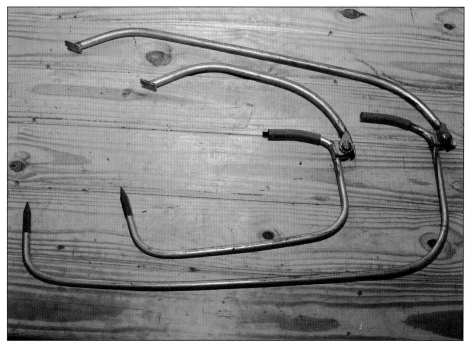

From the gallery of great ideas that just don't work, I offer spring-loaded, automatic Bulls-eye picks. Supposedly, you locate the target anvil over a low spot, and squeeze the handle. Bingo, raised metal. But most situations lack room to fit these clunky devices, and they never strike accurately enough to work.

The Sanding-Picking-Filing-Sanding Metal Finishing Routine

The repair of two small dents in a 1948 Chrysler decklid illustrates the basic sanding-picking-filing-sanding sequence that is used in metal finishing. This process indicates low spots, grinds off high spots, and ensures crown continuity in panels. It is also used to raise and repair small dents.

The first step was to disc sand the paint off the panel, in the area of the two small dents that are the subjects of this repair. Since the rest of the panel was undamaged, and because our plan called for chemically stripping the panel after the dents were repaired, we disc sanded it only in an area that included the two spots. This would allow us to check crown continuity in that area, after we made necessary repairs.

The sanded area revealed the extent of each dent. It was about what we expected, and well within the range of what it is possible to repair by lifting up and filing metal. Our first step was to pick up the smaller spot with a fairly blunt pick hammer. The larger spot was first driven up with a small, highly crowned body hammer, which reduced its size by more than half of its diameter. Then, we used a blunt pick hammer to finish lifting its center.

At this point, the panel was filed with a flat 8-tooth-per-inch body file, held in a slight curvature in a flexible file holder. The first hammering and picking operation

1 *Sanding the paint off this decklid revealed the extent of the two medium-sized dents that were the reason for the repair. Both were perfect candidates for hammering up from the other side, and metal finishing, because both offered good access for that procedure.*

2 *The smaller dent was driven up with a blunt pick to raise its deepest area and, at the same time, to slightly raise the entire area around it. Picking has to be done with the intent to completely level entire damage spots.*

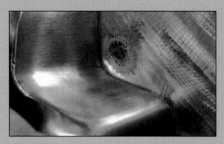

4 *We used a dolly that wrapped around two sides of the dent to back up our hammering. This controlled the movement of the panel area just adjacent to the dent. Hammering was done off-dolly, and the dolly was shifted from time to time around the dent.*

3 *The areas around and between the dents were sanded to bare metal, so that the repair could account for the crown in the entire repair area. The dent on the left is more complex than the one on the right.*

moved most of the metal to level. A little more picking and filing followed. This revealed that the damage was completely removed, and that the panel crown around and between the two dents was consistent and correct.

5 *After the first picking operations, the repair area was filed with a flat body file mounted in a flexible holder. Most of the metal came level at this point, but some additional picking and re-filing were required to completely remove the dents, and to give the panel a consistent contour.*

7 *The filed panel looked like this. Note the filing scratches in the repair area. This repair required so little filing that there was question whether the repaired panel had any badly thinned areas or spots.*

It remained to disc sand the entire area around and between the dents with an 80-grit disc, and then to scuff the area with an 80-grit DA random-orbital sander. This achieved a surface that was smooth, and that had good tooth for primer adhesion.

6 *The repair area was now smoothed with a disc sander, loaded with 80-grit paper. This removed most of the scratches resulting from the paint removal and filing operations. Note the almost flat position of the sanding disc for this procedure.*

8 *After a scuff sanding with 80-grit paper in a dual action (DA) orbital sander, the repaired surface was smooth and had good tooth to hold primer. The completed repair is shown here.*

tends to double the life of a new or sharpened file, and helps you achieve the proper smooth-gliding motion.

Body files are held in file holders made of wood or metal. I tend to use both types. There are also specialty files, like laterally concave and convex, and lengthwise convex ("banjo") files. As well, there are specialty file holders for particular jobs. The most useful general-purpose holder is a flexible metal rig that allows you to custom contour files by adjusting the holder. This is important for working with different crowns, and in some situations where access is a problem.

The instructions for using body files are based on time-tested methods of filing, and are designed to optimize both revealing depressions in metal, and leveling it. The first rule is to always file toward the flattest crown in a panel. This reveals low spots as voids in filed metal, while preventing the file from skipping over features of the panel, like crown changes, as might happen if you fail to file toward low-crown areas.

Your filing stroke should use as much of your file's length, in contact with metal, as is practical. As you file, there are two motions that should be used, beyond pushing the file forward and away from you.

The first is to slide it sideways, about 15 to 20 percent of the distance that you push it forward. This must be done smoothly, or gouging may occur. If you see tooth gouges in the metal, you are doing something wrong. The second motion amounts to a subtle shift of force. It is to rock the file from its front (toe) to its back (heal) as you push it away from you, forward and sideways.

Since, as a child, you doubtless mastered the trick of rubbing your tummy in a circular motion with one hand, while patting the top of your head with the other hand, the filing motions that I describe here should come to you as, well, kid's stuff. If they don't, hours of practice certainly helps to fill any gaps. This combined filing motion is important and well worth mastering. Once you do, it should quickly become natural.

The sideways file shift should be alternated from one side to the other. Say that you start by filing forward, and shifting your file to the left. You may repeat this stroke a few times. Then, you should begin filing the same area to the right, from the point where your earlier file strokes ended. In this way, you cover an area of maybe 1 foot x 3 to 5 inches, always filing toward areas of lower crown.

The Art of Pick Hammering

Here is one of those confidence builders. The first time that you try to use a pick hammer, you will, almost certainly, make a complete mess of it. I know that I did. This is because once their function is explained, people expect pick hammers to be miracle tools that naturally find low spots, and apply just enough hit to raise them to the perfect level for finish filing. Sadly, to date, no such pick hammer has been invented.

The first problem is that without some experience in the matter, it is frustratingly difficult to hit exactly the right spot with a pick hammer. That spot is usually on the other side of the panel from the one at which you are looking, so you are hammering toward yourself. The second problem is that people tend to choose pick hammers that are far too sharp for what they are trying to accomplish. I suppose that these predictably bad hammer choices are

made because sharp looks purposeful and sexy. After all, stiletto heels and sharp features of the human anatomy are said to convey sexual appeal and power. However, in pick hammers, very sharp items are more useful for assault than for serious body work. If very spiked pick-hammers have any good application, it is for very fine work; and then, only in the hands of very highly skilled and seasoned metal workers.

That first problem, locating the place to raise metal, amounts to translating where you know a low spot is from the side of the metal that you can see, to the one that you cannot. There are body workers who do this by hitting tentatively with their pick hammers from the backs of panels, and sensing the hit on the other

side with their fingers, until it is in the right place. Another locating technique is to follow the hammer under or behind the panel and sense where it is located in relation to the side that you can see. This works for locating where to hit metal up. However, it leaves the problem of hitting exactly the spot that you have identified. You might be amazed at how lost that spot can become, between nesting a hammer on it, and then swinging the hammer away from it and then toward it again. Several short, light strokes work best for picking. A short stroke presents less chance of missing your spot. And if you do miss it, a short stroke does less damage than a more powerful one.

After you gain pick hammer experience, you will be able to find

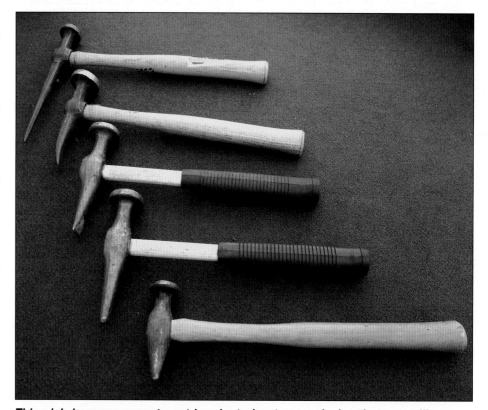

This pick-hammer assortment has just about every device that you will ever need for picking work. The sharp, pointed one (top) has limited application, mostly for very fine tuning operations. The bottom three picks cover most work to raise small low spots.

the right spot on the other side of a panel fairly quickly, as a result of increasing your hand/eye coordination. It is still a good idea to give the identified spot a light tap and feel its location through the metal, to confirm that it is correct. You will learn to see the metal rising each time that you hit it with your pick hammer. This allows you to make small adjustments in your hammering position, as you monitor your results from the other side of the panel. Always remember that you are trying to move metal just a few thousandths of an inch, and that you can correct some inaccuracies in your picking in the filing stage that follows it. Many small, incremental hammer strokes do the job far better than a few heavy ones, and involve much less risk to the panel.

Once you get the hang of picking metal up, it is easy to get carried away, and to try to raise it to Himalayan heights. This is unnecessary and it is destructive. To level metal, you need to pick up low spots to a point just above panel height. This allows you to file it perfectly level. If you raise metal beyond that point, when you file, you need to remove more metal than is necessary to get things level. Always stop picking just after you achieve level, and let your body file or sander do the rest. You make this determination by running your finger tips over the spot that you are picking. It is a good idea to put a smooth, clean rag or tissue under your finger tips when you do this. That prevents the oils and moisture on them from making your fingers grip, drag, or grab on the metal as you feel it, and gives you a much better sense of the topography of what you are feeling.

Left to right: 9- and 7-inch electric disc sanders. Right: a 7-inch pneumatic disc sander. Electric sanders are preferred for metal finishing, because they have more torque. Note the warped disc on the middle sander. It will cause chattering and skips if its disc is not changed for a flat one.

The Disc Sanding Alternative

After you have mastered the techniques of using body files and pick hammers to level metal, the brave new world of disc sanding awaits your discovery. Disc sanding offers an alternative to body filing, but comes with several cautions and warnings. Disc sanding tends to be much faster than body filing and, for that reason, it can damage a panel much faster than filing it. The degree of difficulty in using a body file or disc sander is about the same. Which technique you choose is largely a matter of personal preference. Many body metal workers use both techniques, each in specific situations or in sequence.

Disc sanders come in various powers, speeds, and disc sizes. Most body work is done with 7-inch units, with either rubber or fiber backings behind the abrasive discs. When disc sanders are used for paint removal, an open-coat abrasive disc is preferred. When they are employed in metal finishing, closed-coat, resin-bonded abrasives are best. The 36- and 50-grit sizes are appropriate for metal finishing with a disc sander, while 50-, 60-, and 80-grit sizes have applications for the final smoothing of metal, after it is leveled.

The first phase of using a disc sander for metal finishing is the discovery phase. It involves disc sanding metal surfaces so that the sander skips over depressed areas in a way that reveals their presence.

Proper disc sanding technique, in the discovery phase of the

The final procedure in metal finishing is to disc polish the metal with 50-, 60-, or 80-grit abrasives. This gives it a sheen that makes it easy to spot dimensional deviations. I always dull that finish with a DA orbital sander, for better paint adhesion.

operation, is to hold the abrasive disc against the metal with moderate pressure, tilted about 15 degrees away from it, and toward you, so that the sanding disc's edge bends to contact and cut a narrow swath of surface, say 1 to 1¼ inch wide. The sander is moved sideways, and held mostly laterally flat to the panel, with a very small amount of tilt toward the direction of sideways travel. At the end of each lateral stroke, as the sander's direction is reversed, it is moved the width of its cut swath, up or down. When the sander's lateral direction is reversed, it should be lifted slightly to avoid dwelling too long on the area where the reversal of direction takes place. You also can accomplish this by untriggering and retriggering the

sander, as you reverse its direction, but that is clumsier than slightly lifting it to reduce the pressure on its contact edge. When travel resumes, in the opposite direction from the just completed stroke, the leading edge of the sander should be raised, just slightly, in the new direction of travel, as it was before.

It is critical that the sander always be in motion on the metal. While it is running, it can never stay in one spot. If it does, and if you are lucky, you will only overheat the metal where it dwells, with a very good chance of gouging it. If you are not lucky, you can burn through the metal. A telltale dark bluing of the metal surface under the disc contact patch will warn you that you are burning the metal.

Disc sanding for discovery should leave a series of swirl marks, or shiny paths. Any voids or dull spots in these paths are low spots. High spots may leave visible low voids around them. However, if they are not very high—not high enough to need to be hammered down—they will be ground off by the disc sander as it passes over them, thereby ceasing to be a problem.

The cycle of leveling with a disc sander and pick hammer is the same as for a pick hammer and body file. Sanding identifies low spots and removes most high spots. Hammering, as necessary and preferably with a low-crown hammer, drives down the high spots that are not removed by sanding. Hammering, usually with a pick hammer, picks up low areas. Occasionally, when low areas are relatively large, they need to be driven up with a highly crowned hammer. As with filing, the hammering and sanding operations are repeated until the panel is level and continuous. Also, as with filing, disc sanding removes material and cannot be repeated to the point of excessively reducing the thickness of a panel.

The 36- and/or 50-grit abrasives used in the discovery and leveling phases of disc sanding leave surfaces that are too rough to complete the metal finishing phase of panel work, although 50-grit abrasives are somewhat usable for this purpose. Before metal finishing is complete, the metal must be smoothed for painting. Although filling follows metal finishing, it is bad practice to leave final smoothing for that stage of this work. It should be the last part of the metal finishing operation. That means that when metal finishing is completed, there should be few, or no, ridges or sanding marks that need filling. It also means that surfaces are not so smooth that they lack the tiny nooks and crannies that help paint to mechanically adhere to metal. The 50-grit abrasive disc will accomplish this, but 60- and 80-grit discs are better bets.

In the final smoothing phase of metal finishing, your disc sander is operated somewhat differently than in the discovery and leveling phases. For this operation, it is best to run your disc sander at right angles to the direction that you sanded in the discovery and leveling phases of metal finishing. Your sander should be held as flat to the panel as possible, producing as much disc contact as possible. This creates an averaging effect, and avoids any likelihood of gouging the panel, as might happen if only the outer edge of the disc contacted it.

A good disc cutter is an important disc sanding accessory, one that anyone who uses a disc sander should own. A disc cutter is used to trim the edges off discs used for sanding paint or for discovery sanding. It removes the spent outer inch, or so, from the disc, allowing the good abrasive that is left on the disc to be used. It would be a shame to throw away a disc with only 30 percent of its usable area consumed. A disc cutter allows you to avoid doing this.

The second use of a disc cutter is to allow you to modify a round disc by cutting a symmetrical and balanced rounded-side-and-rounded-point pattern into it. You can do the same thing with a knife or a pair of scissors, but a disc cutter lets you do it faster and more consistently. The object is to cut a shape into a disc that has from three to six apexes. I like a pentagon-shaped disc best, but tastes vary in this matter. The points between the rounded sides also

should be slightly rounded, to keep them from tearing apart too easily in use.

In the final stages of metal finish sanding, these cut, non-round discs should be used exclusively. The reason is simple: When you use them, you do not have a consistently round sanding disc that is always presenting the same edge to the metal that you are sanding. A round disc can quickly cut a groove into metal, particularly when it is moved into an area like the transition from crown to reverse crown. In such an area of changing crown, it may be presented to the metal at very sharp angles that cause its edge to dig in. Damage can occur

in a fraction of a second. However, a shaped, sided disc presents different radii of its shape to the metal as it spins against it, greatly reducing the chance of gouging it.

When metal finishing is completed, your work should have a consistent, silvery appearance, with curves that remain consistent as you move your sight line past them. Enjoy that sight because, after you perform some filling to remove the few minor surface defects that may remain, your work will move on to finishing or refinishing. After that, you will probably never have the opportunity to admire that particular metal surface again.

This disc cutter has two functions. One is to trim off the outer 3/4-inch from used discs, so that new abrasive is exposed for general disc sanding. Its other function is to cut discs into various shapes, with rounded sides and corners, for final surface-smoothing sanding.

WELDING BODY METAL

Automotive sheetmetal and structural welding are vast topics, and it is not possible to give them anything approaching complete coverage here. This chapter concentrates on some of the fundamentals of welding sheetmetal sections, and on a few ploys that that may make this type of welding easier for you to perform, while producing superior results.

It is important to note that welding thin metal sections is very different from welding bridge girders or thick plates. For one thing, welding thick metal pieces rarely involves having to worry about heat distortion and material warping. Thick materials resist distortion due to their bulk, and to their tendency to act as their own heat sinks. The main considerations in that kind of welding are penetration, bead deposit, bead shape, and strength. Concerns like welding through base materials and creating drop-outs are remote. In non-structural panel welding, these issues become paramount, while strength is usually secondary.

You may have great skills for and success with stick welding thick sections, but these do not translate into

In the last 35 years, MIG welding has revolutionized how we join autobody metal. It is fast and efficient, and it provides good quality joints. Oh, that little screwdriver between the fingers of the welder's left hand; read on, and find out why he keeps it there.

gas or electric sheetmetal welding mastery. The skill set for this work is very different, and must be developed separately. If you are familiar with torch and/or electric welding, that may help you to learn sheetmetal welding. But aside from the fact that all of these forms of welding involve carrying a puddle of molten metal down a seam, and fusing it to the metal on either side of the seam, there is no automatic transfer of skills from heavy section welding to sheetmetal welding.

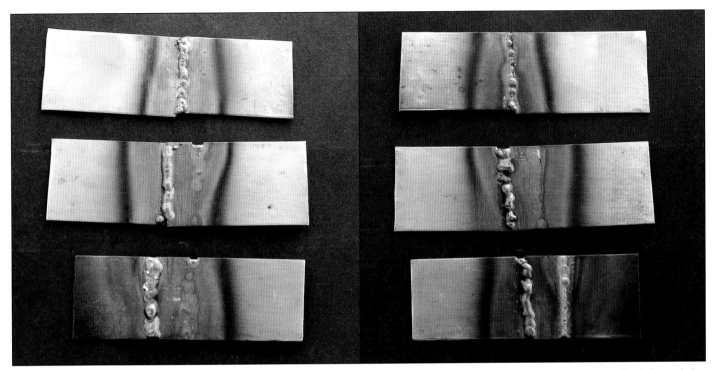

Here are examples (top to bottom) of a butt joint, lap joint, and offset lap joint. The fronts are shown on the left and the backs to their right. These are realistic examples of shop welding done at average levels of quality.

There is one commonality between stick or torch welding thick sections and welding sheetmetal. In both of them, a serviceable weld often, but not always, has a good-looking, even, penetrated, and uniform appearance. Unfortunately, most finished sheetmetal welds are unnoticed because, very quickly after their creations, they are almost invariably ground off and covered over with the likes of filler, primer, and paint. While the skill needed to perform good sheetmetal welds may equal, or surpass, the skill applied to visible welds, like those on motorcycle frames, you are far less likely to attain the fame, accolades, and downright glory with a crowd of the adoring that the makers of those motorcycle welds receive. Still, you will see your raw sheetmetal welds, before they are ground and painted over, so you will have the opportunity to briefly appreciate your great work.

Types of Joints

Panel welding was discussed briefly in Chapter 3. Let's now look at this topic in greater detail.

Welded joints for bodywork fall into three categories: butt, lap, and offset lap. While it would sound democratic to say something like, "…each of these joints has its place in panel work, and each is a good approach," that would not be accurate. Butt joints are the gold standard of welded panel joints. The other two types of jointure, particularly lap joints, are sometimes desirable. This usually is the case when they are used to duplicate factory lap joints. I suppose that it is true that butt joints are more difficult for novice welders to master, but once you learn how to weld them, they are not hard to achieve with good MIG or TIG welding equipment.

Butt joints are made with the edges of the sections butted end to end, against each other, with some amount of gap between them, to provide for expansion during welding. Lap joints are made by overlapping small amounts of metal, and welding the exposed edges of each section to the other, on one, or on both sides. This, of course, creates a double thickness of metal at the joint overlap, something that can be difficult to hide without using excessive amounts of filler.

Offset lap joints require the use of an offsetting tool to flange the edge of one of the sections to be joined. The other section edge is then slipped under the flanged area, and welded to it. This creates the appearance of continuous metal because the double thickness of the lap joint exists on only one side of the joined sections, and, naturally, it is that side that is chosen as the back side, and, therefore, hidden. Again, in offset lap joints, the weld is sometimes made on both edges of the lapped metal to seal the joint.

There are multiple problems with lap and offset lap joints. One is that you may have to weld the joints twice, if you want to seal them. Another approach is to weld the outside (or visible side) of a lap or offset lap joint, and then seal the inner side of the joint with seam sealer. Sealing lap joints is critical to preventing corrosion from forming in the laps, where capillary action invites moisture and electrolytes in for a corrosion bash.

If you double weld these joints, that is, weld them at both seams, you must apply more than twice as much heat to them as you would with a butt joint. In lap welding, one or both welds involve welding an edge to a flat, and this requires more heat than is used to make a butt weld, end-to-end. That extra heat is an invitation to local distortion and panel warping. Another problem with lap joints is that they may later show themselves through filler and paint, as a panel experiences vibration cycles. It takes many miles for this to occur, if it does occur, but it is a haunting possibility. Finally, there is no advantage to using lap and offset lap joints, where situations do not mandate them, other than the misguided idea that they are easier to make than butt joints. The two exceptions are when you are duplicating a factory weld that was originally a lap joint, and when space and access considerations make butt welding undesirable, or impossible.

Butt joints usually return panels more closely to their original format than do the other two types of joints, and are simply the cleanest solution to the issues of laterally joining thin sections of sheetmetal. Certainly, when panel patching is the purpose of welding thin sections, butt joints are preferred.

Welding Smaller Pieces into Large Constructions

Sometimes large, complex constructions are welded up from smaller pieces. Many advanced practitioners of metal forming and fabricating tend to frown on this practice, preferring to make their fabrications from single pieces of stock metal. Still, it can be a useful approach, when limitations of your equipment and/or skills make single-piece fabrication impossible.

It is interesting to note that in the past, some OEM large panels were made from smaller pieces, welded together. While, for cost reasons, this practice is rare or extinct in modern volume produced light vehicles, it was common as recently as 15 years ago. Before that, the side framing panels of many cars were still welded up from as many as 20 separate pieces. That practice was replaced by stamping and roll-forming techniques that made it possible to form these large, complex structures as single pieces.

Early fenders were often fabricated out of more than one stamping. For example, the drop skirt edges of very early automobile fenders were riveted to the bodies of those fenders. Later some large panels, like fenders and hoods, were gas welded, brazed, or electrically welded out of two or three smaller stamped pieces.

When you have to fabricate a panel or structure that is too large or

Some common fixturing tools are shown holding small metal pieces. Left: locking pliers. Center top: magnets. Center bottom: standard Clecos (left) with both sides shown, and Cleco edge type clamp (right). Install tool is below them. Right top: thumb clamps. Right bottom: pressure-type edge clamps and install tool.

complex, or both, for you to form it from a single piece, always remember that, as a last resort, you can form parts of it and then join them.

Fixturing

Of the things that I really hate in life, there are three that stand out: 1) the sound of a horse pulling its hoof out of deep mud, 2) the smell of the inside of a Russian horse doctor's valise, and 3) trying to weld a moving target. It is that last one that I am usually able to avoid.

The way I avoid it is to properly fixture the pieces that are to be welded together. This means two things: providing and maintaining adequate fit-up gaps between them, and holding the pieces firmly in place for tack welding. Once you have done those things, you can tack weld attachments that maintain proper positioning and fit-up gaps for final welding.

There are many methods of fixturing pieces for welding. Which one you choose for your work depends partly on the situation and partly on your personal preference. For example, welding magnets might be adequate for holding a patch panel in place for tack welding, but are probably not the best approach to holding a whole rear-quarter section in position. Of the many fixturing methods, devices, and gadgets out there, the main ones are: locking pliers, welding magnets, edge clips, screw clamps, and various Cleco devices. Each of these represents a class of fixturing devices, and each comes in a great variety of styles, sizes, and configurations. Each also has application to most types of seams— butt, lap, and offset lap.

Locking pliers are often referred to by the name given to this tool by the

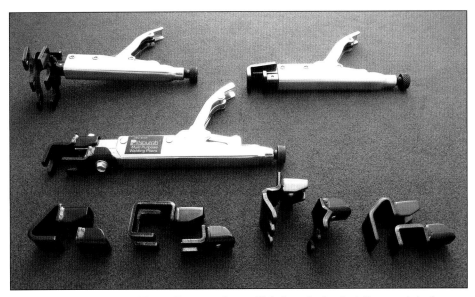

These specialized locking pliers are incredibly handy for holding metal pieces in place, prior to tack welding them. The right-angle configuration of the two sets (top) works in many tight spots. The interchangable jaw set (front) has five sets of interchangeable jaws.

company that first manufactured it, Vise-Grips. Locking pliers are terrific for holding pieces in alignment while tack welds are made. They come in angled, long-reach, and pivoting-end designs, and represent the first line of holding parts in place. Specialized locking pliers devices are also available for many specific purposes.

The main limitation on the use of locking pliers to hold metal in position for welding is the reach of their arms. They may work well for you, when your positioning needs require holding at 12 inches, or even 16 inches, from the nearest accessible edge of what you are welding. But even at that reach, locking pliers tend to be pretty bulky and cumbersome. Beyond that reach, other methods of fixturing must be employed.

Edge clips are limited to holding the edges of panels and patches, but have the advantages of being quick to apply and to remove, and of offering very little obstruction to or interference with adjacent parts.

Wing nut clips can be positioned anywhere in a butt joint, regardless of their depth from its edges. They work well on straight-line joints, and inherently maintain a consistent fit-up gap. However, they do not work along curved joints because they hold edges unacceptably far apart in that application. Still, if you are butt welding along a straight line, these inexpensive clips work impressively well.

Electric Welding

Many welding techniques apply to autobody work. Most of this welding is now electric, though gas welding is still sometimes used. MIG, TIG, and resistance (spot) welding are the main approaches covered here.

Stick Welding

This method was once used to join autobody panel metal, both in production and for repair. This practice involved using small-diameter, coated welding rods that were

Spot welds are not very strong individually, but in numbers they gain strength. The key to making good spot welds is getting the welding duration right, so as to not under-weld weak attachments or burn through with excessive weld times. Clean contact and mating surfaces are also critical.

specifically designed for sheetmetal work. Both AC and DC formats were employed. Stick welding sheetmetal required considerable skill, and yielded results that were often less than great. The main problem was that when stick welding was performed with the machines commonly associated with it, the process produced excessive heat for thin-section jointure, resulting in excessive dropout and distortion. The time required to finish stick welds in sheetmetal was excessive, by today's standards. This practice is obsolete.

Resistance or Spot Welding

This has been a mainstay of automotive construction since the 1930s. It uses no flux or filler, and is accomplished by applying a concentrated short circuit, and strong physical pressure, to a small spot on as many as three thicknesses of body metal to be joined. A combination of intense heat, created by maintaining a very-high-amperage short circuit at the point of the weld for a short interval,

and considerable squeezing pressure on the two outer surfaces of the weld area by the welding electrodes, melts the spot into a fusion weld. Spot welds are quick and easy to make, and reasonably neat and strong. Modern light vehicles depend on as many as 3,000 or 4,000 spot welds to hold their structures together. In recent

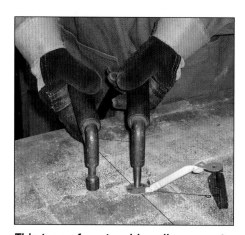

This type of spot welder allows you to make welds from one side of a panel. This can greatly ease access problems. It takes high electrode pressure and clean metal for this type of weld to work well.

years, car manufacturers sometimes supplement spot welds with adhesives and anti-corrosion treatments to add bonding strength, and to protect joints that are welded this way.

Some of the spot welders used in repair and restoration do not squeeze the weld area between two electrodes, but apply spot welding force and heat to one piece of metal that is grounded through the other piece to be joined to it. These devices are particularly handy where access to both sides of a spot weld area are difficult or impossible to achieve. There are also numerous attachments for MIG welders that mimic the strength, appearance, and configuration of resistance welds.

Another technique for duplicating the appearance and function of spot welds is button hole welding. This technique employs torch, MIG, or even TIG welding to join two sections together, one on top of the other, by welding through the top thickness of metal and into the surface of the metal under it. This must be accomplished without overheating the whole area, and ending up with an unsightly and embarrassing hole through both pieces. One trick to avoid this is to do a pseudo-button-hole weld by drilling a hole through the top section, and welding its rim to the metal under it.

Spot welds are often vulnerable to corrosion because the places where they are used are prone to attracting moisture between the joined pieces of metal through capillary action. This problem is made worse by the fact that spot welding tends to vaporize many of the steel treatments, like galvanizing, that are employed to protect sheetmetal. This problem is mitigated by using a weld-through primer between pieces

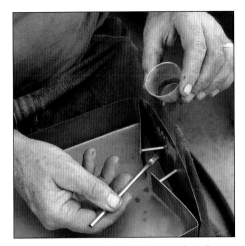

Applying a good weld-through primer to the surfaces between spot welds goes a long way to protecting them from corrosion. This technique can also be used with MIG and TIG welding, but is less effective in those cases than with spot welding.

Today, MIG welding is the mainstay of most autobody welding. It is relatively easy to learn this technique. It is being used here to fill weak spots in a sheetmetal floor.

that are spot welded. Such primers contain a very high percentage of zinc in their solids. This makes them conductive, and thus able to carry spot welding currents, and protects finished welds with ions from the zinc particles in the coating after a weld is made.

MIG Welding

This has become the most common type of repair and custom autobody welding. Its name derives from the term metal inert gas, which is really a misnomer. After all, so-called TIG welding (for tungsten inert gas) is also a metal-inert-gas welding process. Properly, what is called MIG should be called—according to the American Welding Society (AWS)—GMAW for gas metal arc welding. TIG is properly designated as GTAW, for gas tungsten arc welding. I'm glad to get all of that sorted out, thank you. Now, please forgive me, while I continue to use the vernacular terms, MIG and TIG, for no better

reason than that everyone uses and understands them.

In the MIG process, a welding wire is continuously fed into the weld area—the puddle—as it is drawn along the weld seam. The wire carries current, and is surrounded at the weld, by an inert shielding gas that is fed there through the welding hose and gun, along with the wire. C-25 is the most common gas used for sheetmetal welding, in a 25-percent CO_2 and 75-percent argon mixture. The gas acts like the heat-vaporized rod coating in stick welding. It shields the weld puddle and the cooling weld from most of the oxidation corrosion that would occur if the weld was made and cooled in a normal air environment.

The actual MIG process involves a cycle. As the mechanically fed wire contacts the puddle, it creates a direct short circuit with the grounded work piece. The heat generated by the short melts off the wire's end, into the puddle, ending

the short circuit. However, it is quickly reestablished, as more wire is fed into the puddle, creating the short arc cycle that is the basis of MIG welding. This all occurs at about 100 to 150 cycles/second, and produces the famously characteristic frying egg sound that is associated with MIG welding.

The most-often botched aspect of MIG welding is fit-up, the distance between the edges of the metal pieces that are being joined. In lap and offset lap joints, fit-up is not an issue because the joints are overlaps. But in butt welding, it is critical to leave adequate fit-up distance between butted edges. This space is consistently in the range between the thickness of a dime and a nickel. It may sound more difficult to carry a weld puddle down such a gap than down two more closely fitted edges. However, this is not the case.

What is beyond difficult, in fact all but impossible, is to get a good MIG butt weld when edges are fitted up too

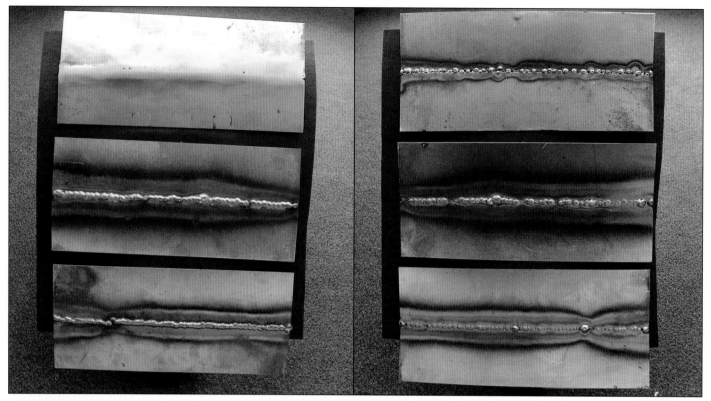

These welds, with their fronts shown on the left and their backs on the right, represent (top to bottom: 1) a finished weld done with alternate tacking and grinding, 2) a bead, welded with trigger on/off segments, and 3) a weld bead comprised of automatically stitch-timed segments.

closely or in actual contact with each other. This is because the expansion from welding heat inevitably distorts too-closely-fitted metal edges so badly that it is very hard to weld them. It is also very difficult to straighten out panels welded that way.

There are several issues to master in order to do good MIG welding. You need to figure out ideal gas flow for your work. This is set with a regulator as the volume of shielding gas delivered. Try to use a two-stage regulator that employs a volume indicator in its second stage. About 10 to 20 CFM (at atmospheric pressure) is a good range in which to work when you are welding body metal with .023- to .025-inch wire. Practice and experimentation are your best guides in this matter.

Amperage settings are critical when MIG welding sheetmetal.

Amperage is set by setting the wire feed speed. Different wires and different thicknesses of metal require different speeds. Manufacturers supply recommendations for this setting with their machines. It is, however, rough data, and you should plan to modify it for your own situations and according to your own experience.

Voltage settings are also critical. The best MIG machines have continuous voltage settings, while less-expensive ones rely on step settings. In either case, the voltage setting in MIG welding is somewhat analogous to how long an arc you hold in stick welding. It controls the format of the weld bead and thus its height, shape, and, to some degree, its penetration.

Somewhere between your general experience and getting frequent practice, you will get the hang of set-

ting wire speed and voltage properly for MIG welding. Some machines set one, or even both, of these variables automatically. While many welds do not allow for practice, some do. If you can duplicate the conditions of a difficult weld with scrap metal that is similar to the material in the sections that you will be welding, and practice your difficult weld, it would be to your advantage to do so.

Some MIG welding machines have fine controls for things like stitch welding, that is, weld time on and time off, and burnback control, which is the time that the wire electrode remains energized after the gun trigger is released. These are handy features that can improve the convenience and quality of work, but they are not essential to doing good MIG welding.

One thing that is essential is to use good wire. MIG welding wire varies in quality. Some wires are junk, barely good enough to weld with, while others are a pleasure to use. Today, most of the major wire brands perform well. Still, different wires often have different features and advantages. For example, one wire may produce welds that are easier to grind, while another may lay down more uniform beads. Again, these are things with which you should experiment.

Other variables, like torch approach (forehand or backhand), distance from work, position, and angle, are best dealt with in manuals and other sources that are specifically devoted to MIG welding instruction.

TIG Welding

This is probably the most skill-intensive type of welding, but presents an odd dichotomy. It can be understood in very complex and technical terms, but it can be performed beautifully with little knowledge of its technical aspects.

Here is an example: Back in the age when TIG welders did not have the modern sophistication of solid-state-generated square-wave forms and slope control, they relied on carbon bundle frequency generators for superimposed high-frequency currents to keep their arcs from stalling at the AC wave turnover point. I knew a man who operated one of those primitive TIG machines. He would not have understood much of the technical sentence above, but with the equipment of that period, he could deposit a uniform and well-penetrated weld bead on the business edge of a razor blade. It was no small feat. He understood little of TIG tech-

TIG welding is probably the most difficult welding technology to master. However, it pays the reward of being the best way to join sheetmetal pieces and panels, when quality is the prime objective.

nology, but knew how to weld with it, instinctively and superbly.

The point is: You can interpret TIG welding in many ways and at many levels, comprehending and mastering as much or as little of the underlying technical issues as the spirit grabs you. Some people revel in the complexities of TIG waveforms and the possible adjustments to them. Others are greatly concerned with the shape of the TIG electrode and/or of its ceramic. Others almost intuitively know or remember how to make the best choices in these matters.

TIG is the most individualistic welding format that exists. Some operators prefer air-cooled torches; others prefer liquid-cooled units. The merits of each are often debated for jobs that involve the same materials and similar welds. Foot controls ver-

sus thumb wheels, and so forth, are hot topics. Also, there is specialization in TIG welding particular metals and alloys.

Unfortunately, is not possible to offer instruction in TIG welding in this book. However, if you are interested in doing ultimate-quality welding work on a variety of metals, from stainless and common steel to aluminum, TIG welding provides the best results. It takes some considerable commitments of money for equipment and of time to learn to use it, but you should at least consider making those commitments if ultimate welding quality is your objective. Don't let the imposing technicalities of TIG welding scare you off if you are interested in this format. You do not have to understand it in technical detail to make

One Way to Reduce Heat Problems

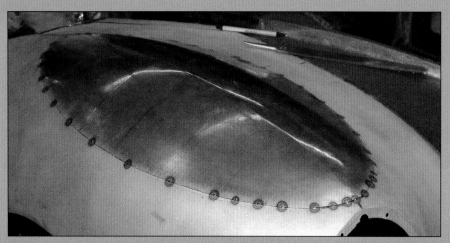

New fender-section metal has been fitted into this old fender with almost no fit-up gap, and TIG tack welded into place. MIG welding would have required a considerable fit-up gap to handle heat expansion, and would have produced much more distortion than did TIG welding.

Keeping welding heat at the minimum necessary for making good joints is critical to joining sheetmetal parts and sections. This limits distortion in the areas of the welds. One way to accomplish this, while ensuring the accurate positioning of pieces, is to make tack welds incrementally along a seam. This works with MIG, TIG, and gas welding techniques. Our example uses TIG, and then MIG, welding processes.

You start by making enough tack welds to position the pieces that you are welding. As you make the first few tack welds, at roughly equal distances from each other, you can make minor adjustments in piece positions by prying them with a small screwdriver. For example, you can keep the edges of the pieces level with each other this way, as you fill in more tack welds along the seam.

When you have filled in most of the welds, that is, enough to absolutely secure the seam, you grind those welds flat to the panel. If you think of each tack weld as a line of continuous and adjacent buttons, you want to make tack welds at every second or third button position in that line. The actual spacing depends on the situation, and on your personal preference. At this point, with the alternate

Tack welds were added between the existing tack welds, until between 1/2 and 1/3 of the seam had been welded. The tack welds were then ground flat to the panel, leaving the seam with a perforated appearance.

welds ground flat, your weld line should look like a perforated tear line.

Now, the entire seam must be closed. This can be done by filling in the gaps between the ground tack welds, and grinding the resulting welds flat to the panel, or by welding a continuous bead over the entire seam. In either case, panel edge position should be perfect, and heat distortion from the whole operation will be reduced from what it would have been with any approach other than alternate tack welding.

The same approach works equally well with MIG welding, although our example lacks the apparent neatness of the same process performed with TIG welding. That is because MIG welding is not as accurate, controllable, or tidy as is TIG welding.

The main point is that this welding technique keeps the buildup of welding heat way below what it would otherwise be, if you attempted to weld continuous beads. This is because it allows more

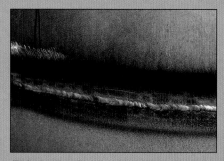

This is the finished weld bead. Note that it is uniform and well penetrated. Also, note how little metal on either side of the bead has been discolored by heat. There is no visible distortion in the original fender, or in the new metal that was welded into it.

After grinding and finishing, here is the completed fender. It required little work to bring it to this point, mostly filing and sanding. The other photos are of the right fender, while this one shows the left. Its repair was almost identical to that of the right fender.

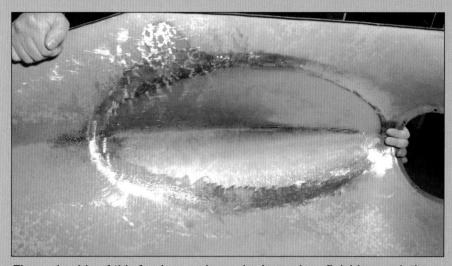

The underside of this fender repair required even less finishing work than its topside. A little, light surface grinding and sanding did the job. This is as close to the perfect restoration of metal as you are ever likely to see. The repaired metal is almost indistinguishable from the original.

cooling and heat-dispersion time between adjacent short welds. When it is used with MIG welding, I prefer to just fill between the ground welds, and not to weld a continuous bead over them, because this involves less heat and distortion.

When you compare these examples of MIG and TIG welding, note the superiority of the welding in the TIG example. This work was done by Wayne, at L'Cars in Cameron, Wisconsin. It represents the achievement of perfection in a very challenging job, from fabrication through welding, and finishing the welds. Some may argue that TIG welding is overkill, in terms of the cost of equipment and time and skill. Maybe so, but it has the potential to restore and fabricate metal that makes it more like original metal than any other welding approach. It finishes more easily and better than any other technique, and creates far less distortion around welds. I don't think that is overkill.

You can use the same type of alternate tack welding approach with MIG welding as with TIG welding. This is illustrated here with a sample that has been welded with spaced MIG welds.

The welds shown in the previous photograph are shown here, after partial grinding. After they were ground flat to the panel, it was tack welded in the areas between the ground welds.

When the seam had been completely welded and ground flat, it was finished with a small orbital disc sander. The result was a strong and good-looking bond. Note that this was a butt-welded joint.

Gas welding is difficult to master, due to the many operator variables involved in its performance. Note the extreme torch angle and the use of filler rod to add metal to the puddle and, sometimes, to shield it from excessive heat. Also note the distortion in this example.

great welds in a variety of situations. As with your personal computer, you can operate a TIG welder without a deep understanding of how it works. A good welding course at a vocational school will have you started down the path of mastering TIG techniques.

Oxy-Acetylene Gas Welding, Brazing and Braze Welding

These are older methods of joining thin metal sections that still have some application in today's world of (mostly) electric welding. In most cases they will prove inferior, in one or more of several ways, to electric welding approaches. But there are times when you may find uses for torch welding and brazing techniques.

The oxy-acetylene flame, generated by mixing oxygen and acetylene gases to fuel a torch, is infernally hot—about 6,300 degrees F at the cone tip of a neutral flame. A neutral flame has a perfect, combustible mixture of oxygen and acetylene for complete combustion of each gas, with no excess of either in the mix. This means that it is possible for that flame, in sufficient size, to melt the surface of steel, which begins to melt at around 2,700 degrees F.

In practice, oxy-acetylene welds are made by moving the flame, with its inner cone near the metal to be joined, angled at roughly 45 degrees to the surface, and oriented in a forehanded direction (the direction that the weld is being made). The torch is moved along with a slightly oval or circular tip motion to make welds that have characteristics indicated by the approved ripple appearance in their weld beads. All of that takes some coordination and practice.

Actually, you can't weld with a torch by melting and carrying a puddle down the seam. The two pieces can't fill the seam without thinning them unacceptably. For that reason, a steel filler rod is applied to, and melted into, the puddle as needed to form a bead, as the puddle is carried down the seam by torch movement in that direction.

All of this is possible and has worked reasonably well for generations. On the other hand, MIG and TIG welding also have worked much better for fewer generations. The first disadvantage of torch welding thin sections is that it requires considerable skill, more than MIG welding, and about the same as TIG welding. Note that the considerations and manipulations of the TIG electric torch and filler rod are somewhat similar to those employed in gas welding.

Torch welding also imparts much more general heat to a weld area than either of the common electric welding formats. This means more distortion and more fun and games chasing collateral damage off the welding scene, after welding is completed. For those reasons, torch welding sheetmetal seams is rarely employed these days. Put simply, you can do better work with much less skill, knowledge, and effort with electric welding techniques.

Brazing and braze welding also have limited use in good autobody jointure practice. Like torch welding, these techniques are performed with an oxy-acetylene flame. In this case, a slightly carburizing flame is preferred. That is, a flame with a slight feather around its inner cone, caused by a richer-than-neutral amount of acetylene in the oxygen/acetylene mixture.

Brazing is somewhat like soldering with tin/lead-based and silver-based solders, but is done at higher temperatures (around 1,000 degrees F) and with filler rod that is a brass alloy or, less commonly, a bronze-based alloy. Note: Brass alloys are based on copper and zinc, while bronze alloys are based on copper and tin. Like soldering, brazing does not produce a fusion joint; that is, the molecules at the surfaces of the metals do not intermingle as they do in true fusion processes, like MIG, TIG, and torch welding. Instead, the brazing material is attracted by capillary action between the sections being brazed together. There is some surface mingling of braze and base metal molecules, but nothing like the alloying action that occurs in true fusion welding.

You might think that brazing is the low-temperature and low-distortion solution to the challenges of joining thin-metal materials. It might seem that all you have to do is bring joints up to a relatively low temperature, and flow brazing rod into the space between the pieces. And because brazing rod is very corrosion resistant, it should automatically seal areas like lap joints.

Alas, it isn't that simple. Brazing materials typically don't have the strength required for making sound butt welds, so their use is reserved for lap and offset lap joints. In fact, in years past, some automobile manufacturers used some brazed lap joints in their original constructions of cars and trucks. However, for most purposes, butt joints are more desirable. That eliminates brazing them.

Even with lap joints, the fit-up for brazing is critical to getting the right capillary flow of the brazing material into the joint. Without this factor, brazed joints tend to be too weak for automotive panel jointure. Maintaining proper fit-up gaps can

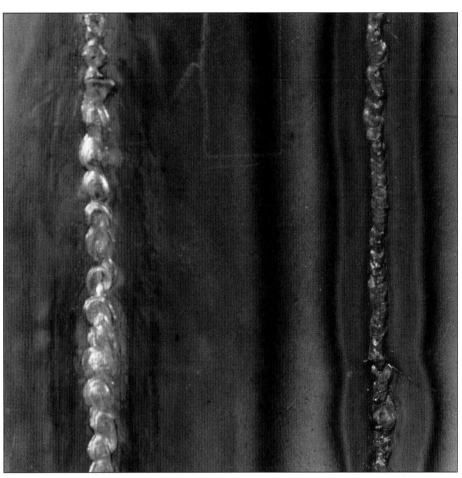

The weld on the left is a pretty good gas weld. The one on the right is a MIG weld. Note how much smaller the heat-affected zone is in the electric weld. This translates into less warping and distortion.

be done in production, but usually is very difficult in repair and custom fabrication situations. Another problem with brazing is the flux that is used. It is most often borax based, and it can be persistently difficult to remove from finished joints. If some is left behind after cleaning, it does not take on primer and paint well. Finally, brazing fluxes have a tendency to cause hydrogen embrittlement in the metal adjacent to brazed joints, and this can cause cracking in that metal, as panels vibration cycle over miles and time.

Braze welding, unlike brazing, goes beyond capillary action and deposits a strengthening thickness (or bead) of brazing material in braze weld areas. This type of joint is stronger than simple brazing, but has all of brazing's other drawbacks, mentioned above. There are some places where brazing and braze welding have application in sheetmetal work, particularly when they are used to repair or to replace factory joints that were originally brazed or braze welded. In the main, however, brazed and braze welded joints are perilously close to being substandard techniques for most panel jointure purposes today. While these techniques once may have seemed attractive, modern electric welding approaches have supplanted them.

Six Welding Shop Tricks and Tips

There are hundreds of little tricks, habits, and minor ploys that will help you make great welds. Some of them are in books devoted to welding, and others in books, DVDs, and seminars by advanced professionals in the sheetmetal and welding crafts. Still others can be garnered by watching seasoned body shop welders at their work. Here are six of my favorites:

Tip #1

The edges of the sheetmetal that you weld are often somewhat jagged, from contact with the likes of saws and aviation-type snips. If you take a minute to run an inexpensive hand-deburring tool over these edges, before you weld them, you will improve your welding results by making them more uniform. It is a small

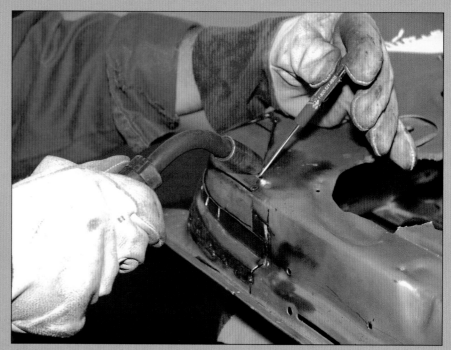

Behold the screwdriver trick for keeping edges in alignment as you tack weld them. The heat from tack welding can cause edges to lose lateral alignment as you add tacks. Some judicious prying with a small-blade screwdriver can reestablish alignment, before more tack welds are added.

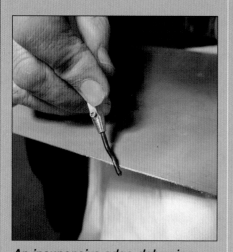

An inexpensive edge-deburring tool can improve your welding when it is applied to the sheetmetal edges that you weld. The tool is drawn along an edge to cut off any minor defects that may have been created when the edge was originally cut.

point, but it is so easy to deburr edges this way that it is a good idea to add this trick to your routine preparations for welding autobody metal.

Tip #2

Sometimes, despite your best efforts to keep surfaces properly laterally positioned to each other, the heat of tack welding or seam welding causes them to move out of position. When this happens, it can be corrected as you go along by prying edges back into alignment with a small screwdriver or other prying tool. I tend to keep a cheap, small screwdriver in my left hand for this purpose as I weld sheetmetal tacks and seams, probably because I am right-handed.

Cooling welds with compressed air, right after you make them and as you go along, reduces heat buildup and hardens the metal in the welds and weld area. Both of these results are highly desirable.

Both sides of welding tape are shown here. The side with the fiberglass bandage is applied to the back sides of weld seams before welds are made. This protects these undersides, and makes for very clean and corrosion-free welds.

Tip #3

One great enemy of copasetic body metal welds is heat buildup that distorts the metal near the welds. To minimize this heat buildup, and to harden the welds, it is good practice to blow compressed air at them immediately after they are made. This holds true for MIG, TIG, and oxy-acetylene welding, and for any joint or bead format that you use, including tack welds, short-triggered-section welds, and long-bead welds. All of them benefit from some forced-air cooling to limit local heat buildup and to harden the welds.

Tip #4

If you want to go fanatical about making quality welds, you should consider using welding tape to protect the backs of your welds from oxidation. Remember, the fronts of your welds are protected by a supplied shielding gas in MIG and TIG formats, by an envelope of vaporized stick coating in stick welds, and by the inert outer envelope of the flame in oxy-acetylene torch welds.

Welding tape is available at high-end welding supply stores. You tape it over the back of a seam to be welded, and then weld the seam in the normal way with MIG or TIG processes. The fiberglass bandage in the stainless-steel welding tape releases inert gas when it is exposed to welding heat, while the stainless-steel tape keeps air away from the cooling weld. When you remove the tape, the back of your weld should be positively corrosion free, even shiny.

Tip #5

Holding metal pieces in position for spot welding can be a great, acrobatic bother. Unlike seam welding, spot welds tend to be made in many different locations, and setting up locking pliers, magnets, and other fixturing devices can be difficult and cumbersome. If you try to hand-hold pieces in place for spot welding, you will quickly wish that the human anatomy included a third arm and hand assembly.

One solution is to buy or make a foot-pedal-operated spot-welding setup, so that you have two hands free to position metal, while one foot closes the spot welder's arms and turns it on.

One particularly frustrating spot welding afternoon several years ago, I made the foot-operated device for my spot welder. I fabricated it from things that were lying around my shop. It has served me well, ever since. Note that it is very easy to remove the spot welder from the device, if its service is needed for mobile applications.

This homemade, foot-operated spot-welding setup frees both hands for holding and positioning the pieces to be welded. This device was designed to allow for good foot travel at a reasonable level of applied foot pressure.

Tip #6

I saved the best and most important welding tip for last: Always weld clean metal. If you try to weld over rust, paint, plating, or anything else but base metals, you get inclusions of these things in your welds. That compromises their quality. Abrasive blasting, sanding, grinding, filing, wire brushing, etc., clean metal adequately for welding if it is done completely. Chemical stripping also accomplishes this purpose. Whatever method you use, make sure that any metal that you weld is as clean as you can get it before you try to weld it.

FILLING

I don't expect to work in a body shop any time soon, but if that should come to pass, I would like to do collision metal work, bumping, and metal finishing damaged panels. If am ever employed that way, it will be one of my main objectives to give the paint-prep guys as little to do as possible. I have nothing personal against them, or their employment. It is just that good metal work should require little or no filling before it is coated with primer and paint. This is the last stage of metal work and, as far as the eye can see, probably the most important.

However, like many other issues in metal work, the decisions of when, where, and how much filler to use are matters of degree. At some level, it is almost always possible to do enough metal finishing, without using fillers, to serve up panel work that needs nothing but primer and some light contour sanding to pass the muster of the highest standards. The question becomes, "What does it take to get the metal to that point?" At the very least, it means hours spent adjusting surfaces to perfection.

There comes a point of diminishing returns when you are making such

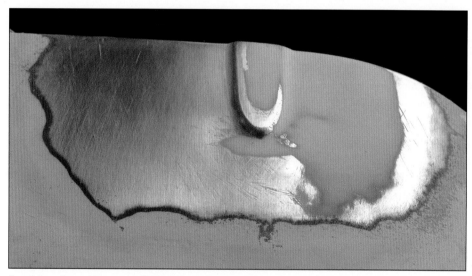

Looking from the panel's back toward its front, you can see the completed repair of a decklid's left-hinge mounting relief area. For demonstration purposes, the left side of the repair area was filled with body solder material and the right side was filled with plastic filler.

adjustments, a point at which they may create other problems, sometimes elsewhere in a panel. That can mean backing up and doing creative destruction to your work, to try to eliminate that last niggling defect. That process may create other problems that have to be solved, often with great difficulty but without success.

Put simply, the issue becomes one of practicality, and of knowing

when to quit and to use some filler to complete a job. Knowing when to quit is among the hardest disciplines to acquire in any line of work.

Body filler has a place. That place is as a corrective for minor surface defects, and for very small shortcomings in shape. If it is used within those limits, it is a full-fledged and respected member of the metal finishing family. If it is gobbed on to cover sizeable flaws in metal work, or used creatively to produce what amounts to sculpture, it is misuse.

The Secrets of Lead Work

An extensive example of lead work is included in Chapter 12, and in the photos and captions in the first part of this chapter.

Lead was the unquestioned filler of choice in body work from early automotive times into the early 1950s. This was true because it was the only known, practical body filler. Then polyester fillers were introduced and, over the years, have almost completely eclipsed lead fillers in this work. Polyester fillers enjoy many advantages over lead. By comparison, the material is much less expensive, and far less skill intensive and time consuming to apply. Unlike lead particles and fumes, exposure to airborne plastic filler particles is not particularly hazardous, though it is always a good idea to wear a protective filter mask when you sand plastic fillers. Modern polyester fillers are purported to be as durable as lead. They are also claimed to be at least as workable as lead when it comes to being filed and sanded to perfection.

I know that I am swimming upstream on this one, but I still prefer lead filler. Basically, I take issue with both of the last two points, stated above, that favor plastic fillers. While polyester fillers have evolved enormously in the last 50+ years, I continue to doubt that they have the durability of properly applied lead fillers. I also question that they can be finished as accurately. My reasons for doubting their comparable durability to lead is that plastic fillers remain somewhat water absorbent, even with the modern components that are now

added as solids to their resins. They also lack the adhesion to base metal of properly tinned lead filler. Despite their improvement in these two areas, I think that they remain behind lead in both regards. However, that is only a personal opinion.

The earliest plastic fillers were resins filled with talc. Over the years, many other, less-moisture-absorbing substances, like marble spheres, have been combined with greatly improved polyester resins to make plastic fillers. The result is plastic fillers that greatly outperform the original issues of this type of product.

The bottom line for me is that tin/lead based fillers are metal. Applied to sheet steel, you have fillers that are somewhat similar to the base metal to which they are applied. Tin/lead fillers are far softer than the base metal, but they file, sand, and finish more like it than do plastic fillers.

You can decide for yourself which type of filler you favor in your work. I discuss both of them in the example that follows.

The decklid hinge mount area in the photograph at the beginning of this chapter shows damage that has been bumped back into its roughly correct shape, and then filled and metal finished, using both tin/lead body solder and plastic filler, in different areas of the repair. In the photograph, the tin/lead application is on the left side of the hinge-mount relief, while plastic filler was used on the right side of the relief. You can follow both processes, applied to similar situations, in the photos and captions that follow.

The Project

The panel used as an example here is the decklid from a Triumph

TR-3, year not known. There was minor damage to the left-side hinge-mount area of this decklid panel.

Note: The convention of describing damage from the perspective of looking from the back of a vehicle forward should always be followed. Thus, in nautical terms, the damage described here was to the port-side decklid hinge-mount area.

The damage extended from the hinge mount's center relief to the outer edge of the decklid. Put simply, the outer edge of the hood was sprung out in the hinge-mount area, and the hinge-mount area itself was canted down and to the left.

Before this repair was begun, the panel repair area looked like this. This photo was taken from the front of the panel. Note that the relief area was pushed down on the left, and the metal beyond that was sprung up and out from its edge.

The nature of this damage, and how it was removed, is not central to this account of using body fillers, but a little information about it provides some useful background for that discussion.

The decklid arrived with its hinges removed. My guess is that it was caught in an open position by strong wind, or some other force, coming from the car's right rear. This

Decklid Panel Repair

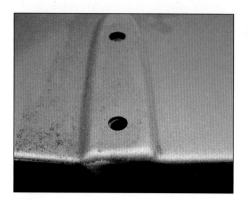

1 After light abrasive blasting with silica sand, the damaged area looked like this. The damage is more obvious with the paint and rust removed from the panel. You can see a reinforcing plate through the front hinge-mounting hole in the hinge-mount area.

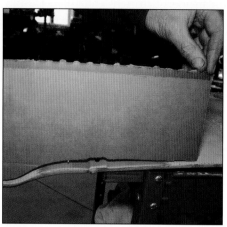

2 A cardboard template was made from the undamaged side of the decklid. Then it was turned around and fitted over the damaged area. It indicates the exact location and extent of the panel deformation.

3 Twisting the hinge-relief area sideways, up and away from the decklid's edge, while lightly tapping the metal beyond it with a body hammer, returned the metal to its correct format. Two incremental applications of this procedure bumped this area back into proper shape.

4 Filing the repair area began to reveal high and low spots. Body files are usually held with both hands, and slid forward and sideways, with a toe-to-heel weight shift as they are moved. Shown here is a one-hand filing motion, used to isolate a particular high spot.

5 About halfway through the initial filing, the panel looked like this. Note the low spots along the right side and to the front of the hinge-mount relief area.

probably resulted in breaking the right hinge, while forcing the decklid panel up, and to the left. This would have bent and canted the left-hinge-mount area because the right hinge was no longer attached to the panel, and could not restrain its movement. The left-front lip of the decklid prob-

ably contacted and engaged the decklid jamb, springing the metal outward from the hinge-mount area. The visible damage to this panel was consistent with this scenario, but other sequences are possible.

The deformation of the metal, immediately to the left of the hinge-mount area, was sufficient to release the paint there. Then, exposure to moisture caused that area to rust. After cleaning the damaged area with

a very light blast of silica sand, a cardboard template of the hinge-relief area was cut from the undamaged right side of the decklid panel. Then, it was turned around with respect to the car, and applied over the damaged area to determine the exact nature and extent of the damage.

The repair was accomplished simply, by fitting a large monkey wrench over the damaged hinge-relief area, with a small wooden pad under the relief and a large one on top of it. Then, the wrench was pulled sideways, away from the damage, while the metal beyond it, to the left, was tapped lightly with a medium-crown hammer. This combination of steady pressure and light impact almost completely restored the panel to its original format in one planned operation that was repeated twice. Correct contour was confirmed by checking the repaired area against the template that had been made from the undamaged hinge-mount area on the decklid's other side. After the second operation, it fit perfectly.

The strength of the repaired panel was checked by attempting to physically twist it in various ways, while observing the repair area. No movement in the repair area was observed. There appeared to be no weakness in the metal, and with two correctly mounted hinges, it is doubtful that it will show any tendency to lose its shape in the repaired area. Since the hinge-mount area can be highly stressed when the trunk is opened, it is interesting to speculate whether the greater adhesion and strength of the lead part of the repair gives it better durability than the plastic part of the repair.

The repaired area was filed to indicate any low or high spots. Some low areas were found and partially corrected by picking them up, off-dolly, while using a shot bag for backing. At this point a few very shallow depressions in the metal remained, most prominently behind the hinge-mount relief area and to its immediate left. It might have been possible to raise these areas to level with more pick-hammer work, but their depth was so shallow that filling them seemed like a better approach.

Applying Lead Filler Material

The first step in applying lead filler is to clean the area to which it will be applied with a good, degreasing solvent. The adhesion of the tinning solder that bonds the lead filler to the panel is compromised by any traces of rust, paint, oil, or grease. Always degrease any area that you plan to fill with lead. This is done by wiping it down with rags, doused in solvent, and then wiping the area

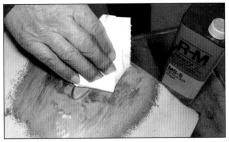

6 Before the repair area could be tinned, it was repeatedly wiped down and dried with enamel reducer. This removed any grease and oil from it, as well as any filing particles that remained on it.

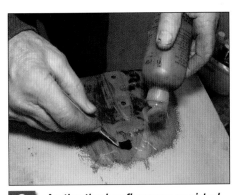

8 As the tinning flux was squirted onto and brushed around the repair area, it sizzled and steamed. This was a good indication that it was doing its job. The purpose of flux is to clean base metal and to promote solder flow.

dry. This should be repeated until the solvent-wiping rags and drying rags come up clean.

It is usually a good idea to lightly sand or blast the metal to be tinned with a fine-grit abrasive paper or blast media, to remove oxides and protective coatings. This should be done before it is solvent washed, so that the solvent washing removes sanding debris.

Although metal may look clean after sanding and solvent washing, it still has oxides and contaminants on its surface that interfere with the proper adhesion of the tinning sol-

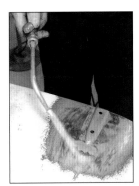

7 The metal in the repair area was now heated, in preparation for 50/50 tinning solder application. Low and high spots, left by the filing operation, are clearly visible. The low spots were shallow, and numerous enough to justify applying lead over the whole area.

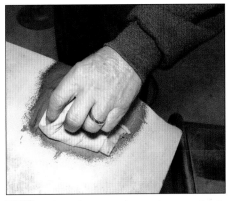

9 After the panel repair area had cooled a bit, excess flux was wiped off. It is important not to wipe all the flux off, or it cannot do its important job.

der that is used to bond lead filler material to it. To remove these adhesion-robbing contaminants, and to perform other wetting and adhesion-promoting goals, apply a flux to areas to be leaded. There are many types of liquid, powdered, and paste fluxes on the market. Some of them include solder particles in their formulations, and make fluxing and tinning a single-step process.

I prefer to use a straight liquid flux that is designated specifically for autobody lead work. This is available from many autobody and catalog sources. It is applied to metal that has

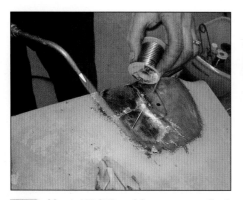

10 *Next, 50/50 solder was applied from a coil to the fluxed, heated metal. Note that the torch was not applied to the solder directly, but to the panel metal. You can see a completely tinned area behind where the solder is being applied.*

11 *The solder was applied from the coil, and complete tinning was achieved by using a rag to rub it around on the panel's heated area. You may accidentally singe a few rags as you are learning to do this.*

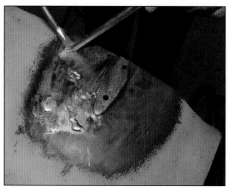

12 *It takes some practice to stub lead from a bar onto tinned metal. The trick is to keep the tinned metal hot with the torch's outer flame, while softening the end of a solder bar enough with its inner flame to twist it onto the panel.*

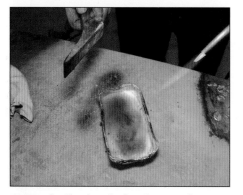

13 *As the lead-shaping work began, the paddle was lubricated, to keep it from sticking to the lead as it was spread. To do this, we liquefied the surface of the tallow with the end of the torch flame and dipped the working surface of the paddle into it.*

been heated to the point that it sizzles off the liquid flux, when it is sprayed or dripped onto it. Flux application turns the metal a light gray color.

The best flame to use for fluxing, tinning, and applying body lead is one from an air-acetylene torch, often called a "plumber's" torch. This type of torch produces a flame that is long, and graduated in temperature along its length. There are

inexpensive air-draw tip attachments for oxy-acetylene torches that convert them to air-acetylene operation. These are a bit clumsy, but they do work. Note that an oxy-acetylene flame is much too hot for performing lead work. Propane torches are sometimes used for this work, but their flame is not as long and graduated as is the air-acetylene flame.

After the target area has been fluxed, it is a good idea to scrub off any excess flux residue with a rag and/or spun-nylon pad. These residues may appear as heavy, brown, gummy deposits, or they may not be present at all. Be careful not to scrub down to bare metal because a flux coating is necessary for adhesion of the tinning solder that you apply over it.

Tinning is accomplished by keeping the fill area hot with your torch, while melting enough 50/50 tin/lead solder from a coil onto the metal to cover the area when that solder is spread uniformly over it. It is important to use the middle-to-end part of your torch flame to keep the metal hot enough to melt the

solder onto it, but not to overheat it by getting it much hotter than that.

Never apply your flame directly to the solder from the coil. As you melt solder from the coil onto the base metal, keep playing the torch over several square inches of the area that you are tinning. Then, when you have deposited enough solder to do the job, spread it out with a rag until it thinly and consistently covers the heated area. The solder should have a shiny appearance as it bonds to the metal. Be careful to wipe it lightly when you spread it, or you will remove the solder completely, rendering your tinning procedure useless.

After the entire area to which you plan to apply lead is tinned, it is time to apply the body lead. My preference is to use 1/2-pound bars of 30/70 body lead. Appendix I shows the transition temperatures for various tin/lead solder alloys, from solid to paste to liquid. My experience tells me that 30/70 is the best alloy for most body lead applications, with some minor exceptions, like sealing seams, which may be better

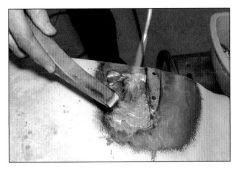

14 *We worked the lead with the end of the torch flame to heat it uniformly to its paste state. We did this slowly enough to heat through the entire filler thickness, not just its surface. Note that while the lead was being heated, the paddle was held at the ready.*

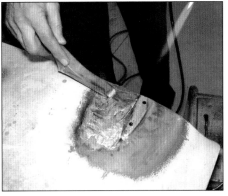

15 *We repeatedly tested the lead surface with the paddle, to indicate when it reached a plastic state. A short time after it first become plastic, it was ready to work with the paddle.*

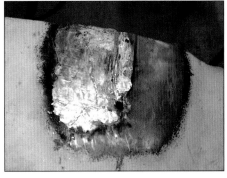

16 *The paddled lead in this example looked like this when its application was completed. The dark residues on its surface are tallow lubricant and flux residues from tinning that worked up through the lead.*

17 *The tallow and flux residues were removed before filing began. To do this, a metal conditioner was wiped onto, and scrubbed off, the leaded surface. This removed these contaminants.*

served by using a 20/80 alloy. A 30/70 lead bar has a plastic state of about 130 degrees F. As long as you keep it in that temperature range, it will have a consistency something like peanut butter. In this state, it is easy to work with leading tools.

If you overheat lead, it goes to liquid and, likely as not, ends up on your shoes and/or on the floor. At the very least, when body lead is overheated to its liquid state, its tin and lead components tend to separate. Trying to re-soften separated body solder, after it has re-solidified, does

no good because the tin and lead will no longer be alloyed. Without the tin/lead alloy, there is no plastic state in which this material can be formed with leading tools. Of course, if you allow your lead to cool too much, it becomes solid, and resists any attempts to shape it with paddles.

Before you try to form lead, you have to deposit it on the area where you are going to use it. You do this by heating—but not overheating—the tinned area of the base metal by playing the last few inches of your torch flame over it. As you are doing this, hold a lead bar against the panel in an area where you want to deposit lead filler, also keeping the end of the bar warm with the torch. Slowly attack the base of the lead bar with flame that is nearer to the hot inner cone of your torch flame, until it begins to soften. You will see and feel this happening. When the lead on the end of the bar (about 1 inch or less) is soft enough to deform easily, twist it off and onto the panel. Then, move to another spot and deposit another stub. Continue this stubbing process until you have

deposited enough lead where you need it to accomplish the filling.

At first, it is likely that you will deposit more lead than you need. Later, with experience, you will learn to deposit the right amount of lead filler for your filling purposes.

The chief obstacle for novices is overheating their work areas, and liquefying the lead. This is a common problem with a simple, but not obvious, solution. Overheating is made worse because people tend to move their torches sideways when they sense that it is occurring. That simply results in overheating another area, one adjacent to the area that was the original problem. The answer is to move your torch in-and-out from your work, not to the side, to control heat. This approach helps you to maintain your 30/70 body solder in the 130-degrees-F range in which it is plastic. It takes some time to perfect this somewhat unnatural torch manipulation but, after a while, it should become quite natural.

The best lead-working tools are paddles made from seasoned hard maple, boiled in mutton tallow.

18 *A body file in a flexible holder is my favorite general filing tool, my first choice of weapon for small and large body-solder filing jobs. It is versatile and accurate. That setup was used here to file the leaded surface.*

19 *As filing continued, areas of base metal appeared through the body solder. Correct filing technique ensured that the continuous contours being filed into the repair area were the correct ones. It is always a good idea to file across as much leaded area in one operation as possible.*

20 *Panel edges should be filed with a very delicate touch. Light pressure, accurate file position, and constant monitoring of shape are essential when you file panel edges. Any inattention can result in damage to a panel.*

Mutton tallow is also the preferred working lubricant for these tools. Other popular lubricants, like beeswax and chassis grease, cause all kinds of problems and should never be used. To apply fresh lubricant to a maple paddle, you play the end of your air-acetylene-torch flame over the surface of a tin of mutton tallow, until it melts to a depth of about 1/2 inch. Then, dip the work contact surface of the paddle into it. Let the excess tallow drip off the paddle, back into the tin. The paddle is now lubricated.

To work, or form, the lead that you have stubbed onto the work area, you use your properly lubricated paddle to spread it onto the areas where you need it. Deposit the lead a bit thicker than the approximate thickness to which you will finish it. Keep the lead soft by playing the end of your flame over it. While you keep it in its plastic state, it is easy to form it with your paddle. Of course, all of this takes some practice, but, with the benefit of some experience, it is not difficult to master.

Some situations may require leading tools that are not readily available. For example, if you need to

lead a 1½-inch-round shape, it will be possible, but difficult to accomplish this work with a flat or convex lead-paddle working surface. The solution is to make your own tool for this purpose. It's just too inefficient to try to do the job with an incorrectly shaped tool.

In the example above, I would take a stick of kiln-dried hard maple, say 2 x 3/4 inches, and form a radiused, chamfered, and tapered end on it, starting at about a 1¾-inch-round diameter. Then, I would boil the new tool's working end, for an hour or so, in a tin can with about 2 inches of mutton tallow in it.

This step is often left out of the leading process and which, when omitted, results in endless later grief. It is critical to kill lead at this point; that is, right after it is applied to metal and paddled into preliminary shape. Killing, in this case, means removing flux and lubricant residues from your work. If left in and on the lead, such residues would later raise havoc with primer and paint adhesion.

Chemicals used to kill lead residues have ranged from ammonia,

vinegar, and other household substances, to the metal conditioners used to prep metal for painting. A good metal conditioner is your best bet for neutralizing contaminants in worked lead. Phosphatizing conditioners are among the most effective chemicals in this class, and are readily available from body shop supply outfits. A good move at this point is to use a nylon scrubbing pad with your metal conditioner, or other killing agent, to scrub off any visible tallow residues on your paddled lead filler surface. Flux residues from tinning that may have worked up through the body solder may not be visible but if they are there, and if you file them into your lead, they will cause trouble later.

You will need to perform the killing process again, when your lead filler has been filed into final shape. That is a precaution to make sure that these residues are completely removed from your work. The best time to remove them is now, when you scrub and neutralize them out of the paddled lead, before you file it.

Lead filler is shaped with body files and hand-sanding devices.

21 *While you can accomplish most filing jobs with a flat body file in a flexible holder, some jobs and areas require file shapes different from that. The side of the decklid hinge-mount relief required some filing with both round and square files.*

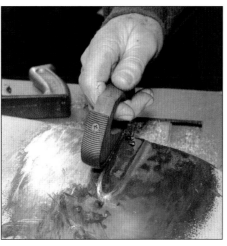

22 *This specialty bull-nose body file was very helpful in getting the correct taper next to the hinge-mount relief. Unfortunately, files like this are no longer manufactured.*

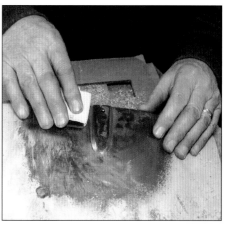

23 *After filing the repair area, it was sanded. The first sanding application was with 80-grit paper, backed by a hard-rubber pad. Note that the area to the right has not yet been filled.*

Never, never, try to shape lead with any power-sanding or power-grinding tool. Lead can be absorbed through the pores of human skin, and ingested in saliva. It is very deadly in airborne and small particulate form, which is the form that it attains when it is power sanded. If you work with lead, be careful to avoid its fumes and small particles that contain it. Be particularly careful to cover exposed skin, particularly arms, wrists, and hands. I also highly recommend wearing a particulate face filter. The symptoms of lead poisoning do not appear quickly, but the effects of lead poisoning are extremely debilitating, even fatal.

The theory behind line filing and board sanding filler is that a series of somewhat random motions will average the surface that you are filing or sanding into the continuous contours that are the basis for flats, simple curves, and crowns. This works because lead and plastic fillers are softer than the metal to which they are applied, so that metal sets the overall shape that is filed or sanded over it. It does this by providing hard contact points that guide filing and sanding.

This theory places two requirements on the use of files and board sanders. First, they must be used in random patterns that vary slightly in position, direction, and application pressure with each stroke. Second, after rough filing is completed, that is, the basic shape that you are trying to achieve has been cut into the filler, you must be very careful to remove very little material with each successive, random stroke. If you follow this practice, you file continuous flats, simple curves, and crowns that are guided by the metal under the filler. As filler is filed off, and that metal appears, it guides your file into cutting correct contours. For this to work, the metal under the filler that guides your file has to be accurate before you attempt to file it.

Remember, filler is not meant to create the shape of what you file. It is designed to do only what its name implies, to fill low areas, and to help to reproduce exact and valid contours by allowing you to make very minor corrections to them. Once rough filing to remove excess filler is completed, fine filing creates final shapes and contours.

Specialty files are often helpful in dealing with complex shapes, particularly the transition areas between different crowns. The rules for using them are the same as those for flat files and files, like adjustable curve files, with simple end-to-end curvatures.

The proper filing motion with body files is described in Chapter 7. In summary, it is a forward motion, away from you, with a lesser side-sliding movement and a shift of weight from the front of the file to its back. This motion promotes desirable, continuous contours.

Once lead filler has been filed smooth, and very close to final shape, finish it with sanding procedures. Never attempt sanding with your bare fingers. If you do, you are more likely to disrupt desirable surface configurations and put inaccurate depressions into your work than you are to improve it. Always

24 *Specialized sanding tools, like this one, aid in sanding fine detail into some panel shapes. A 180-grit paper was used to sand detail into the side of the hinge-mount relief area. Fine abrasives cut slowly, thus helping to avoid going too deep into lead filler.*

26 *Major shapes and contours were fine tuned with a board sander fitted with 180-grit abrasive paper. The general contour of the panel was blended with the hinge-mount relief area that earlier had been detail sanded.*

back up abrasive papers with something like a rubber pad to give them some rigidity and some consistent pressure. Such pads vary from soft foam to pretty hard rubber. Sanding boards use fairly hard foam pads to directly back abrasive papers. This helps them to average contours, and to avoid gouging filler.

In some situations, you may need a specialized sanding tool to create a special shape or detail. This can be formed by anything from wrapping abrasive paper around a tapered file, to making a specialized wooden sanding tool to sand the detail that you seek.

After lead is filed, you can rough sand it with an 80-grit paper. This gives pretty fast cutting, while avoiding the creation of deep scratches. Finish the lead sanding with papers between 120- and 180-grit, depending on how far you want to go. Whatever sequence of filing and sanding you use, it is important that each stage of it removes any stray marks and scratches that are left over from the previous stage of your work. I always try to do a final board

sanding of as much area as I can access with a long board sander. I do this after I have filed and sanded all of the details that I need.

As you file and sand filled surfaces, check them visually and by feeling them through a rag. One great advantage of lead filler is that as it is filed and sanded, it becomes shiny enough to reflect light reliably. This means that by looking at a contour and changing your sight line as you do so, you can watch reflections move across or along that contour. These indicate any defects in flats, curves, or crowns that may still exist. These reflections should move consistently, and without much change in basic distortion, until they encounter changes in crown.

For example, if the fluorescent tubes in an overhead light fixture are the reflection that you are tracking, they will be distorted by the curvatures of the panel from which you see them reflected. As you move your head with respect to that panel, the tubes will seem to move along it. The tubes will appear to be distorted, and

the distortion in this reflection changes as you change the place from which you view it, and as the crown or curvature of the panel changes. But if you see a sudden change, particularly one in just part of the reflection, you may be looking at an undesired change in the panel's contour that was a result of your metal finishing work to the panel or to the filler. Sudden changes should only occur in areas of fairly steep crown changes in the panel. Make sure that they occur only where they belong.

After a panel is finished in deep lacquer or glossy enamel, defects like the ones you can see in reflections stick out like warts on the heads of bald men. When you are evaluating your filler and metal finishing work, it is important to catch defects while they can still be corrected relatively easily.

Applying Plastic Fillers

A detailed example of a repair area that was filled with plastic filler is described in Chapter 13. What follows is a discussion of the theory of and best practices for using this type of material.

Probably, you already have the idea that I prefer lead filler to plastic filler. Despite my preference, the world has gone almost entirely to plastic fillers. Still, even if you never intend to use lead filler, you should read the first part of this chapter on that topic—the one that you may have just skipped to get here—because the shaping techniques and tools used for both types of filler are very similar in many particulars.

One great advantage of polyester fillers is that they are easier and faster to shape than lead fillers. On large jobs, they can be grated quickly

Applying Plastic Fillers

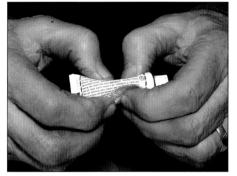

1 It is important to thoroughly mix the components of polyester filler separately, as well as together. Tubes of hardener should be kneaded, and cans of filler should be stirred with a screwdriver or putty knife, depending on their size.

2 Mixed filler, deposited on a steel sheet, was spread with a putty knife onto the fill area. It is important to work filler into base metal, to ensure its adhesion to that metal.

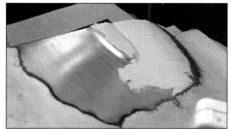

3 The filler was then shaped onto the repair area with a flexible plastic spreader. At this point, it was important to avoid creating air bubbles in the filler, and to work out any air that may have become trapped in it.

4 The filler was then allowed to cure to a semi-hard state. The time needed for this to occur varies, largely depending on the proportions of hardener and filler that you mix. In this case, a timer was set for 15 minutes, which turned out to be just about right.

into rough shape, before they fully harden. After they cure, they can be worked with power tools like disc sanders, DA orbital sanders, and air tools with grinding burrs.

With proper metal preparation, plastic fillers have excellent adhesion. What they do not have is much ability to resist water molecules. After you complete work with plastic fillers, it is important to protect filled areas from moisture and humidity by coating them with waterproof primer, and/or primer and top coats that provide moisture-barrier protec-

tion. Those poor souls you see driving around with bare filler showing on their cars' bodies are in for a world of hurt, particularly after they paint over that moisture-saturated plastic filler, and trap the basis for future corrosion under the paint.

Preparing metal properly for polyester filler involves having it as clean and grease-free as possible. All visible signs of paint, rust, and flying smut should be removed from the substrate metal. Its surface should be given good tooth to hold the filler. That tooth is the crags, crannies, nooks,

and other interlocking shapes that lock filler to the metal surface. The adhesion capabilities of plastic fillers are purely mechanical, not chemical.

Abrasives in the 50- to 80-grit range provide good tooth. Below that range, you leave scratches that are problematic because they tend to promote sand scratch swelling in paint applied over them to the metal adjacent to your filler. Above 80-grit, metal lacks the tooth to adequately bond plastic filler. I have seen people who fanatically polished filler and metal with 400-grit, or greater, abrasives before applying primer to them. This is a bad idea because the primer will find little to grab onto in such a metal's surface.

The first rule of using plastic fillers is to use a good-quality material. Some brands of filler are better than others. Reading product brochures and experimenting with different materials informs you on these issues. The second rule is to mix the components thoroughly, with themselves and with each other. When mixing them with each other the mixing proportions are not terribly critical, but stay within the

5 *After the filler had reached its semi-hard state, it was grated with a cheese-grater-type file. This process can remove material very quickly, so you have to avoid over-enthusiastic grating at this stage.*

6 *Plastic filler is filed in much the same way as lead filler. The same body files used for lead can be used with plastic fillers, with one bonus: There is less tendency to accidentally file lateral grooves into plastic filler.*

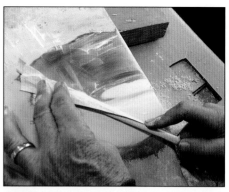

7 *A round, tapered file, wrapped in 80-grit abrasive paper, was used to file detail into the hinge-mount relief area. Later, a tapered, square file, wrapped in abrasive paper, was used to further refine the shape of this area.*

8 *As with lead filler, the mainstay of sanding this plastic filler was a board sander fitted with 80-grit paper. You can see how the board's position has been shifted slightly with each stroke, so that the same stroke is never sanded more than once in the same location.*

range of proportions stated by the material's manufacturer. This is sometimes expressed as the color of the mixed components.

Unlike lead, polyester filler is inexpensive and comparatively fast to work into desired shapes. Also, unlike lead, polyester filler can easily be added on top of itself to raise low spots that may be revealed by filing. Adding it in three or four stages is common. With lead, such additions are difficult. It is a bad idea to use plastic filler to a depth of much more than 1/8 to 1/4 inch, and generally less is better. Do not allow the easy layering capability of plastic filler to encourage you to build up excessive thicknesses with it.

Polyester components should be rigorously mixed individually, to uniform consistencies, by kneading or stirring. Then, they should be mixed with each other on a hard and non-absorbent surface like sheet-metal or shiny plastic. They should not be mixed on surfaces like cardboard or on any waxed surface, such as waxed cardboard. In the first case, the filler components can be selectively absorbed into the cardboard, unbalancing the chemistry of the filler. In the second case, the wax tends to mix with the filler and mess up its density and adhesion.

After the two components in polyester filler have been combined, they should be mixed thoroughly, and I mean thoroughly. Basically, you should mix them with your choice of mixing tool as completely as possible, and then mix them some more. When combined in the correct proportions, curing times are leisurely enough to avoid a problem with their setting up too fast.

Apply the fully mixed filler to the target area, and work it into its metal, again with your choice of tool. A flexible putty-knife blade or plastic spreader works well for this. After the filler has been applied, it should be spread with a plastic spreader and smoothed out into approximately the contours to which it will be filed. As filler is spread this way, it is important to not trap air bubbles in it, and to work out any air inclusions that may have occurred when it was applied. It should be left on the panel with a smooth, continuous appearance.

The curing of filler is a chemical reaction that will vary in speed with several factors. Among these are the ratio at which the filler's components were mixed, the ambient temperature, and the thickness of the filler. Manufacturers of these materials supply rough data on set times.

When plastic filler reaches a semi-hard state, which can be determined by checking a sample of what you

9 A shorter board sander was used to blend the detail from the hinge-mount relief into the adjoining panel filler. Note that the abrasive paper has been purposely positioned over the side of the sander, to let it ride up the relief.

10 Some hand sanding with 80-grit paper, backed by a hard-rubber pad, was applied to the back edge of the panel to give it shape. This was followed by sanding the area with 180-grit paper.

11 The final step in this repair was to treat the bare metal in the repair area with metal conditioner. This is important because, without protection from airborne moisture, the bare metal could begin to rust in a few hours.

applied by impressing one of your fingernails or a tool into its surface, it is time to grate it. This is done with a cheese-grater-type file. The purpose of doing this is to save time later, by removing what is obviously excess filler more quickly and easily than would be possible with power or hand filing and sanding approaches. Be careful not to go too far in removing material at this stage, or you may have to add more filler later to make up a deficit. While this would not create any quality problems, it does waste time and effort.

After the grated filler is fully cured (roughly, after lunch), it can be filed into exact contours, using the filing techniques discussed earlier. As noted, it also can be disc sanded to remove material and to bring it very close to final shape. The next adjustments and detailing of shapes should be performed with body files, using similar approaches to those used for this phase of this work for shaping lead. Again, as

with lead, final shaping is done with abrasive papers backed with pads of varying hardness.

The final step in using plastic fillers is to treat exposed metal, adjacent to the filler, with a good metal conditioner. Unlike lead filler, plastic filler does not present the problem of flux and lubricant residues. Therefore, there is no need to kill or neutralize these contaminants. However, it is still a good idea to apply metal conditioner to exposed metal in areas where all filler has been filed or sanded completely off a panel. The best way to protect this metal, as well as to protect the metal under the filler from attack by moisture is to prime the entire panel or vehicle with a waterproof, etching-type primer, very soon after completion of final shaping and sanding. This provides the soundest possible surface for later coating with sandable primer and paint top coats.

Note: If you choose to use a metal conditioner, you should not

use an etching primer over it. The two are incompatible. Use one, or the other. Over lead, it doesn't really matter which you use. With plastic filler, the etching type of waterproof primer is the best choice because it deals with the lack of moisture resistance and moisture-absorbing potential of the plastic filler.

The photograph at the beginning of this chapter shows the completed repair of the decklid hinge-mount relief area. The area on the left, in the photograph, was filled and finished with body lead filler, while the area on the right was repaired with plastic filler. The panel is destined to be fully stripped and refinished for use on a car that is now in restoration. In the future, if this panel is ever again stripped for refinishing, someone will probably notice that half of the left-hinge-mount repair was made with lead filler, and that the other half was filled with polyester filler. I wonder what that someone will think.

 WABASH CARNEGIE PUBLIC LIBRARY WABASH, INDIANA

SPECIAL PROJECTS AND PROCEDURES

As in most other endeavors, in autobody metal work there are many special projects and procedures that are needed to move work along, and/or to complete it. Some of these are huge and daunting tasks like fabricating a complex assembly. Others are jobs that must be done repeatedly and routinely, like hanging and aligning doors or decklids. This chapter details some of these projects and procedures, starting with a very difficult and impressive example of this kind of work.

The Project

At first, as I watched Matt, a metal crafter at L'Cars in Cameron, Wisconsin, fabricate a reproduction splash shield for a vintage Ford military amphibian vehicle, I was amazed that what he was doing could be done at all. Parts of the job, like patterning and cutting, were straightforward and familiar to me, but other parts of it stretched my concept of what is possible to accomplish when custom forming sheetmetal, without using stamping dies.

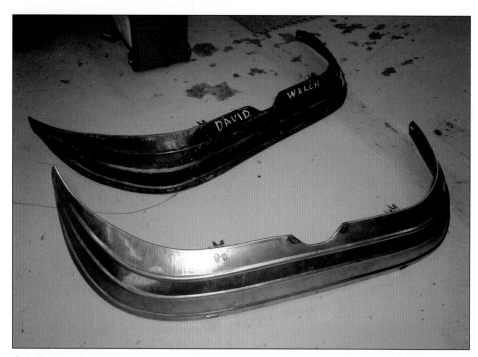

Original and duplicated new splash shields for a vintage Ford amphibian vehicle are shown here. The reproduced item, in front, was formed and outfitted in a little more than a day, using no significant specific tooling to produce it.

As I continued to watch Matt work on this project, two more forms of amazement joined my first sense of awe. I found it incredible that he could progress as quickly and certainly as he did, and I found the quality and precision of his results quite beyond anything that I had expected to see, or even thought possible. At times, his dexterity with the metal was so great that I had to remind myself that he was working with 21-gauge mild-steel sheet stock, and not a sheet of some kind of malleable

Fabricating a Splash Shield

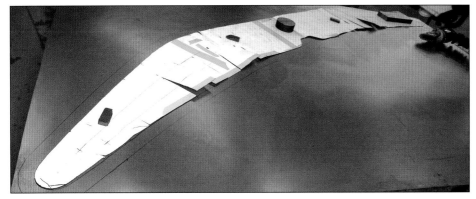

1 *This paper pattern has almost magical 3-D capabilities. Here it works flat, to outline the shape of the new splash shield. Later in this project, the cuts in it will allow it to indicate specific areas of the new part's shape, in three dimensions.*

2 *At this point, it was not necessary to cut out the metal from which to make the new splash shield very accurately. The part would be trimmed to exact dimensions, later. Still, Matt made his cuts accurately because that is the standard to which he works.*

3 *These Steck forming dies, mounted in a Pullmax, form very quickly. The dies' back areas impress V-shaped grooves into the work piece. Then, as it is drawn forward, through them, the dies' crowned front surfaces flatten and upset the V-shaped grooves, shrinking, and forming the metal.*

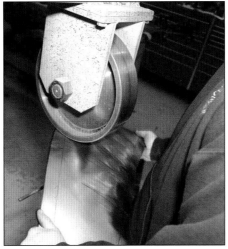

4 *The Steck die operation left the metal pretty uneven, but with shrink areas in the right places. Next, a large English wheel was used to smooth out the metal. Note the area below the forming wheels that was made uneven by the Steck process.*

5 *These Eckold shrinking heads were used to produce very compact, local shrinks, and to smooth the metal. They work by mechanically gathering the metal between them in a controlled upsetting pattern. The result is the ability to create very specific local shrink areas.*

plastic. The metal seemed to willingly respond to his every action.

Matt began the job by selecting material similar to that in the original splash shield that he was copying. He created an elaborate paper pattern of the original shield by outlining it on paper, and then cutting reliefs, sideways into the paper, so that when it was deformed to close

them, the paper took on the shape of the original, amounting to a three-dimension-capable template. This was not done so much for checking his final result with the splash shield, as it was to make it possible to check specific sections of it as he went along. Of course, he always had the original shield that he was copying to

check his finished result against. The paper template served when he had questions about a particular bend or

7 *At times, Matt stopped to compare his work piece to the original splash shield. You can see that at this point, he still had a long way to go. He had created the basic contour of the piece, and the beginnings of some of its crowns.*

6 *The early stages of this job required plenty of human intervention between machine operations. As the piece evolved, Matt used the Steck, Eckold, and English wheel devices to make his bends permanent. He did this by relaxing the metal into the shapes that he wanted it to take.*

8 *As work progressed, the piece's crowns began to appear. Matt used the English wheel to smooth areas disrupted by the Steck heads. Note one of these areas under and to the right edge of his left hand.*

9 *This paper pattern is being used to indicate one of the work piece's corner crowns. As the grooves in the paper are closed, it bends into three dimensions, indicating other angles of the crown that are supposed to be in the metal under it.*

contour, as he was forming the new piece from rough. Essentially, it was used to guide his progress.

A rough outline of the fabricated item was marked on the metal, leaving plenty of extra border material for later trimming and wire edging operations. The outline was cut out of the stock metal with an electric hand shear, along its straights and looser curves. Aircraft snips were used in its tight radius areas, its ends. All of this was pretty routine. Then the fun began.

The shape of the splash shield had been indicated roughly on the metal, with marked vertical lines at

some of the cuts in the paper template. Different distances from each line to the next, and the lengths and angles of the lines, indicated curvature in the panel crosswise and, at its corner bend radii, lengthwise. Starting with the corner bends, which had curves in both directions (amounting to crown), these areas

were worked into the metal with Steck forming tools, mounted in a Pullmax device.

As the Pullmax cycled—closing, separating, and closing again—the Steck shaping dies on the metal, the Steck dies' front area impressed considerable V-shaped bends into the metal—bends that stopped short of stretching it. Then, as Matt pulled

10 *The paper template indicated excessive crown in the marked area on the panel. Adjustment to the required crown in this area was too small for the Steck dies, while the crown radius was too tight for the Eckold heads. Another solution to shrinking and forming it had to be found.*

11 *The solution to upsetting and shrinking the mild inboard excess of crown was to push the metal through this cycle press, with a domed, steel-bottom die and a hard-rubber, flat, upper-die receiver (a hockey puck). This action put small, domed impressions in the metal.*

12 *The domed impressions were then hammered flat from both sides, and wheeled flatter in an English wheel. The result was to slightly upset the metal, causing local shrinks. This left it smooth, and in the correct crown.*

the metal back through the Steck dies, their slightly crowned front area flattened the bends that had been V-bent by their rear area, creating an upset in the metal, and shrinking it. This also shaped it. It took a combination of skill, judgment, and experience to use this device effectively, but armed with these attributes, it is incredible what Matt accomplished, in a relatively short time, with the Pullmax and Steck dies. It was equally amazing that there was almost no collateral damage—surface abrading, tearing, stretching, or cracking—to the metal that he was forming.

A comparison of the Pullmax/Steck combination to a less advanced method of rough shaping metal, like the good old plastic mallet and shot bag routine, might go like this. It would be like the comparison of a sport utility vehicle to an F1 racing car—they are both vehicles designed for transportation, but one of them gets you there much faster if you know how to drive it.

The Pullmax/Steck combination moves metal incredibly quickly but, understandably, it does not leave a smooth surface. To smooth his work and, to a lesser degree, to provide additional forming, Matt used an English wheel to work the area that he had shrunk and formed with the Steck dies. He employed a diagonal approach, from two directions, to smooth away the roughness created by the Steck dies.

The above-described operations were repeated several times, until the basic shape of the finished splash shield was pretty well established in the new metal, including the crowns that were inherent in its shape. As work progressed, Matt added the use of Eckold shrinking heads to his tooling routine. The Eckold heads were mounted in a press that cycled them toward and away from each other, pressing against the metal inserted between them. The Eckold device firmly grips sheetmetal, and then compresses it laterally. Think of this as a mechanical gathering action. The surfaces of each head's halves grip the metal as they compress it, and then move toward each other a small distance. This creates a small, compact upset—a defined and local shrink. The operator can control the amount of the shrink in several ways, in particular by adjusting head pressure—the

13 *Behold the rare and lovely Magee Wire Edger. It uniformly wraps sheetmetal edges around wire cores. It can handle mild curves in three dimensions. That amazing feat qualifies it for my list of the Seven Sheetmetal Wonders of the World*

14 *The next step in fabricating the splash shield was to roll the first of three lengthwise beads into it. A tape line was pulled in the position of the first bead, and marked on the metal. The bead was rolled slowly and accurately with a hand-operated bead roller.*

distance between the heads in their repeated strokes—and how many cycles he or she allows the metal to be compacted in a given area.

Do not think that all of this sophisticated tool work was occurring untouched by human hands. As Matt alternated use of the Pullmax/Steck operation with wheeling on the English Wheel, and Eckold head shrinking, he also did some good, old-fashioned hand bending, to make the piece go into the correct curvatures. Once he had the right contour in his work piece, he used the machines to refine it and to make it permanent. Because Matt's shaping approach involved sequential force and stress relieving operations, the panel acquired impressively little stress and hardness as he worked it. He also avoided producing any thin spots.

I have seen metal worked with conventional hand tools in dimensionally smaller amounts than this, and become so brittle and stressed that it cannot function as it is supposed to, without springing out of shape, or even cracking. By comparison, the metal in Matt's panel remained supple and resilient throughout the process.

Of course, Matt checked his evolving fabrication often against the original piece, as his work progressed. As the crowns and curves in the new piece became more and more regular and authentic, its surface became smoother. It began to look finished.

No matter how good the piece looked, however, it was critical to its dimensional correctness to keep checking it against the paper template. Those comparisons provided better and more useful indications than could be derived from comparisons to the original splash shield. To verify specific areas of the new piece, checking against the paper template informed exactly where the new fabrication might be off, because it was possible to position the paper template exactly over any particular area in the work piece. At one point, the paper template indicated excessive bulge in the crown at the new shield's corner bends.

To correct this, Matt performed some radical cold shrinks and reshapings where the metal was bulged. This was done with a cycling press that impressed the metal between a domed steel tool, and a hard rubber surface, basically a hockey puck. The result was then upset with a body hammer over a shot bag, and smoothed out on an English wheel. This corrected the last major dimensional deviation in the basic shape of the fabricated part. More work with the Eckold heads and English wheel fine-tuned minor areas of the piece, until it very closely approximated the original item when compared to the paper template.

The original splash shield had most of the length of its edges wrapped around a wire core, the exception being the attachment areas at its ends. To duplicate this configuration, Matt used a Magee Wire Edger. This was a common production tool, from Model T days into the

15 With the first wire edge installed, and the first bead rolled into the metal, it took on a new firmness. Matt now did some manual shaping. Note the contour outline marked on the floor for checking the piece's shape. The first rolled bead is clearly visible.

16 The second and third beads were now rolled into the splash shield. A little re-rolling touchup in a tightly curved and crowned section of the third bead is shown here.

17 At this point, the Eckold heads were used to shrink and smooth a small buckle in the edge of the metal. This was in preparation for installing the second wire edge in the work piece.

18 The second wire edge was rolled into the metal, using the miraculous Magee Wire Edger. While this machine makes this look simple, it takes skill, judgment, and experience to achieve good results with it. The hardest part of using the Magee is setting it up correctly for a job.

19 With the second wire edge completed, the piece was in its final form. It remained only to refine some of its details. Here, Matt is fine tuning one of the beads. Later, he uses a body hammer and a die that he had fabricated to make the beads' ends uniform.

20 The Magee Wire Edger couldn't follow the sharp bends. After shaping and welding in wire, Matt bent the edge of the metal over the wire with locking pliers. He had to anneal the metal once to finish this bending job.

1940s. Somehow, Bob Lorkowski, the amiable proprietor of L'Cars, has resurrected one of these extremely rare machines for use in his shop's restoration work. A sheetmetal edge, not necessarily a straight edge, is fed into the machine along with a piece of core wire. The Magee bends the edge of the sheetmetal uniformly around the core wire, with absolutely no fuss or visible distortion. It is an amazing process to behold.

With the first of the two wire edges on the work piece formed, Matt and some helpers used a bead roller to roll the bead nearest to the wire-cored edge into the work piece. This required the use of a deep-throat bead roller with a manual drive. The bead was rolled slowly enough to precisely follow a tape line that Matt had marked on the metal for guidance.

The rolled wire edge gave the piece strength, and the first rolled bead added to that strength. Now, Matt manually bent the piece into final shape. Up to this point, it still had been too floppy to hold its final shape. Now it did.

The other two beads were rolled into the piece, with dimensional checks and small corrections made to it along the way. The Eckold shrinking dies were particularly useful at this point for stabilizing the metal in its correct and final shape.

What If You Don't Have a Magee Wire Edger?

Over the years, in production, many automotive items, like fenders, hoods, and running boards, had their edges wrapped around wire cores by a Magee Wire Edger. If you have to duplicate this format in a fabrication, it is possible to do so without using the original Magee machine and tooling. However, this is difficult and it is doubtful that any manual process for wire edging will achieve the perfection of the Magee results. Hint: If you talk to Bob Lorkowski at L'Cars nicely, he might perform this process for you with their Magee, on a fee basis. That would definitely be my first choice for accurate wire edging.

For years, restorers and fabricators have had to do their best at approximating Magee results. There are several ways to approach this job, depending on your equipment and imagination. None that I know of are particularly pretty for long runs, but at least some of them can be made to work.

My first step in wire edge wrapping is to roll the narrowest half-round bead that I can, about 1/4 inch in from the edge of the piece that I am wire edging. I use the smallest-bead-diameter bead rolling dies that I have, about ³⁄₁₆ inch. This procedure produces a rounded bead with a little flat metal beyond it.

Next, I use a brake to gently roll the bead over on itself. I do this incrementally, pulling the rolled bead through the brake, and braking it slightly in several positions to tighten the bend's radius. It takes some experimentation to make this work—preferably on scrap metal—because dimensions vary with the thickness of what you are wire edging, the diameter of the wire that you use to core your edge, and the tooling that you have available.

After flattening the metal beyond the edge radius with a square-faced body hammer, I tamped the remaining metal flat to the panel with a hammer and a piece of bracket steel.

If the edge that you are creating is not straight—it rarely is—you have to form it in sections, using cuts between short, straight runs to accommodate curvature, and then beading the sections individually, before closing them with a finger brake or pliers. I warned you that this procedure wouldn't be pretty!

The third step in this procedure is to hammer the wrapped edge down, flat, over the wire core with a square-faced body hammer. This closes the edge around the wire. Finally, I hammer the edge flush with the back of the panel with a tamping tool. A flat piece of thick strap iron works well for this last operation. A wire-cored edge that is made this way obviously lacks the perfection of a machine-rolled edge, but it can be made to work acceptably. If you are dealing with a curved edge, it is necessary to weld shut the cuts that you made, and to use discreet amounts of lead or plastic filler to finish the welded lateral cuts that you used to create curvature in your wire-cored edge.

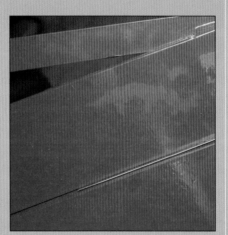

The first step in my home-style attempt to wire edge this piece of 22-gauge steel is to roll the narrowest bead that I could, about 1/4 inch in from its edge. Wire edging a curved edge presents another set of problems, and is much more difficult to accomplish.

The second step in my home-brew wire-edging process is to radius the edge metal, beyond the rolled bead, into a 3/4-round shape. I did this in a brake, in several small actions against the open edge, until it remained open only wide enough to insert my wire core.

21 *Matt fabricated these shield mounting brackets from flat stock, and spot welded them onto the splash shield. Talk about detail! Even the brackets that he fabricated were faithful replicas of the originals.*

With the third bead rolled into place, and the metal checked and rechecked for fidelity to the original piece, the second wire edge was added. At this point, the piece became quite strong, while showing no tendency to want to spring or oil can into and out of shape. The metal contained little stress. Metaphorically, it seemed happy and at peace with itself. Maybe you just had to be there to sense this.

The second wire edge was added to the new splash shield, and minor corrections were made to the rolled beads, and to the metal around them. The ends of the beads were made uniform with a hammer and a special die that Matt had fabricated for this purpose.

Finishing details and features were added to the new splash shield. Two three-dimensional strap holes were formed near its bottom edge. Wire edging was completed around an indent in its top edge, which contained turns that were too sharp for

the Magee Wire Edger to follow. This was done manually, by welding in a shaped piece of wire that followed the contour of the indent, and rolling the splash shield metal around it. Annealing heat was used to soften the metal in this area to allow completion of its severe deformation around the wire. Top brackets were fabricated to duplicate the originals, and then spot welded into place. Finally, mounting and reinforcing plates for the splash shield's ends were formed to duplicate the originals, and spot welded to the splash shield.

The authenticity of Matt's fabricated duplicate piece was superb. This was one of the most difficult metal forming jobs in steel material that I have ever witnessed, and it was done with an exactness of shape and detail that is at the far limit of what can be accomplished in fabricating sheetmetal. Note that when the finished fabrication is put into service, it will be visible from both sides. It will be subjected to severe service, in terms of impact, vibration, exposure to weather, and possibly to corrosive sea water. Surviving these factors made it impossible to take the easier route of fabricating it from welded-together sub-sections.

It also is impressive that the whole process of making this piece took less than a day and a half, and that included considerable time that was spent answering my questions, and stopping work so that I could photograph it.

Making Panels and Trim Fit

From replacing quarter panels to making grille or headlight trim surround pieces fit properly, autobody panel work constantly requires adjust-

ments of the dimensions and positions of parts, to make them to work together properly. This is a continuous battle in this work, with no simple, or general, attack plan available. Sometimes early-on minor mistakes, or botched details, can cause big problems in fitting things together later. Other times, what may appear to be big problems are surprisingly easy to solve. The following photos of a range of fitting operations were taken at Muscle Car Restorations, Inc., in Chippewa Falls, Wisconsin.

The only general advice that applies to these things is: You minimize the potential for big problems when you attend to dimensional accuracy as you go along.

Quarter-Panel Replacement

When it is done correctly, quarter-panel replacement can be a long job. This is work that can be done very well or very badly. Doing it well involves making everything fit nicely, while avoiding forcing fits in any major way. Such forced fits can cause distortion in the finished job.

The first step is to plan exactly what metal you want to remove and replace. In large part, this is dictated by the damage that is the cause for having to graft in the new metal. It is tempting to replace all of the old metal that is included in the new panel that you are installing—after all, you paid for all of it—and often, this is the best way to go. It all depends on the soundness of the old quarter panel, the quality of the replacement panel, and the logic of where you have to weld in the new metal. It is possible that there are features of the old metal that are sound, making them superior to their counterparts in the replacement

Quarter-Panel Replacement

1 *Part of this quarter panel's lower section had already been removed to gain access for a structural repair to part of the unibody. Now, tape was applied to it to indicate the cut line for removing the rest of the quarter-panel metal that would be replaced.*

Cutting out a quarter panel with a plasma arc torch is fast and accurate. With a car stripped as far as this one is, there is no reason not to use this technique for this job. **2**

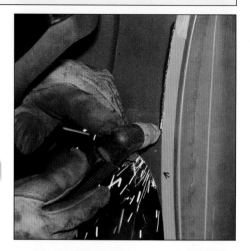

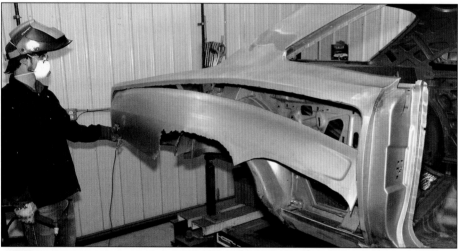

3 *The almost-removed quarter panel is shown here, dangling (just for my photograph) from the rest of the body. Note that the worker is wearing gloves, a welding helmet, and dust mask. That kind of protection is a very good idea when you use a plasma cutter.*

4 *Even a good quarter panel can have problems. It pays to correct the obvious ones before you install it. This panel has bulges generated by stretched metal. Shrinking the metal with a shrinking hammer saves time later, when it will be more difficult to gain good access.*

panel. This may be the case with regard to the positions of character lines, or of accessory mounting points that have to match other features in surrounding panels. Every partial panel replacement has its own logic and imperatives. Where you cut and weld in new metal may be an easy decision, or it may take considerable forehead-wrinkling thought.

Any of the metal cutting techniques described in Chapter 4 may

have a place(s) in your approach to cutting out an old quarter panel. One that is not described there, the old air-chisel method of separating large metal sections from panels, is pretty obsolete, but sometimes has a place in cutting out areas in some quarter-panel constructions. Plasma arc cutting is often the fastest and best way to sever old quarter-panel metal.

Any supporting structure behind a quarter panel that you replace must be repaired if it is damaged. Areas

like inner wheel housing attachments must be confirmed for alignment and contact, before you weld in a new quarter panel. It is much easier to correct structural issues before a quarter panel is mounted than after. In most cases, any supporting structure behind quarter panels is at their edges. The exception is monocoque quarter panels, where a skin is stretched over structure during manufacture to give rear vehicle quarter areas added

5 *Here, you can see how rough this panel is. Unfortunately, there was no other choice for this application. Reworking this panel, before it was installed, saved time.*

6 *It is best to cut a temporary line into either the old or the new panel, for a trial fitting. After that, you can refine the fit of your seam and make your final cuts.*

structural strength. An example of this construction is the Jaguar XK-E.

Although it is almost impossible to duplicate monocoque construction in repair or restoration work, dealing with it does dictate the use of special measures that are beyond the scope of this book. Just remember that if you ever encounter monocoque construction, you have to account for it. Semi-monocoque rear quarters are fairly common. However, the amount of structural strength contained in the outer metal in these units is relatively small, and they can be repaired or replaced using conventional techniques.

A key to performing successful rear-quarter-panel replacement is the sometimes disappointing realization that reproduction quarter panels are manufactured to varying standards of accuracy and quality. A few are impressively good, while others are nearer to the junk category. It is necessary to know how accurate your replacement panel is, and to begin to correct any deficiencies in it, before you try to weld it into place. It is far

easier to correct many of these problems before you attach new metal, rather than after.

Good panel fit is critical, before you attempt to weld in new quarter-panel metal. Usual practice is to hang and position the new quarter panel in place with Clecos, and then to weld it with lap (or occasionally with butt) welding techniques to the old metal. Your choices of welding technique and joint type depend on your situation, and on your skills. At the high end, this joint is performed as a butt joint with TIG equipment. In the middle range are lap joints welded with MIG equipment. And, at the low end are spot-welded lap joints that have to be slathered with filler to hide them. Chapter 8 describes the relevant fixturing and welding techniques for quarter-panel replacement, in detail.

No matter how careful you are in fixturing and welding in new quarter-panel metal, there is always cleanup shaping work to do, after it is welded into place. The best way to minimize this work is to control heat

buildup in your welded joints. Some of the tips in Chapter 8 help you to avoid unnecessary welding heat buildup. Anything that you can do to reduce it saves you time, by limiting metal distortion. This also improves the quality of your work.

Shrinking and stretching are often needed to make a quarter-panel replacement work. Remember, quarter-panel replacement is a fairly advanced job, one that should only be attempted after you have mastered basic metal working and panel welding skills.

Door Re-Skinning

Door re-skinning was once a fairly common procedure in automobile repair and restoration work. About the third time that I re-skinned a door, I did it right, and was able to complete the job acceptably and in a reasonable amount of time. Those first two times…well, I don't want to talk about them. Let's just say that a Three Stooges comedy routine has nothing on them, except possibly being funny.

In recent years, door skinning has become pretty rare in collision work, but it is still performed sometimes in repair and in restoration work. The reasons for the decline of this procedure will give you some idea of the problems with it. The first is the availability of decent new door skins. The ones made by OEM manufacturers tend to be expensive. They also can be hard to find for older vehicles. The door skins sourced from aftermarket suppliers are often more trouble than they are worth. Simply put, they frequently do not fit very well. It can take enormous amounts of labor to make them fit properly and look good. Due to their

After all fold-over flange spot welds have been ground, or otherwise broken, a pair of door de-skinning pliers like this one helps to remove the skin. This works best after the edge of the skin has been ground or sanded through. Then, the pliers remove the remaining folded-over metal strip. (Photo courtesy of the Eastwood Co.)

light construction—an emphasis on weight reduction—modern doors are often damaged in collisions to the point that re-skinning them is uneconomical. It requires so much work to straighten their frames, (or cores, as they are called in the industry), that the labor cost in these jobs makes replacement with new, or salvage doors, look pretty good. That, at least, is increasingly often the conclusion of most insurance companies. In many cases, they simply will not pay for door re-skinning.

Door re-skinning is still done in restoration work, but many restorers prefer to use salvage doors if they are available in reasonable condition. If rust is the reason for re-skinning a door, it is likely that the core requires so much work to make it sound that a salvage door looks like a better alternative. Still, there are times when door re-skinning is the best or only way to go.

The first imperative in this work is to start with a good door skin.

Avoid economy skins like the proverbial plague. After you have removed the subject door and stripped it of all removable parts—trim, door handle and latching mechanism, window regulator, window tracks, wiring, etc.—it is time to remove the old skin. After you have removed the spot welds that secure the skin to the door by grinding, drilling (with a spot-weld cutting drill), or disc sanding them away, you are ready to remove the original door skin. This can be accomplished by various methods, including edge grinding, seam chiseling, or seam prying. Special pliers-type devices that are sold to remove door skins work well to unfold door skin edges from door cores.

Carefully grinding the fold-over edge of the old skin is often a good gambit for starting the skin's removal. A grinding wheel or a disc sander outfitted with 24-grit abrasive is a good setup for this job. If you go this route, be careful to stop grinding or sanding just as you go through the old skin's folded edge. If you work slowly and watch carefully, you should be able to see a dark, early separation line appear in the folded metal as you cut through it. Be careful to stop grinding before you grind into the core's flange area.

Spot welds between the core and skin in the door handle area are common, so look for and remove them. Some doors have internal bracing, particularly in their upper areas near the window edges. The spot welds that attach these braces to the door skin will have to be broken. Grinding carefully through the skin is one way to get at them, without destroying metal that will be needed later to attach the new skin. Sometimes these attachment points can be cut

apart from the top, after windows and their trim have been removed.

After the old skin is removed, either by grinding its flange or by prying its edges back, all metal and weld residues must be removed from the core's flange areas. They should then be straightened, ground flat, and smoothed, as necessary.

The new skin should be held in the door opening and visually checked for contour match against, and fit to, the metal that will surround it. Then it should be checked against the core. If you discover any damage to the core, it must be corrected before you try to fit the new skin to it. If the skin does not position on the core naturally and easily, you have to determine whether the problem is in the skin, in the core, or in both, and correct it.

Almost all skins come with the 90-degree closing bends already formed at their bottom and side flange edges. A skin of this type may have a top bend that slips over the core, or it may not be configured that way. In either case, a good skin should slip into place over its core easily and authoritatively. Some skins allow for limited adjustment of

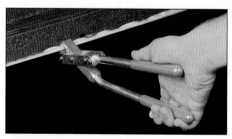

These door-skinning pliers do an accurate job of folding the edge of a new skin over a door's edge flange. Always begin folding the skin edge at its center and work out toward its corners, alternating from side to side from the center, as you go. (Photo courtesy of the Eastwood Co.)

their positions on their cores. These allow some movement of the core within the skin's edge bends, after those edges are partially or fully closed over the core. This movement is only possible before they are welded, or otherwise permanently fastened, to their cores.

Skins of this type have to be positioned in the door jamb before they are fully attached to their cores. This usually is done by temporarily hanging these doors, before final flange closing is completed. At this point, it should be possible to move these skins on their cores vertically, laterally, and diagonally by small amounts, to make them fit properly in their door openings and to make character lines align. You will not have much movement to work with, but there should be some. These types of skins are moved on their cores by very carefully tapping their edges with soft tools. Hammering on wooden blocks held against them, or tapping them with plastic mallets, often works well for door skin final positioning.

To close the bottom and side skin flanges over the core, you make your bends; working from the center of

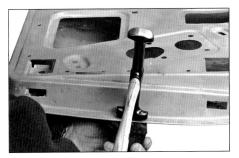

Hammering a door-skin edge over and flat is the old way to do this job. I wouldn't recommend it for installing a new door skin, but it is very helpful for touching up the seams that you have flattened with pliers, pneumatic crimpers, or rolling tools. (Photo courtesy of the Eastwood Co.)

each area, outward, in both directions, to the door's corners. That sequence helps to avoid distorting, buckling, and stressing the installed skin.

In some configurations, the tops of skins are positioned and secured by the bracket areas that you may have ground through when you removed the original skin. In these cases, the new skin will have brackets or flanges that mate to them. These may be adjusted for skin-to-core gap, and then secured with sheetmetal screws or by welding them. Once this is done, the door skin flanging can be completed. There are several ways to do this. You can move re-skinning pliers along skin flanges to close them. This gives you finer control. There are also pneumatic crimping and rolling tools available that are much faster than closing pliers, but offer less control as you move along with final seam flanging.

No matter how good your flange closing tools are, most re-skin jobs still involve limited use of the granddaddy of all closing tool sets, a door skinner's hammer and a dolly (or block of wood) to finish and refine some of the areas of your flange.

There are two possibilities for bonding a door skin to its core: You can spot or plug weld it into place, or you can use adhesives to bond and seal it.

Modern practice is to use adhesives to attach skins to cores. These adhesives are special two-part materials that are designed to adhere skins to cores, and to seal them. They should be applied to both sides of the core's flange, that is, to its outside before it is lowered into the skin, and to its inside flange before the skin is crimped or bent over it. These adhesives have reasonably friendly

cure times, but don't plan on any extracurricular activities too soon after you have applied them. Door skinning that is performed this way often involves two or three people, and those people tend to move pretty fast, once the adhesive has been applied. Multiple tools are often employed to bend the skin's edges over its core.

The other method of adhering skins to cores is to weld them in place on their bottom and side edges, after those edges are fully closed. This can be done with spot, MIG, or TIG approaches. Attachment welds should be made at intervals of every few inches, along each bottom and side seam. No prizes are awarded for making excessive numbers of welds. In restoration work, the number and spacing of welds should be as close as possible to the original configuration. While it is possible to spot weld skins to cores, this requires special equipment, and has no particular advantage. Plug welding is often used in restoration work to secure skins to simulate the appearance of original factory spot welds.

New skins come primed on both sides. Be sure to paint the inside of any skin that you mount with a waterproof and resilient paint, before you install it. It is critically important to remove all rust from the flange areas of cores, and to paint them, before you install new skins over them. I recommend a good weld-through primer for this application. Also apply seam sealer to the critical folded area of the skin, after it is installed.

Hanging Doors

Over the years, there have been so many different ways that door hinges and latches have been configured and

Most doors are heavy, bulky items that must be adjusted to fine dimensions to look right and to work correctly.

Many of them require or benefit from a crew of two or more to mount them.

A straightedge, calipers, and thickness gauges are useful tools for confirming proper door alignment. A piece of string drawn tight is also very helpful. To use these items effectively, you need a good eye, or someone with a good eye, for dimensions, spacing, and symmetry.

adjusted that it is impossible to describe all of the major ones here. Door hanging has aspects of art and science about it. I have no statistical proof of this, but I have noticed that the people whom I have known in body shops who were really good at this job—hung it perfectly right on the first or second try—also tended to be excellent pool players. Like pool, hanging vehicle doors involves manipulating several variables in your head, simultaneously. This is because every adjustment that you make may not only change the factor that you are adjusting, but one or more other dimensional factors, as well.

The first step in adjusting doors is to understand the logic of the particular system that you are adjusting. Basically, you usually have two hinges to adjust. In the best situations, each can be moved in, out, up, down, and back and forth. This can be done with threads, washers, shims, cams, or sliding plates, among other possibilities. With welded hinges, after you run through the possibilities on the removable side attachment, your options may be limited to bending the metal that supports the welded attachment side. When both sides are welded and only hinge pin removal is provided for door removal, bending the hinge-mounting metal becomes your only recourse.

Older door systems used threaded fasteners and moveable mounting plates to secure doors to their hinges, and hinges to their body posts. Add some shims as needed and you can make any adjustment that you will ever require. Modern, welded hinges are not as convenient or forgiving.

The same motions and movements that are used for adjusting hinges are possible for adjusting door latches and latch receivers, with similar configurations of their hardware. And that is only the beginning of the possibilities. In older cars, body shims between bodies and frames were often used in making doors fit properly. That's right, you sometimes had to reposition the hinge and latch posts, themselves, to make things line up correctly.

Most door fitting involves making multiple adjustments to hinges and latches, to have everything properly lined up. Each adjustment should improve one factor, generally reducing misalignment there, until perfect

This alignment problem is not as bad as it looks. That's why the installer is feeling the gap with his right hand, to assess its extent. Despite appearances, the problem is not the jamb panel contours; it is door alignment, which is much simpler to correct.

alignment is achieved when all factors are accounted for and properly adjusted. At every stage of these adjustments, this puts a premium on knowing exactly where things are in relation to where they were, and where you want them to be.

Any technique that you can make work for sensing alignment makes the job easier. This may involve the use of reference tools, like straightedges, to check surface alignments. Or, it may require eye-balling, or feeling surfaces, to spot deviations from proper alignment.

One of the problems in making door and other panel adjustments is that as you come closer to a final result, the necessary changes become

Although door-alignment adjustments are perfected in small increments, the ways that you make them often look heavy handed. Since any adjusting operation runs a pretty good chance of overshooting its target, scribing position lines at each stage of the adjustment helps to determine the next move.

This grille section needs to be perfectly aligned with everything around it: the headlight surrounds on either side of it, the metal panel under it, and the hood on top of it. Any misalignment in the visible surfaces of these items will be painfully visible.

Trial grille mounting revealed that the substructure center-attaching point needed to be moved forward. Using this large slide-hammer and robust hook end was a good way to exert the force needed to modify the grille-mounting substructure.

Ever finer adjustments are the routine in most trim-mounting procedures. Here, the heavy slide-hammer adjustment has given way to a finer, hammering adjustment. After the grille is in place, there is a final slotted-screw adjustment for fine tuning its center's fore-and-aft position.

If this grille is slightly mis-positioned, mating the headlight surround trim to it puts that piece out-of-position, as well. In trim work, one error can lead to another error, and another, until there are no more ways available to hide the errors, and the job still looks bad.

smaller and smaller. Most adjustment systems do not particularly accommodate very fine, incremental adjustments. It may take several attempts to make an adjustment right, without destroying some other aspect of panel alignment. It all takes clear thinking, good manual technique, and even a bit of luck. Luck isn't absolutely necessary, but when you have it, it speeds this work along.

Mounting and Adjusting Trim

Mounting trim has the same, basic consideration as hanging panels—you want to make everything line up. Over the years, in the quest for invisible ways to attach trim, manufacturers have developed and adopted a dizzying variety of methods for affixing trim to panels. Some are pretty straightforward, while others range from amusing, cumbersome, or difficult, to downright stupid. Modern trim is often affixed with adhesives, which has the distinct advantage of not puncturing paint and metal, thereby removing a

potential source of rust. Otherwise, various types of plastic or metal clips, threaded fasteners, expanders, and the like have been, and are, used to attach it. Snapping, sliding, and pivoting motions often are required to affix and to remove it.

Small adjustments to trim position can involve modifying trim clips, or other attachment items, by bending, filing, or grinding them. Where new metal is involved, it is necessary to puncture it for most trim clip attachments—the exception being the attachment of trim to the edges of panels.

Some trim attachments are adjustable, with slotted bolt-through configurations, and other methods. At times, after structural and panel repair, adjustments of this sort do not provide sufficient range for proper alignment. In those cases, either the adjustment or the mounting point has to be modified to make trim fit properly.

As with other alignment propositions, final fit must be determined visually, by feel, and by the comforting sense that everything looks right.

BEFORE YOU PAINT

The moment of truth has arrived. Your repaired, restored, or fabricated sheetmetal masterpiece is completed, and ready to be finished. That means that it will soon be hidden for nearly eternity, as far as you are concerned, under an opaque coating. Whatever type of finish is applied over your work—solvent-based paint, water-based paint, or powder-coated plastic—it will have an index of reflection that will reveal any defects in your work to a degree that the sanded metal that you now see never could. In fact, its coating will scream out any defects in the surface over which you have labored so long and so diligently. And no, painting it in flat, crackle, wrinkle, or hammertone black probably is not a practical workaround to avoid that shiny, painted reckoning.

That is what makes this the moment of truth. It is when the quality of your results with skills like bumping, metal finishing, and filling are about to be put on display for all to see, and in the harshest possible way—under highly reflective paint. Then, it will have the opportunity to pass the first of the two pertinent

Someone had begun to repair this front fender before it came to me. The cause of the rust-out was a Y-configured rubber seal against its inside, in the area where the repair was made, and where the factory didn't apply paint. Adequate coating and undercoating should cure that problem.

This isn't a final panel check, but the technique is the same. By feeling through a rag or tissue, much of the friction of your moist, oily skin is eliminated. That allows you to feel minute imperfections that your eyes might not catch.

tests applied to metal work: How good does it look, and how long will it look that good? It takes a while for the results of the second test to become known.

As you think about it, it is reassuring to remember that if you did everything right, made all the right decisions and moves, the quality of your metal work has built on itself at every stage. And it will pass that first test now, and the second test later.

Think of it this way: Great panel work involves the massive accumula-

tion of favorable details. If there are 100 things—big to small—involved in a job that can be done between very badly and almost perfectly, and even perfectly, it is your mission to capture as many of those 100 things as is possible, as close to perfectly as is feasible. In almost all cases, this depends on the validity of the basic concept(s) that you used to approach your work, and on how many of its tasks you performed near flawlessly. If, from basic concept to small details, you did everything very well,

The trick of posting a stationary light source, and then watching it appear to move across a panel as you move your head, shows you defects in panel shapes that are difficult to spot in unreflective metal, but very easy to see under shiny paint.

Here's a way to locate small defects in crown. Rock a straightedge, with a light source behind it, in several places and at several angles, across surfaces that you want to check. You will be able to discern minor deviations in crown in the light shining under the straightedge.

you will have produced good-to-great work. Of course, small missteps can ruin a job, but it usually takes more than a single slipup to botch everything.

If you bumped or fabricated metal to very good approximations of final shapes, leaving little for filler to fill, this helps. If you attended to shrinks and stretches in the metal, as you formed it into correct shapes, you are a long way toward making its final format stable. If you avoided putting stress into the metal by forcing it harshly into position, and then welding it there, this helps some more. It is okay to slightly fine tune an edge with a small screwdriver, persuading it into perfect position for welding. However, if you made things line up with pry bars and 2-pound hammers, that will invite big problems, later.

If your metal finishing achieved perfect contours, as revealed by careful visual and tactile inspections, the odds in favor of it turning out between very well and perfectly are increased. If you made your filler application over metal that was completely cleansed of all traces of rust and other contamination, you have another considerable advantage.

If you used no filler, or used it very sparingly and in very minor thicknesses, you have a definite benefit. If you used lead filler, and were careful to neutralize all traces of flux and tallow residues as you went along, that is a big plus. If you used plastic filler and were careful to thoroughly mix its components, individually and with each other in correct proportions, that removes two more possibilities of failure at a later date.

Whichever kind of filler you used, if you were meticulously careful to sand out all file marks, and then to use abrasives with escalating grit numbers to erase all deep scratches left by previous and coarser grits, until you had produced a surface free of visible individual scratches, you have won the battle against sand-scratch swelling in the finish that will cover your work. If your last sanding was with an abrasive that left both metal and filler surfaces with good tooth for primer adhesion, you have headed off another potential issue that can plague metal work. If you cleaned your finished surface with solvent, and then blew off all loose debris

with dry compressed air, you are another step toward perfect results.

If you protected your finished surface from corrosion with the one-two punch of a good metal conditioner, properly applied, followed quickly by priming and top coating, you have eliminated a whole class of failings and blemishes that can haunt metal work. If, instead of using metal conditioner, you went the other good-surface-protection route and quickly, after its completion, covered your work with an etching, waterproof primer, you have made a good move to exorcise the rust demons that can lurk on metal, under coatings.

As I said, if your basic approach was right, and you supported that by getting all, or an overwhelming majority, of the pertinent tasks and details of your work right, it should rank at or near the highest possible grade. It should look good and last long, and that is a substantial accomplishment, one in which you should take considerable pride.

The Danger from Behind

There is one more critical detail that accompanies the completion of metal work, before you paint it yourself or turn it over to the paint guys. It is the consideration of protecting the back side of your work from attack by moisture and the corrosion that inevitably follows prolonged contact with moisture. If your work fails at some future date, due to corrosion, it may be difficult to determine the source(s) of that failure. Perforation rust can originate on either side of a panel. When you do great metal work, protecting the back sides of your panels makes great sense. It won't happen unless you do it or pay to have it done.

The bolting flange at the bottom of this front fender is problematical because it traps moisture and dirt. Aside from keeping it clean, the best in-service protective measure is to coat it with a strongly bonded, dense paint, followed by a good rust-proofing agent.

Your first chance to deal with potential corrosion is when you design a sheetmetal structure, or work on one that has obvious problems in this area. In the main, areas that trap water or, worse, water and dirt, and hold them against metal are places where corrosion is likely to begin and increase rapidly. Dirt tends to absorb water, and hold moisture against metal, long after just water would have left the scene due to evaporation, passing air, or by the momentum generated by vehicle movement.

One major corrective step that you can take is to avoid designing structures with moisture traps that hold water, and small openings that can use capillary action to draw moisture into narrow spaces. If you can imagine some of its features acquiring and/or trapping water when you look at a structure, you should try to prevent this from happening or to figure out a reliable way to cause them to drain.

At this point, you can very easily run into the law of unintended conse-

quences, a variant of Murphy's Law. My favorite formulation of Mr. Murphy's dictum is the statement that "nature always sides with the hidden defect." When dealing with corrosion prevention in sheetmetal structures, you have to identify all hidden defects and take countermeasures to overcome them. Then, you have to make sure that none of your countermeasures created new hidden defects along the way. If this happened, you have to take countermeasures against the flaws in your countermeasures.

For example, take the matter of sealing structures from the intrusion of moisture. Consider something like a headlight module system in failure, with fog coating the inside of its lens. It was designed to keep moisture out but the design not only let moisture get in, it actually trapped it there by preventing its exit. That is why it remains there. Another example is the seals on some bearings. They were designed to keep lubricant in, and dirt and moisture out. How many times have you seen such bear-

ings hopelessly contaminated with what was supposed to be kept out and, due to their seal designs, all but impossible to relubricate? You have to be vigilant to avoid creating your own versions of these counterproductive situations. Providing for factors like drainage, venting, and cleaning access usually helps.

Consider the sealing systems that wipe against and seal car door windows. They are designed to keep water from seeping into doors, as windows are lowered, and rusting them out at vulnerable seams. Those vehicle door-window seals keep most of the water that could enter that way from leaking into doors. Unfortunately, they also help to seal in the moisture that does get past them and that arrives from other sources. Then, when the sun beats down on the outsides of these doors, with the potential to heat their cavities, evaporate the moisture there, and drive it out, those same wiper seals help to prevent this desirable outcome from occurring. The holes and vents in door bottoms that are designed to let water out often foul with dirt and debris, blocking its exit. Over the years, a few automotive body cavities have been fitted with vents designed to work on the Bernoulli principle—to use passing air to create a low-pressure situation to extract water from their insides. This works until some small bit of debris changes their configuration, and then becomes useless.

In many situations, keeping moisture away from metal is a very tricky proposition. I don't care if they say that something difficult is like making water run uphill. Take my word for it, water will run up hill enthusiastically, when it senses that it can find something to rust by going there. Okay—I haven't actually seen this happen.

Failed anti-corrosion designs and features are not hard to find. They are all around us. Just check out any junkyard.

Still, you shouldn't be overwhelmed by the odds against taking perfectly effective action to prevent rust from mortally attacking your sheetmetal work someday. Just try to put that day off for a century or so. You have a big, last chance to make your final moves just before your project is painted. Later, you may have a few more chances to inspect, detect, and correct problems, but remember that corrosion looks for ways—24/7 and holidays—to destroy your work.

What You Can Do

The good news is that there are things that you can do. First and foremost, you can try to keep water from seeping in. This means designing seams and joints that are, and remain, tightly sealed against moisture. But that is not enough because moisture is pernicious; it can enter areas in airborne form, and condense into liquid. Even in airborne form, it can start and promote corrosion, without ever becoming a liquid.

Keeping water out is a noble aim, and should be pursued. But do so with the certain knowledge that your success with it will be partial at best. With that in mind, there is a second line of defense that you can pursue. If the structure that you wish to protect is one that you designed, you can eliminate obvious water traps like shelves and other enclosures. You may include drains for areas that might otherwise possibly trap water. You can vent potentially vulnerable areas, so that moisture has a chance to escape, or is extracted from them. You can make your vents and drains large enough to not plug up with debris.

Seam sealer is a terrific way to protect vulnerable joints, such as this door skin joint, if it is applied over scrupulously clean metal and in a reasonable thickness. It is also possible to abuse seam sealer applications in ways that cause them to do as much harm as good.

The third line of defense is sealing and coating the unseen sides of your work. It starts with removing all traces of paint, rust, grease, and oil from the back sides of your metal work. After that, apply a good seam sealer, particularly to the back sides of lap and offset lap joints. Body caulk should be used in areas that are too wide open for seam sealers to fully close them. Back side metal should be coated with a waterproof and very dense (in the molecular sense) coating like moisture-cure urethane. Applied to steel, moisture-cure urethane aggressively draws water molecules from both of its surfaces, the one exposed to the environment and the one facing metal. That means that it removes all moisture from what is under it—a considerable advantage in fighting rust.

The molecular structure of a moisture-cure urethane coating is so dense that even the relatively small, frenetically active H_2O molecule has great difficulty penetrating it. While moisture-cure urethane's surface characteristics, and its lack of robust resistance to ultraviolet light, make it inappro-

priate for finishing vehicle topsides, it is ideal for protecting their undersides. It clings to properly prepared metal tenaciously, blocks the transit of moisture, and remains resilient for decades after it is applied. This means that it is unlikely to crack under the assault of flying gravel and other things kicked up by vehicle wheels.

After you have completely sealed the back side of your metal work, go for some extra insurance. Remember, anyone who wears both a belt and suspenders is unlikely ever to suffer the embarrassment of lower wardrobe failure. The extra insurance is to coat the painted underside of your work with a flexible and resilient corrosion-protection agent. This could be a hot-sprayed, paraffin-based rustproofer that contains anti-corrosion additives, or a rubberized undercoating.

Finally, you should check these measures, after their applications have settled, to make sure that there are no gaps or other flaws in them. For example, be sure that you applied the undercoating consistently. And

Hot paraffin-based rust-poofing material is great for protecting most undercarriage surfaces, where the impact of gravel and stones is not a problem. Where it is, a good rubberized undercoating works best. The coatings shown here are applied with the air sputter gun, shown in the can on the left.

be sure that it didn't flow downward, potentially creating gaps, and possibly clogging or blocking critical drains and/or vents.

With all of those measures, you may still fail to provide your work with perfect, or even adequate, protection against rust. This is true for both custom work and for modifications that you may make to improve the corrosion resistance in existing vehicle designs. Sadly, in the end, rust always triumphs. The real issue is what we can do to deny it that victory for the longest possible time. If we gain some valuable time against the rust enemy, that alone is worth celebrating.

What I have written on this topic indicates how tricky rust prevention problems can be, and how carefully you have to develop and deploy your countermeasures to them. Here is one last example: In early 1977, I took delivery of a new Honda Accord, the car that arguably established Honda as a major player in North America. Immediately after delivery, I took the car to have it undercoated by a friend who operated a Ziebart rustproofing establishment.

When I returned to pick it up, my friend said, "Matt, I want to show you something." He produced a memo from Ziebart's home office in Connecticut, noting that their franchises were required to advise their customers that the standard Ziebart warranty would not apply to the front fenders of Honda Accords sold in the United States and Canada. In fact, Ziebart would provide no warranty at all on the front fenders of these cars.

The memo went on to state that the design of these fenders made it impossible to protect them with the Ziebart rustproofing process. As it happened, my friend had another

Accord in for rustproofing that day. He walked me over to it, drilled an access hole in its right front fender door-jamb-facing surface, and inserted his undercoating wand through the hole. He told me to watch the metal on the top of the fender, near the cowl and hood, as he shot undercoating at it. Then, he triggered his spray wand and withdrew it through the drilled hole, spraying high-pressure, hot paraffin undercoating from its nozzle at the fender top's underside. As I watched, I saw the metal in the fender's top deflect slightly, from the pressure of the undercoating hitting its other side.

"Wow," was all that I could say. My friend agreed, and noted that he had never seen anything like it. Honda's die-stamping process had drawn the fender top metal so thin that it could be moved by an undercoating spray.

Worse, that thin metal flexed so much during the car's operation that Ziebart had determined that any coating applied to it would tend to fracture in short order. Ziebart further concluded that once the paint fractured, it would pull in moisture and would quickly rust. The rust would expand and release the coating, leaving the thin steel bare and wide open for corrosion.

It got worse. Because the air under the fender tops exchanged with the air in the engine compartment, moisture would condense from there, as that warm area cooled when the engine was shut down. Cyclical engine-compartment cooling and condensing moisture is a natural occurrence in many climates. This predictably happens when an engine is shut down at the end of a day.

Ziebart was right. Its corrosion engineers had foreseen a situation

that Honda's designers and engineers had not. Within a few years, almost every early Accord that one saw in northern climates was either rusting about its fender tops, or sporting replaced fenders. Honda even offered replacement fenders for little or nothing, if the customer would pay for installation and painting. This offer was kept open for a long time after the original warranties on these cars had expired.

I tell this story to make several points. Honda had very good body engineering in that period, but failed to foresee this problem with the Accord. Ignorance of the North American climate and salt use here probably contributed to creating this design flaw. Besides, these kinds of failures are usually far from obvious. In this case, the actual problem involved a sequence of factors and events that worked together to produce a perfect corrosion storm. Corrosion failure is rarely attributable to a single cause or fault. Later Accord fenders looked very similar to the early ones, but did not suffer any unusual or premature corrosion problems in their fender top areas. These problems can usually be solved fairly easily, once their exact causes are known.

The best action that you can take to prevent back side-initiated corrosion from ruining your work is to consider the possibility that it can happen, in every action that you take. Think about it when you decide on joint design, or when you seal the backs of your joints. Consider it when you paint your work, or instruct someone else on how you want it painted. In sum, be aware of any factor, series of factors, or combination of factors that might result in a successful corrosive attack on your work. Then take the best countermeasures that you can.

MINOR RUST REPAIR TO

A FENDER EDGE

This chapter is about a real-world repair. Specifically, it details removing and replacing rusted metal in a lower-edge wheel well area in the front, right fender of a 1986 Jeep Comanche. This type of repair is called sectioning and is a frequent task in the real world of autobody metal projects.

The cause of the rust damage? The plastic trim that covered it trapped water, salt, and dirt, holding them against the sheetmetal above it. As a result, the fender's metal surface corroded, pitted, and rusted through in some places.

While fender replacement might be an economically preferable alternative to repairing this panel, this demonstration project shows what can be done to repair this kind of damage and how to do it. Another alternative, finding a used fender that is strong in this area and transplanting metal from it, might also be an attractive approach. However, finding such a fender probably would be difficult. The trim configuration that caused this damage would have caused it in identical fenders in most climates. There are

The first step in any rust repair job is to determine the extent of the damage. Picking and wire brushing are good ways to separate the sound metal from the weak metal.

always multiple valid approaches to any sheetmetal repair. The approach taken here is one of them.

The Approach

Two aspects of this job are uncommon: Traditional metal sectioning and finishing techniques are applied to a fairly modern panel. These techniques are usually reserved for panels in older vehicles because those panels are thicker and softer (contain less carbon) than is the case with this 1986 Jeep fender.

But because this panel will be fitted with modified trim that will not completely cover the repaired area, this area must have a fully finished appearance that was not part of its original configuration. That is why older and more time-consuming techniques were chosen to restore it.

Many people believe that these older metal-working techniques cannot successfully be applied to modern sheetmetal because it is too thin and too hard. That is partially true. Modern, thin autobody panels do not weld as easily, or file as well, as

Hand or power wire brushing near the visible rust released loose paint, revealing additional weak areas lurking under the finish. This is essential knowledge to have before you begin repairs.

Mild abrasive blasting poked holes through areas where the metal was weakest. This procedure also began cleaning the metal in the repair area for later steps, like welding, tinning, and filling.

Once the repair area was lightly blasted, some additional picking and hand wire brushing revealed the apparent extent of the rust damage.

the panel steels that were in use before the 1970s. The older techniques of sheetmetal work can be applied to modern panels, but only with great skill, time, patience, and often with somewhat compromised results. The approach, taken here, to this job requires intermediate to advanced skills.

The First Step: Evaluation

Cursory inspection of this fender revealed that the area was suspect for structural rust damage. Picking at it with a scriber, and hand brushing it with a carbon-steel-bristle brush, indicated that the metal could be punctured easily in this area. The same probing of other areas did not go through the metal.

Light abrasive blasting of the weak area and other suspected areas seemed to reveal the true extent of the damage. More probing and brushing followed.

When the full extent of the metal to be excised in this area was determined, it was marked for removal. It is always a good idea to remove metal beyond the actual sus-

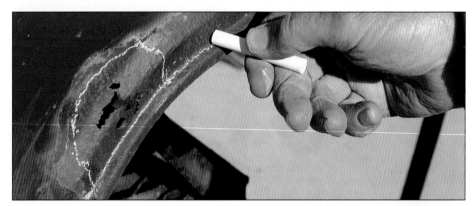

Knowing the likely extent of the damage to this part of the fender, the next step was to mark it off so that a repair strategy could be formulated and followed. The marked area represents the shapes and sizes of the patch parts to be fabricated.

pect area, to ensure having sound steel to which to weld new metal.

Early in any sectioning project, where new metal will be fabricated to replace old metal, it is always advantageous to start an indexing system that will help you to accurately position the new metal. In this case, simple index marks were chalked onto the fender, for later transfer to templates and to new metal.

This photo shows the boundaries of the metal that needs to be cut out of the panel, and replaced with new metal. Note the vertical index markings: These were used later to align the new, fabricated metal with the rest of the fender.

Removing the Bad Metal

There are many ways to remove metal from panels. Popular among them are: hand and power saws, nibblers, air or electric shears, grinding wheels, and plasma arc cutting. Different methods have different advantages and drawbacks in various situations. The object in this kind of cutting is to do as little collateral damage as possible, and to create as little distortion as is practical.

For this project, a very straightforward approach was favored. An entryway was ground into the fender with an air-driven muffler-cutting wheel. Then a small reciprocating saw blade was inserted into the cut and moved along the cut line. This was done from both ends of the cut line.

Small air-driven reciprocating saws are handy for this kind of work. They are inexpensive, very maneuverable, and reasonably fast cutting. In this case, the entire removal operation took less than 10 minutes, producing a clean separation with no physical damage to the fender

1 *The first incision into the panel was made with an air-driven 3-inch muffler cutter. This allowed entry of the next tool, a small air-driven, reciprocating metal saw, used to cut the diseased metal out of the panel.*

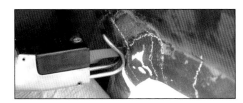

3 *The reciprocating saw can make turns that a grinding wheel cannot, but it causes some vibration and shake in the panel. While one hand is used to guide the saw along the chalked cut line, the other stabilizes one of the panel's edges.*

2 *This saw cuts more slowly than the grinder, but is easier to control and guide accurately. It cuts cleanly and without any damaging heat buildup, making it ideal for this job.*

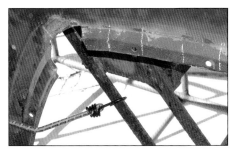

4 *The panel has the diseased metal removed. The excised material was in a high-stress area of the fender that included compound curves and strengthening creases, to deal with that stress. A good repair has to be structurally robust.*

Planning and Modeling the Repair

With the bad metal removed, a sketch was made of the part needed to replace it. We decided to make the new part from two separate pieces and join them together, after each was tack welded into the fender. This approach was selected largely because each separate piece could be accurately and easily fabricated on a metal edge shrinker, a tool that was available for this job. Fabricating a patch from a single piece of metal would be more difficult, and would offer no particular structural or cosmetic advantage, beyond some bragging rights.

Good modeling is a critical step in sectioning work. It allows the metal worker to gauge and confirm the shapes and/or dimensions of new pieces to the ones that they replace. There are numerous ways to model any surface. The simplest is often the most useful. In this case, uninsulated copper electrical wire was used to model the format of the fender's vertical edge. The more gradual curve of its horizontal (wheel arch) edge was transferred to a piece of insulated copper wire. Forming the uninsulated modeling wire to the fender's vertical edge was easily accomplished by hand

1 *Planning a repair process, minutely, is one key to reducing the likelihood of unpleasant surprises. A sketch of what the repair patch will look like is a good first step.*

---

bending with a needle-nose pliers. Uninsulated wire is best for accurately capturing small detail. Insulated wire bends naturally into long curves. The latter was used to capture the gradual curve of the horizontal fender arch in the sectioned area. The lateral indexing marks on the fender were transferred to it for later use.

2 When bad metal is removed from a panel, it is critical to have some type of pattern or template to record its shape and contours, so that new metal can be formed accurately to replace it. This piece of 14-gauge electrical wire is easy to form and retains its shapes well.

3 The wire is shaped, checked, and reshaped, until it fits the panel edge perfectly. Because the removed metal was too deformed to use as a pattern, an adjacent area was modeled. This worked because the feature being modeled is consistent and continuous.

4 A lengthwise model was made from another piece of 14-gauge electrical wire, this time with its insulation on. This wire is marked with indexing from the fender that will later help to fit the panel patch accurately.

Cutting and Forming the Metal Patches

The tool chosen to perform the bulk of the forming work, an edge shrinker, is one of the most useful and versatile tools in the metal worker's arsenal. It simply and easily shrinks metal on the edge of a piece by compacting it laterally, between two sets of jaws. In this case, a flat piece of 23-gauge body steel was cut to rough dimensions in a shear, and formed into roughly a right angle in a small sheetmetal brake. At this point, its format resembled that of a small piece of very light angle iron.

As the metal along one edge of the piece was compacted in the edge shrinker, the body of the piece began to curve. This curvature was constantly monitored and checked against the insulated wire template, until it was very close to the template's shape. Then, it was indexed to the marks on the fender, and checked against the fender opening into

which it later would be welded. After some fine tuning with the shrinker, a very good fit-up was attained.

Using the relevant index markings, the new piece was positioned in the fender opening and marked for approximate cut-off length. A little extra length was allowed for final fitting, and the piece was cut with aircraft

1 This tool, a metal edge shrinker, is perfect for forming the long edge piece needed for this repair. As the surface between the jaws of the tool is laterally compressed the piece curves to accommodate the shrunken area, creating exactly the kind of curve needed for this repair part.

2 As the new edge piece was formed, it was repeatedly checked against the wire template and modified accordingly. Although this edge shrinker has a foot control, using the hand lever gives the operator better control.

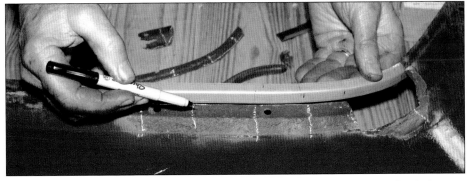

3 As the repair piece approached the shape of the template—its final shape— it was checked against the cut-out area, and indexing it was completed. It could not be fully and accurately indexed until it came close to its final shape.

4 The last check of the repair piece against the cut-out area revealed the need for slightly more curvature in the repair piece's long section. This was applied.

5 When the repair piece perfectly fit the contour of the cut-out area, it was marked for lengthwise termination. The index markings were very helpful in accurately positioning it in the fender metal.

6 Simple aircraft snips cut accurately enough to trim the long repair piece close to its final length dimension. Final length was adjusted by grinding. At this point, it was important to leave a little extra length, to allow for accurate, final fitting.

7 The cutting operation slightly deformed the end edges of the long repair piece. These were easily straightened by gently tapping them against an anvil with a low-crown body hammer.

8 A small disc grinder was used for this piece's final lengthwise trim. Because metal expands at welding temperatures, it is critical to trim repair pieces to provide expansion gaps—between the thickness of a dime and a nickel—to prevent their expansion from causing and locking in permanent panel distortions.

9 Final fit for this piece was now checked and approved. In a repair like this, time invested in getting good fit-ups will be repaid many times over in time that will not have to be spent correcting a variety of problems.

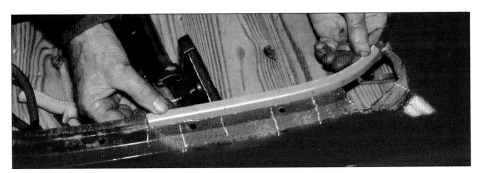

10 *A piece of patch metal, cut to rough dimensions, was checked against the space that it will occupy between the panel and the long repair patch piece. Note the line on the short patch piece that represents the location of its center crease.*

11 *The short repair piece's center crease was formed in a finger brake. The angle of the bend exactly duplicated the crease in the fender flange to which it will be fitted.*

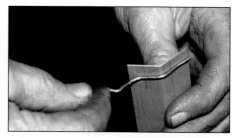

12 *The copper wire template that was made of the fender edge shape was then used to check the bend in the repair piece. Rechecking and bending were performed until the match was perfect.*

13 *With the patch piece bent to the correct angle, it was now roughly indexed to the long repair piece, and given preliminary marking for final dimensions. These dimensions could not be confirmed until the piece was near its correct, final contour.*

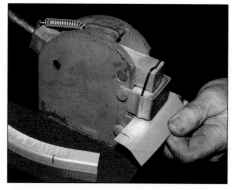

14 *Once again our old friend, the edge shrinker, was the perfect tool for forming the contours needed in this part. The visible mark near the edge of the patch piece roughly indicates where it will be cut, but this may change as it is formed.*

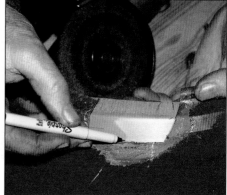

15 *Careful use of the shrinker yields a patch part that is remarkably close to the needed dimensions. Here, it is being marked for fitting between the fender and the long repair piece.*

16 *The marked lines were then joined, freehand. This was the preliminary cut-out shape for the final patch, but extra metal was left on every edge for final fitting.*

shears. Slight deformation from the shearing was removed by lightly tapping the piece's ends with a body hammer against an anvil. Then, the piece was ground to a final fit with a 4½-inch electric disc grinder.

With the long patch piece that would form the edge of the fender completed, attention turned to forming the short patch piece that would replace the metal cut out of the flat part of the fender. After determining the rough dimensions for this part, a piece of body metal that was a little larger than the actual area to be formed was sheared from stock and checked against the opening into which it would fit. A line was drawn on the piece to show where it would need to be creased.

It was then bent in a finger brake to the angle indicated by the copper wire template, and marked on its edges for rough fitting into place, between the fender metal and the fabricated long edge piece.

Again, the edge shrinker was used to form it into the correct arc. Some fine adjustment to its surface curvature was made by hammering it lightly with a high-crown body hammer against a corrugated-cardboard backing. The piece was then positioned under the opening in the fender into which it would be fitted, and marked for final trimming.

Final Fitting

The big issue in final fitting is to fit the parts without excessive gaps, but not so tightly that the heat generated in welding them causes them to jam against and distort themselves and adjacent metal. The long piece in this fabrication presented few problems in fit-up. However, the short piece had the potential to distort its neighbors when welding heat was applied to it.

To avoid this, the edge of the piece that butted up against the side of the long piece was ground to give it some reliefs. This provided room for the metal there to expand under welding heat without creating damage. The reliefs were bent, individually, to create a straight edge for the welded piece. As welding progressed, the reliefs were welded over and closed.

Welding Considerations

The choice of welding technique and equipment to join the newly fabricated pieces to each other, and to the panel, was pretty obvious. The first decision was to make butt joints (edge-to-edge joints) where the fit-up involved butting edges. The only other choice would have been to make lap joints, with one edge overlapping the other. These joints can be easier to make and to weld because they require less fit-up precision and they tolerate more heat without burning through. However, they are difficult to level, and can suffer severe attacks by corrosion. The joint between the two fabricated pieces is a right-angle joint, not a butt joint, and was welded in right-angle configuration.

To weld the butt joints and the right-angle joint, there are only three

Final trimming and fitting were accomplished by grinding. Here, the inside edge of this patch piece, the one that will mate to the fender metal's edge, is being slotted to allow bending this edge to the right contour and position.

The short metal tabs were bent with a small pair of locking pliers. Note that this edge is formed in three dimensions. The slots that were cut into it allow for the expansion that occurs in welding, without excessive distortion.

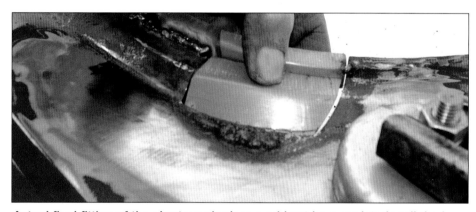

Actual final fitting of the short repair piece could not be completed until the long piece had been tack welded into place. That fitting is shown here, after one tack weld was made in one end of the short patch piece, to keep it in place.

practical welding techniques available: oxy-acetylene torch, TIG, and MIG. As covered in Chapter 8, MIG (metal inert gas) welding is technically called GMAW (gas metal arc welding). TIG (tungsten inert gas) welding is more properly designated GTAW (gas tungsten arc welding).

The oxy-acetylene torch method was the traditional way of performing panel welding. In most autobody applications, it was replaced by MIG techniques and equipment during, and after, the 1970s. MIG welding requires less skill and experience than oxy-acetylene welding, and produces as good a weld in sheetmetal. It also produces much less distorting local heat. MIG welding equipment has become very inexpensive over the last 20 years.

TIG welding has been around since World War II, and is used for

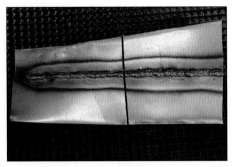

It is usually impossible to make practice welds in the actual body panel materials that you will weld, but you can make them in materials of similar thickness. The welds shown here are in 23-gauge sheetmetal, the same thickness as that in the repair fender.

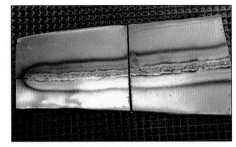

The critical underside of the practice weld fully penetrates the metal. The object is to achieve that penetration, without excessive heat that burns through, or distorts, the panel and patches. Practice welds allow you to optimize welder settings and to perfect technique.

The best test for penetration is to cut through a weld, and look at its cross-section. Such a cut is shown here, with the bead tops facing each other. The lacerations in the cuts are the marks left by the band saw that separated the pieces.

extremely fine work on materials like sheetmetal. However, TIG equipment is still quite expensive, and the skill required to use it is beyond that needed to do good work with MIG welding equipment. While TIG welding can be used at very low heats, with little distor-

tion, it is also a very slow welding technique.

Following the above considerations, MIG welding was chosen for this job. Before performing the actual welds, several practice welds were completed on sample pieces of 23-gauge steel, the same thickness as

the patch pieces that were fabricated, and the same thickness as the steel in the fender. The results of the practice welding were encouraging.

Cleaning, Positioning, Fixturing and Welding

The area of and near the site of attachment of the new metal to the panel was now disc sanded, so that good, clean metal would be available to weld. Cleaning weld areas generally makes it easier to see what is happening in areas adjacent to actual welds, when welding heat is applied. The long patch piece was secured in place with locking pliers, and a final visual check was made of its alignment with the fender edge. This piece was then tack welded into place, rechecked for final position, and seam welded to the fender. Our welder's stitch timer function was used to switch the arc on and off for brief intervals during the welding, so that the bead was actually an accumulation of short welding pulses.

The timer device on our welder allows setting on and off times, individually, for the arc. The advantage of using this approach is that the

1 *Prior to welding in the patch pieces, a disc sander is used to strip the weld area of most paint, contamination, and corrosion. Care was taken not to snag a metal edge with the sanding disc.*

short, interrupted welding intervals reduce the amount of heat buildup in the metal. This lessens the chance of burning through the metal, and

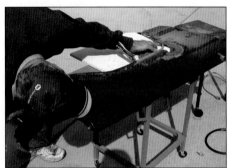

2 *A final check of lateral alignment was made for fitting of the long repair piece to the panel. Once welding starts, it is difficult, or impossible, to make any very major adjustments in the positions of the pieces.*

3 The long repair piece was tack welded into place with a MIG welding torch. The tacks held the pieces in place, while they were being joined into a continuous weld.

4 *Joining the tack welds between the long patch piece and the fender into a continuous weld is shown here. The welder's stitch timer feature was used to pulse welding current on and off, between short weld segments. This somewhat mitigates heat buildup and distortion in areas near the weld bead.*

5 Now, the short repair patch was tacked into place. Note the panel gap between it, the fender, and the long patch piece metal. Magnets were used to hold this piece in place for tack welding.

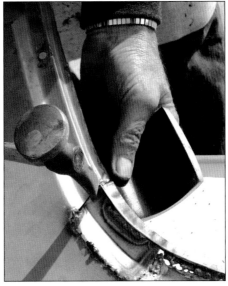

6 As welding progressed, panel alignment was checked, frequently. Here, a minor adjustment to the edge alignment of the short patch piece and the fender is made with gentle hammer tapping.

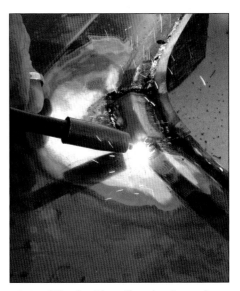

7 *After tacking, the short repair patch piece was welded into place, between the long patch piece and the fender. There was a problem: The metal near the fender seam was unexpectedly weak, and required re-welding to repair blow holes. This caused exces-sive heat distortion, generating a bulge in the fender metal.*

helps to control excessive distortion near the weld seam.

With the long patch piece completely secured to the panel, the short piece could now be attached to it and to the fender metal. After tack welding the short piece into place, one of its edges was tapped lightly into final alignment, and it was seam welded into place.

Unfortunately an evaluation mistake, made early in this project, led to a miscalculation that became evident when the short patch piece had been welded into place. The metal in the inner body of the fender that attaches to the short patch piece was weaker than had been thought. That resulted in blowing holes through it with the welder, while

attaching it to the fender metal. The man making the weld somewhat instinctively over-welded the area to fill the holes, putting so much heat into the weld area that the metal bulged in the patch piece and adjacent fender.

This bulge was caused by the heat expansion of an area bounded by unheated metal that restrained its further lateral movement. The only place for the overheated metal to go was into a bulge. It did so in the direction that the metal was already formed, causing the bulge. After everything cooled, the bulge remained.

This situation is typical of the kind of errors that sometimes occur in projects like this. Would it have been better to have not made this mistake? Of course it would. Should attention be turned to hand wringing and cursing providence over this situation? Of course not. Mistakes happen, and the only productive thing to do about them is to solve the problems that they bring and to move on, resolving to learn from them and to avoid them in the future. In this case, the correction was relatively simple.

8 *The welded-in patches are shown here. The over-welding and adjacent bulge are visible. The bulge will have to be dealt with later. If the repair had been extended 1½ inches farther back into the fender metal, where it was sounder, the over-welding and bulge problems would not have occurred.*

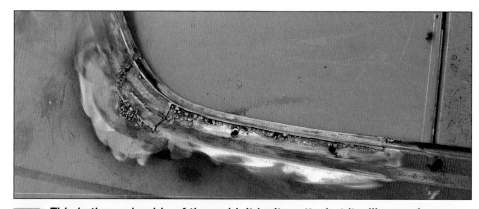

9 *This is the underside of the weld. It isn't pretty, but it will never be seen. A little time spent leveling the area improves its appearance. Then, it will have to be protected from corrosion.*

Grinding the Weld Beads and Shrinking the Bulged Area

While the underside of this weld will not be visible in use, it is an issue of craftsmanship to give it a neat appearance. On fenders configured with their undersides more visible in this area, a more finished appearance would be mandatory. Here, the issue is one of choice—how far do you want to take the job? We opted for a neat but not-so-finished appearance.

Our priorities were to leave the underside of the repair area clean and sound for coating with various anti-corrosion treatments like etching primer, resilient paint, and undercoating. It was important that the area be left smooth enough to

accept paint uniformly, and that no features that could trap water and debris were left there to initiate or to encourage corrosion.

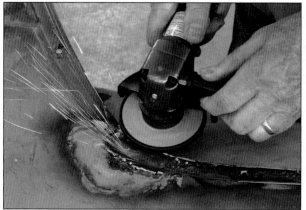

Next we attended to correcting the bulge that the welding had created in the short patch and fender metal. A couple of applications of

1 *Leveling was accomplished with a 4-inch air disc grinder. Its small size and considerable speed make it ideal for this job. It is easy to maneuver, and small enough to work around intricate features, without accidentally grinding them.*

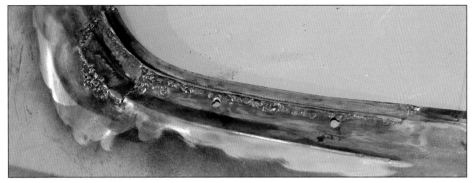

2 *After grinding, and some other abrasive stripping work, the underside of the welded area is ready for anti-corrosion treatments. Unseen areas, like this one, do not require much finishing and remain stronger if they are not leveled too extensively.*

3 *Excessive heat in the over-welded area created a bulge in the patch and fender metal. This area was brought to cherry red with an oxy-acetylene torch, and hammered down in two operations that shrunk the metal, and relieved the bulge.*

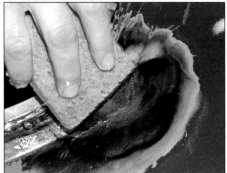

4 *While the metal in the bulged area was still hot, it was worked with a hammer-off-dolly technique to push the bulge farther down and to raise sunken areas around it. A low-crown hammer was used.*

5 *A final step in the shrinking process was to quench the heated area with a wet sponge. This produced controlled shrinking action. Knowing exactly when and where to apply the quenching action requires some experience with this procedure.*

shrinking technique resolved the bulge problem completely.

The shrinking technique, in this case, involved heating the most distorted part of the bulge with an oxy-acetylene torch to a temperature between dull and cherry red. The area heated this way was a little larger than 1 inch in diameter. This caused further local bulging. The torch was then safely stowed, and the heated, bulged area was hammered down without any backing. This created an upset, literally a compacting of metal in a small area that exchanges lateral dimension for a locally thickened panel area.

The second shrinking operation was performed at a lower heat (dull red) and over a slightly wider area.

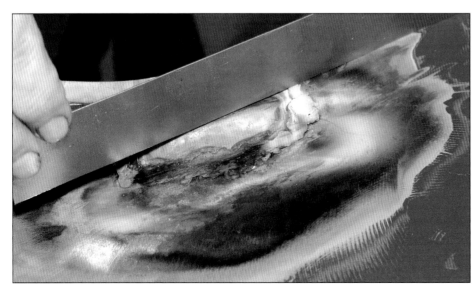

6 *A check with a straightedge indicated that the shrinking operation was successful, and that the metal in the formerly bulged area was now within the range required for a good final result.*

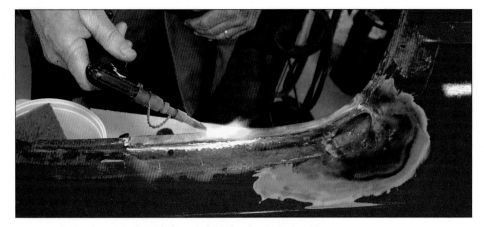

7 *A little bowing in one area of the outer edges of the long repair patch needed to be shrunk. That area was heated to dull red with an oxy-acetylene torch.*

8 *After heating, the bowed area was hammered down, off-dolly, to upset the metal there. That means exchanging some of its lateral dimension for thickness, which amounts to compacting, or shrinking, its surface area.*

This time, the hammering was done off-dolly, and the dolly rebound under the fender was used to raise some sunken metal around the bulge.

In this application, the metal in the formerly bulged area was quenched with a wet sponge to enhance and control the extent of the shrinking. The area was checked with a straightedge.

Measuring indicated that the bulge had been completely eliminated, and that the area now had the correct shape. Some distortion in the fender-edge repair patch metal was now removed by heating and hammering that area, gently, off-dolly.

Final Steps before Filling

The weld beads were now leveled to the fender by grinding, disc sanding, and filing them almost level with the surrounding metal. In the battle to level welds, it is fair to use any tool or device that helps do the job. In this case, we even used a rat-tail file and a die grinder.

After leveling the weld beads, the surface was inspected. No low or high spots were found that were beyond the range of modest filling and filing. A few low areas were raised slightly with a pick hammer, completing the metal finishing of the repair area.

The topside of the repair area was now completely cleaned and stripped to bare, healthy metal. All visible corrosion was removed. This operation was left until now because welding tends to create scale and debris that have to be removed before filling. Final cleaning after welding is the best approach, since removing every trace of contamination from the entire area before welding it would be a waste of time; it would just have to be done again.

The nylon disc-stripping wheel is a particularly useful tool for getting into the surface intricacies of metal and removing lightly pitted contamination from them. Following mechanical cleaning, the repair area was wiped down with solvent and blown dry. This was repeated until the wiping rags came up clean.

1 *Various grinding and disc sanding procedures were then applied to the surfaces in the repair area to clean, level, and prepare them for the next step: filling with body lead.*

2 *Final leveling of some of the welds, in some areas, required a variety of approaches. Good, old fashioned filing with a rat-tail file is very useful for some of this work.*

3 *A high-speed, air-driven, right-angle die grinder was particularly helpful for leveling some weld areas like the one shown here. This tool cuts quickly and accurately, and is easy to control.*

4 *At this point, it was important to clean the entire repair area for the next steps, tinning and leading. Rotary and hand wire brushes, and other devices, sped this job, as did the grinder-mounted nylon/carbide wheel, shown here.*

5 *Before moving on to the next step (tinning), the entire repair area was wiped down with solvent, and blown clean and dry. This procedure removed abrasive and chemical residues from the surface.*

Tinning

We decided to fill the repair area with body lead to correct any low spots, and to allow us to file the surface to exactly the contours that would make the repair area indistinguishable from the rest of the fender.

The first step was to tin the area to be leaded. It was pre-heated with an air-acetylene torch to about 300 degrees F. Tinning solution was then dripped onto it from a plastic squeeze container. At these temperatures,

1 *Tinning compound was dripped onto torch-heated metal in the repair area. The heat was supplied by an air-acetylene torch, and held to roughly 300 to 350 degrees F. The air-acetylene torch produces much milder heat than the oxy-acetylene torch, previously used for the shrinking operations.*

2 *The tinning compound was brushed around on the hot metal with an acid brush, while more heat was applied to it. A visible, brown residue formed on the metal. This was a good indication that the tinning compound is doing its cleaning job.*

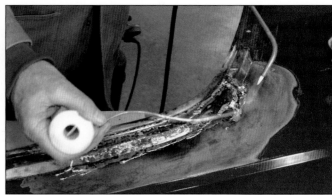

3 *The 50/50 (tin/lead) solder was then unspooled from a coil and melted onto the surface. The torch was played over the area to keep the base metal hot enough for the solder to melt and flow onto it.*

tinning solution chemically cleans base metal, preparing it to accept and adhere to tinning solder. As the tinning solution hit the panel metal, it sizzled on the hot surface, leaving a brownish film. That is the proper appearance for the application of this product.

Next, 50/50 (tin/lead) solder was uncoiled from a spool and run onto the metal's surface, as the air-acetylene flame was played over it to keep it hot. After sufficient solder had been deposited on the entire area to be tinned, a rag was used to spread it evenly across the surface. During this operation, the air-acetylene flame was played on the surface to keep it hot enough to maintain the solder in its liquid form.

A few spots that resisted the solder's flow and adhesion received small additional applications of tinning flux. Then, the solder was brushed into them with a small stainless-steel-bristled brush. This worked, completing the tinning process. The whole area to be leaded was now covered with a uniform coating of tinning solder.

4 *While in a liquid state, the solder was spread on the metal surface with a rag. The tinning solder must fully cover the metal. However, rubbing it too hard with the rag may wipe it away completely, resulting in spotty bonding of the lead filler material.*

Applying the Lead Filler

The most outstanding characteristic of autobody lead—the one that makes it ideal for filling depressions in metal work, while providing a medium for filing contours—is that it is a metal applied to a metal. With correct application, the bond achieved with the metal substrate is unequalled by that of any other type of filler. However, paddling lead onto a properly tinned surface is about as difficult as making water run uphill.

1 *Lead from a 30/70 body solder bar was then stubbed onto the tinned surface. The end of the bar, and the metal around it, were heated until the lead started to soften. Then, a lead stub was twisted off the heated end of the bar, and onto the panel surface.*

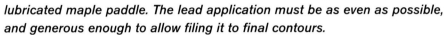

2 The lead was softened to a plastic, bubble gum-like, consistency with the end of the torch flame, and spread on the repair area surface with a lubricated maple paddle. The lead application must be as even as possible, and generous enough to allow filing it to final contours.

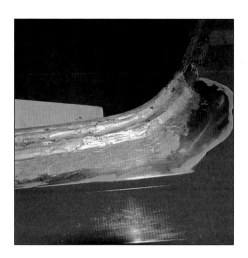

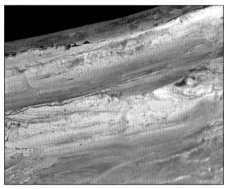

3 These two photographs show the repair area surface after the lead application was complete. The apparent roughness of the surface is not a problem, because body lead is a soft material and files easily into desired contours.

Our first step was to stub a 30/70 (tin/lead) body solder bar onto the tinned surface. This was done by heating the end of the body solder bar, while playing the end of the air-acetylene flame over it and the tinned surface. The lead material has a plastic state at between 100 and 150 degrees F, depending on its composition. In this peanut-butter-like state, it can be twisted off in short stubs, onto the tinned surface.

After enough stubs were deposited, we spread them into a consistent layer of filler with a lubricated maple paddle, much as you might spread peanut butter with a small putty knife. While the filler looks somewhat rough, it was easy to file it into a smooth and accurate surface.

At this point, we killed the lead. That term describes neutralizing chemical residues from the flux used in tinning, and from the lubricant used to keep the maple leading paddle from sticking to the lead. While the killing process will be repeated on the panel after it is filed to its final format, as the last step in leading, it is also critical to do this before any filing is done. Otherwise, residues will be filed into the lead and it will be difficult, or impossible, to fully neutralize the finished surface.

4 The panel surface was wiped as clean as possible, and treated with metal conditioner. This step was repeated after filing and sanding were completed, but it is important to do it at this stage, to avoid filing contaminants into the filler, making them harder to remove later.

5 After the metal conditioner had reacted with the metal in the repair area for a few minutes, it was wiped off. This step, and its repetition when the surface is completely contoured, prevents the loss of paint adhesion that can occur if these steps are omitted.

Shaping the Lead and Finishing the Job

Filing lead filler is not very different from grating and shaping plastic filler, except that different tools are used to do it and the shaping operation feels very different. We began shaping the lead with a bull-nose body file, and then switched to a flexible file holder and file to work on the flatter surfaces. Several different shaping tools were used.

During the filing process, the panel surface was constantly monitored, visually and by feel, to make sure that it was smooth and continuous. Some filing was solely in the lead filler material. In other areas of the repair, lead and steel panels were filed and blended into a continuous surface. Care was taken not to file too deeply in any area. Lead can be added to areas where it has been filed too deeply, but this is a tricky fix and care should be taken to avoid having to resort to it.

After filing was completed, the surface was sanded with 80-grit abrasive paper mounted on sanding boards. These boards place somewhat soft rubber backings behind the abrasive paper, and tend to further average and blend the surfaces on which they are used. Paint sticks, wrapped in abrasive paper and without flexible backing, were used to sand some fine details into some areas of the lead and steel surfaces. Final sanding with 120-grit abrasive paper completed the surfacing phase of the job.

The entire repair area was again neutralized (killed) with metal conditioner, completing the repair.

1 *A variety of body files was used to achieve final, correct surface contours. This bull-nose file has a convex lateral format, and was perfect for removing material quickly and accurately in the concave area of this fender.*

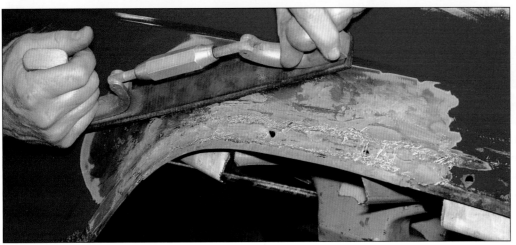

2 *This flexible file holder and file can be shaped to match desired surface contours. Most of the lead shaping and leveling was done with this setup. A good, sharp body file removes both lead filler and body metal, allowing the blending of both metals into a continuous surface.*

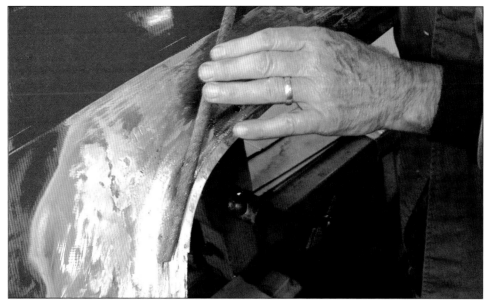

3 Other files, like this round bastard file, are useful for getting into tight areas, where flat files might tend to cut destructive channels and ridges into the lead filler and body metal. Filing requires great concentration, and involves both feel and visual inspection as it progresses.

4 As the filled surface was filed, it was important to constantly feel surfaces and check for any depressions or raised spots. Proper filing technique employs files to blend raised spots into desired contours, and to avoid creating or lowering depressed areas.

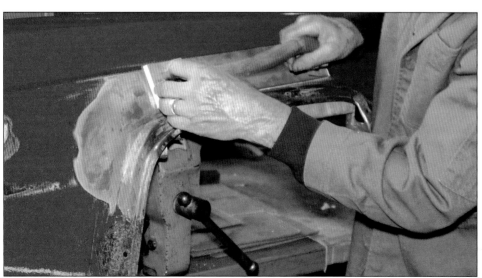

5 Filing was followed by board sanding. This board sander has a somewhat soft rubber backing under the abrasive paper. That helps to achieve continuous surfaces that have no unauthorized high or low spots or areas.

6 Final sanding can be a finicky operation. Here, a paint stick was used to back abrasive paper. The surface warping of the stick is used to create a mildly concave or convex sanding tool, as required to contour and level the surface.

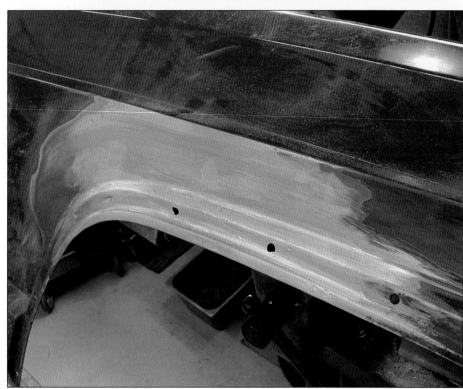

The final, repaired surface is shown here. It is not perfect. Very minor applications of spot putty will be needed in a few places to fill small depressions in the lead.

REPAIRING COLLISION DAMAGE IN A DECKLID

This job is to repair the lower area of the rear decklid from a 1937 Chevrolet sedan. The original panel was punched in by impact from another vehicle hitting it from the rear. Most of the damage was to the right side of the decklid, but some damage also occurred to the center and on the near left side of the lower panel.

The damage amounts to a series of related and unrelated deformations in this decklid's skin. This combination results because most of the damage was indirect; it was forced into the metal by direct impact against the heavy trim pieces attached to the panel. The impact from the second vehicle was primarily against the trim, which in turn pushed the decklid skin in from several points of the trim's attachment to the panel. In some areas, one dent created or modified another. Some areas of the damage are quite unrelated to each other.

There was one small but particularly significant area of direct-impact damage. This small area was hit directly by the second vehicle, and has severe direct damage that is locking in a large area of undeformed

This is the starting point for the metal straightening, finishing, and filling job. It amounts to correcting several related and unrelated dents in the decklid of a 1937 Chevrolet sedan. My good friend, Herb Statz, is shown working in many of these photos.

metal that will begin to return to its proper shape and position when the direct damage is removed.

After removing the trunk lid's trim and body gaskets, we obtained a better idea of the type and extent of the damage. Damage is revealed by close inspection, and that inspection is aided by removing anything that interferes with viewing and feeling the damage as minutely and directly as possible.

This photo illustrates a subtle but important point: The innocuous-looking scrape between the two white arrows was the only area of direct impact that deformed this panel. The other damage was done by impact against trim, which also deformed the panel. Understanding this is key to repairing the panel.

As hopeless as it may look, always remove body gaskets and trim carefully, as if you will have to reuse them, because it may just come to that. If you don't have new items in-hand before you remove the old ones, keep the old ones for patterns, just in case.

This is important because the point of direct impact damage is locking in a tremendous area of metal that can be released when it is relieved. Then the locked-in metal in the panel will be on the way to assuming a shape that is pretty close to its original format. A little work on the direct damage, on the ridges surrounding it, and on the indirect damage will produce dramatic results.

This job divides into three major areas of damage, and a few smaller ones. First the trunk lock and associated trim pushed in the panel metal under them when they were hit. That damage was evident on both sides of where the latching mechanism was mounted.

Second, the damage traveled upward, pushing in the license plate bracket, which may also have sustained some direct impact. That deformed the trunk panel into a second area of damage that extended up to and slightly beyond the top mounting point for the license plate bracket.

A third, separate, area of major damage was evident on the lower right side of the trunk. This was caused by direct impact in the center of the dent. It produced a deep and severe rolled buckle, upward from the point of impact. A less serious rolled buckle extends to the right of

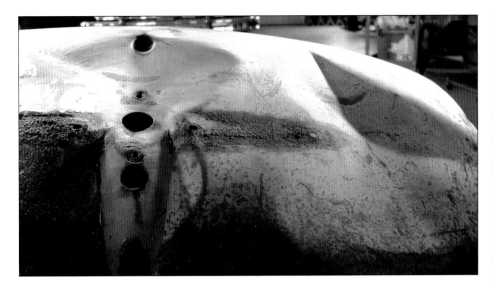

This view and lighting shows the nature of the damage particularly well. Three distinct damage areas are easily visible. The direct damage point is obvious, as are the deformations caused by the trim and bracket items. It is easy to see where and why the damage stopped moving through this panel.

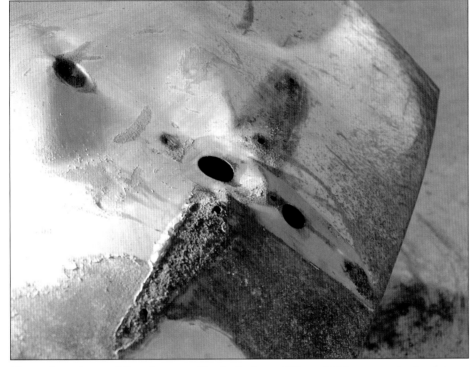

These two views of the damage illustrate how different things can look when seen in different light, and from different angles. Only by examining damage from several viewpoints, and manipulating the light on it, will you fully understand it.

the direct impact point on the panel. Metal was also deformed and displaced downward from the point of impact. The damage in this dent was stopped by the crown of the metal at its top, and by edge substructure at its bottom and to its right.

As is usually the case with collision damage, there is good news and bad news. The good news is that the supporting structure of this decklid held its shape. There is no overall dimensional deformation in this panel, in the sense that it still perfectly fits in and aligns with its jamb. Its diagonal measurements remain exactly symmetrical.

If there was no substructure behind the decklid skin, it would be relatively simple to rough the damage out of it. Some hammer-off-dolly and hammer-on-dolly work would successfully remove the buckles and ridges, and relieve the relatively small areas of damage that are locking most of the out-of-place sheetmetal into its presently deformed state.

Now the bad news: The decklid's substructure prevents direct access to the areas where almost all of the corrective work needs to be done. The exception to this dismal situation is that there is good access to the back of the center dent's upper area, behind the license plate bracket.

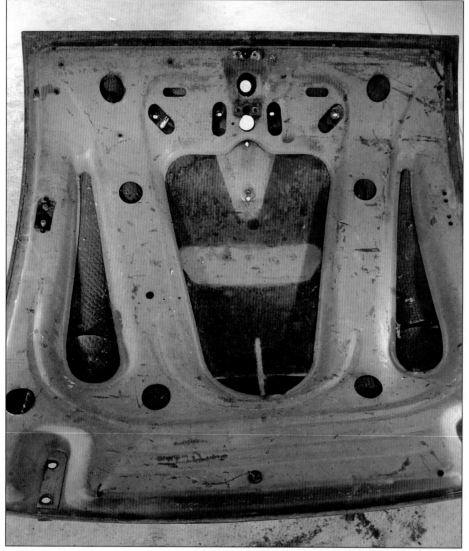

The substructure under this decklid panel severely limits access to the panel's back side, making it much more difficult to work on. Actually, there is great rear access to many areas that do not need attention, and very poor access to most that do.

The Approach

There are two possible approaches to repairing this damage. One would be to cut away enough of the decklid's substructure to gain access to the critical areas on the back of the panel, and then approach the job with conventional hammer-on-dolly and hammer-off-dolly work in those areas. With this approach, after the metal in the panel had been returned to its original format, the removed substructure would then be welded back into place. This way of doing this job would probably be faster than any other way of accomplishing it, such as the one that we decided to use. Also, it would yield a panel surface that would require little metal finishing and filling. The panel surface could be brought pretty close to its original format easily and quickly.

The other approach—the one that we used—is to leave the substructure in place, and to work around it with pry tools and other specialized tools and techniques. This is a much more cumbersome and time consuming way of doing this job, but it has two distinct advantages. First, it maintains the shape and alignment of the trunk lid. If substructure members were removed to straighten the panel surface, it would be almost impossible to maintain the shape of the decklid, and a difficult refitting process would be required. The fact that this decklid is still in near-perfect alignment with its jamb is an advantage that should not be ignored.

The other major problem with removing and replacing substructural members for access is that it would require considerable time to re-weld and refinish them. This would probably offset and possibly cancel out any time saved. Finally, the substructure around the lower and right edges of the panel could not be removed without severely disturbing and deforming the panel in those areas.

For all of these reasons, we decided to work around the substructure, rather than to remove it. Please note: The decision to work around the decklid's substructure does not change the basic approaches to removing collision damage, outlined in earlier chapters. The theories and sequences of damage removal remain the same because the elements of cause and effect in working damage out of the sheetmetal do not change. What does change is some of the tools and techniques used to accomplish the job.

The Early Steps

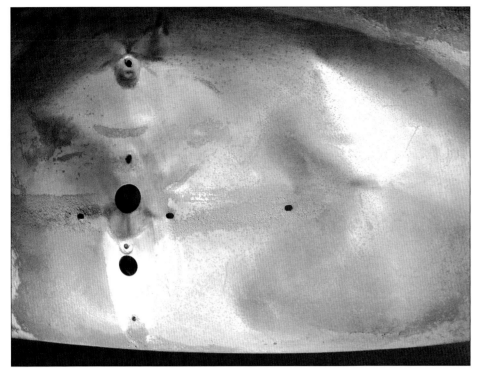

1 *After chemically removing the paint and scuffing the loose rust with coarse steel wool, in the lower-left part of the panel, its surface looked very different. It was then much harder to spot the area of direct impact.*

Coming up with an effective strategy for dealing with collision damage requires seeing the damaged area clearly. In this case, applying some paint stripper to the decklid, and removing the loose rust with coarse steel wool, revealed previously invisible detail in the lower-right part of the panel.

It would be difficult to overstate the importance of using all of your relevant senses to understand impact damage. We'll pass on smelling and tasting it, but feeling damage and looking at it from many different angles are necessary to gain enough information about it to formulate a good plan to repair it.

Analysis of the damage in the right dent suggested that it was caused by direct impact. A key to unlocking the damage in the entire dented area is to gently work out the

2 *Feeling damage with your fingers often divulges information beyond what your eyes can see. Tactile data can be as important as visual data in planning approaches to removing collision damage from autobody metal.*

3 *While the outside of this panel revealed what needed to be done to repair it, its underside showed how difficult it would be to gain access to several key areas. It is always best to understand the extent of such problems before you begin to work.*

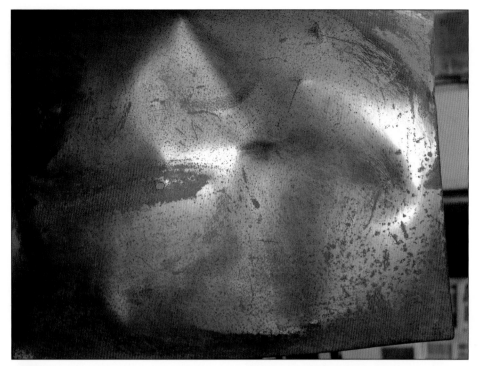

4 *We started with a plan. First, we would correct the direct damage. Then, we would push and hammer out the long, vertical V-channel above it, while hammering down its rim. Similar strategies were planned for the rolled buckles on the right, below, and to the left of the direct damage.*

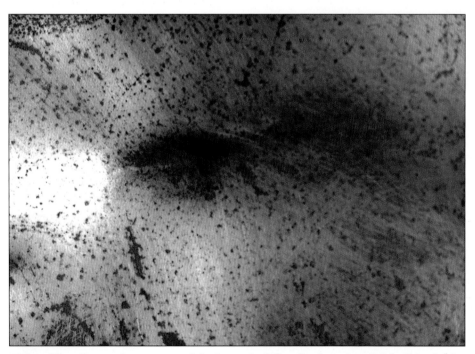

5 *After the work was completed, most of the displaced metal in this dent was released. Then, with a little underside persuasion with mallets, the metal returned to normal. The key to this result was in understanding the role of the small area of direct damage, and relieving it.*

crease that is evident at the impact point. Following this, apply gentle pressure against the dented area, while lightly hammering on the ridges that surround it. This will be difficult at the right and bottom edges of the panel because there is supporting structure behind the metal in those areas.

The favorable factor in this dent is that most of the metal in the large damaged area is not badly deformed. It will spring back into its approximately original and correct positions,

6 *Usually, feeling the back of a panel reveals where things are. However, in this case, substructure interfered with feeling the knot of direct damage under it. To ensure accuracy in prying it out, we used a large set of calipers to precisely transfer its position to the decklid's back side.*

7 Next, a line was drawn to indicate the exact position of the direct damage, under the sub structure. It is along this line that force was applied with a pry bar, against the decklid skin, to work the direct damage out.

8 The prying was done with the bent part of a pry bar, inserted through the sub structure hole in the center of this photo. The pry bar shaft was marked for depth of insertion, indexing it to the left edge of the hole.

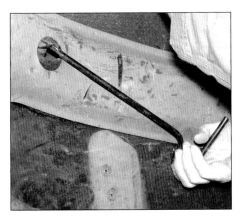

9 Once the pry bar was positioned, the bending operation was accomplished by twisting it. After several attempts, the chalk mark on the pry bar smeared, but we could feel the proper depth of insertion by then, and did not need to see it.

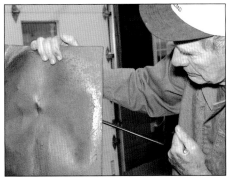

10 It was critical to watch, and to evaluate, the effect of each pry bar twist. A second worker sometimes provided another set of hands, stabilizing the panel, while hammering lightly on the rim of the direct damage dent, as Herb applied prying force to it.

Once the small knot of direct damage had been pried out, we **11** went to a broader prying tool, to force out the area of metal surrounding it. That look visible on Herb's face is genuine teeth-grittin' determination.

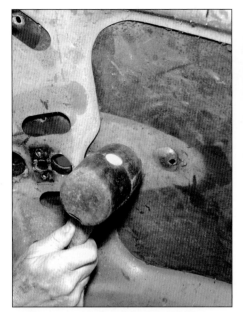

12 *With the locking factor of the metal in the direct damage relieved, a soft-rubber mallet was used to push out the un-deformed metal that comprised most of the area of the dent. Access to this area was refreshingly good.*

13 *Some areas of displaced metal resisted movement by our soft-rubber mallet. A dead-blow plastic shot mallet proved ideal for persuading these areas back into place. Both the rubber and dead-blow mallets were used more to remind the un-deformed metal where it belonged than to form it.*

once the relatively small areas of deformed metal that are holding it out of position are removed.

It is critically important that the attempt to pry the direct damage area out, and to release the metal that it has locked out-of-place, be made with the greatest possible accuracy. A near miss would create a serious problem that would have to be corrected. For that reason, we transferred the exact position of the direct damage line from the front to the back of the panel with a large pair of calipers. Then, we made a chalk mark, indicating the exact area under the decklid's substructure, from where the prying force would have to be applied.

We selected a suitable body-prying tool, and marked its depth behind and into the substructure hole. We then inserted it through the hole to accomplish the prying

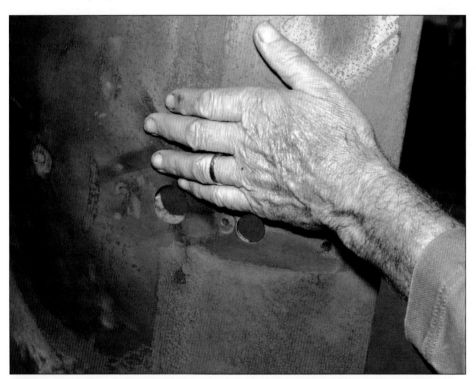

14 *As the straightening work progressed, Herb kept feeling the surface of the panel to confirm its progress toward its final format. The importance of checking work by feeling it cannot be overemphasized.*

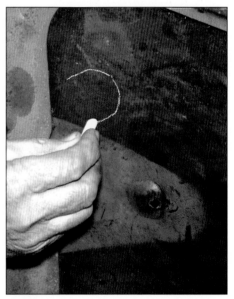

15 *It is always useful to mark areas of a panel that require straightening work. As Herb tapped lightly on the panel's topside, he felt and marked where he was tapping on its reverse side, identifying an area that still needed to be lifted.*

maneuver. The whole process was performed as carefully as possible, since one false move could worsen the damage. The initial move in this job was to work out a small but strongly deformed knot of metal, as a first step in releasing the damage. This meant applying considerable but very accurate force to a very small spot. The twisting motion of a pry bar was ideal for this purpose because it confined the applied force to a small area.

The prying was done very slowly, and in many small, incremental steps. It was critical to watch the metal that was being pried move, from the outside of the panel, to determine when it had been moved far enough to accomplish the first stage of restoring the panel to its original format.

The actual amount of movement in the direct damage area was so small that a photo of it would be hard to distinguish from a photo of the area before prying force was applied to it. Nonetheless, that small movement of metal in the panel released the locking force at the point of the direct impact. Next, we applied broader force with a large, curved prying spoon. This worked out the larger area of metal around the direct impact area.

The back of the panel was then lightly worked with a rubber mallet, and with dead-blow mallets. During this work, a dolly was held against the ridges on the outside of the panel at the edges of the dent. In some cases, the buckles at the end of the damage—where the panel finally stopped the deforming metal from advancing during the impact— were hammered down lightly, as the panel was reshaped with light pries and soft blows on its back side.

16 *Pry bars are useful for raising broad areas of low metal when you cannot access them directly. Here, Herb lifted a shallow dent. He lightly hammered the ridges surrounding it, on the other side, while lifting its central crease with pressure from a pry bar.*

Additional areas of panel damage were located visually, and by feeling the panel, and were marked and hammered out with appropriate tools.

This work requires imagination in how best to use tools in ways that will accomplish your goals. You look at a problem and try to find a tool, or tool combination, that will solve it. We used several different prying tools to remove this damage.

Sometimes, the best tool to do part of a job isn't in your collection. When that happens, you have to improvise—imagine what is needed and then create it.

Sometimes a simple maneuver, like inserting a small block of wood under a spoon and hammering it through a hole in substructure, will accomplish what is needed. Small, specific solutions that accomplish tasks that address the right problems are critical to doing autobody damage repair work efficiently and well. In this work, the simplest and most direct approach is often the best approach.

In a relatively short time, we accomplished a dramatic improvement in the panel. After the initial roughing out of the dents, we felt the damaged areas, and located and relieved a few points that were still locking in displaced metal. Then, we applied mild force to move the undamaged metal out, and into its proper positions. Those few operations greatly improved the panel. However, we were still far from finished with this job.

By its nature, autobody panel work is incremental. It takes many well-planned steps to accomplish goals. Each action should improve the result. Each action, when possible, should be small enough to be

17 *Inserting this little scrap of wood between the back side of the decklid panel and its substructure allowed two other tools to accomplish a job that they could not have done without the wood block. Because the wood was soft, it did not leave its outline in the metal.*

19 *The solution was to use a rod, and to hammer down on the back of the spoon. A few strong blows were enough to do the job. Three simple tools, used together, accomplished what, in this case none of them could do individually.*

18 *A spoon was inserted over the wood block to apply force to it. However, using the substructure above the spoon would not work for a prying fulcrum. The structure was not strong enough.*

reversible because some moves may not achieve their desired results and may need to be undone. Many small actions are often far better than a few big ones.

The area of damage in the right side dent has been greatly reduced.

There is some overwork in the area of the original impact damage, where it was pried out, but this can be corrected later.

Next, our priority was to remove the remaining big ridge in the right dent area. This was done by

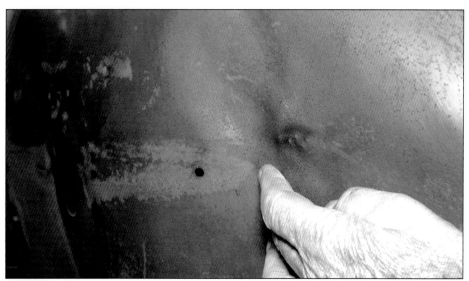

20 *At this point, the panel showed marked improvement. There was some overwork on the direct damage crease, just above Herb's fingers. And one buckle above that still had to be worked out. The mild dent, below and to the left of the buckle, was pried out easily.*

21 *Working through the substructure, behind the panel, required innovative uses of tools. The action replaced simple blows with a body hammer with very heavy blows struck against a body spoon's shank. This is not a good situation, but it sometimes comes with the territory of panel work.*

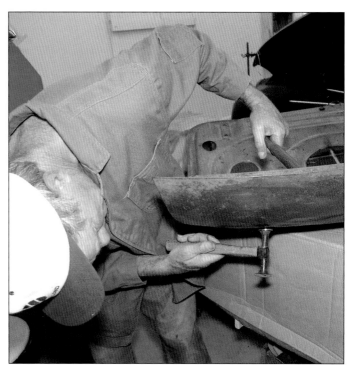

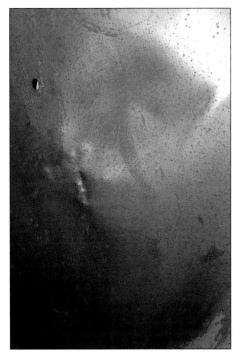

22 *In this view of the panel, you see the ridges and buckles that were still locking what was left of the dent. With good access to the back of the panel, it would have been easy to hammer the V-channels out, off-dolly, while supporting the buckle ridges with a dolly.*

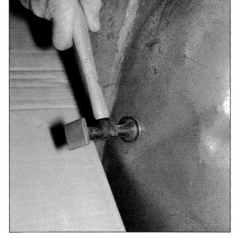

23 *Pressure, applied against the main V-channel in the lower-right dent with a big, curved body spoon, combined with light blows against its surrounding ridges on the panel's surface, allowed much of the metal locked in this dent to move back into place. Body metal has a long memory. If you can identify and correct the deformations holding damaged metal out of place, you can rely on that memory to return much, or most, of the metal in a damaged area to its correct positions.*

hammering down its locking edges, while applying pressure to the back-side of the V-channel through what access points were available. It would be far better to hammer directly on the V-channel, off-dolly, but limited access prevented this approach.

Similar prying work was applied to the rest of the major dents in the panel, until most of the metal in it was in roughly the correct positions.

Mapping damage helps to keep tabs on the amount of work that remains to be done, and may suggest sequences for attacking it.

The major crease in the right dent area was mapped on the reverse side of the panel, so that it could be driven out by hammering against it on a curved body spoon. It was important to back up the area of the crease to limit the deformation by the spoon that was being hammered against it. This was done by placing and backing up the panel on a resilient surface made up of several layers of corrugated cardboard.

24 *The damage map, chalked on the remaining damaged areas of the decklid, indicates where metal still needed to be raised (minus signs)and two areas where it had to be lowered (plus signs). Areas that are particularly obvious, like the area of the direct damage, were not mapped.*

At this point, the major metal moving had been completed, and it remained to work out several small areas of damage, the ones indicated in chalk on the panel surface. A small dent in the edge of the decklid jamb area was corrected with a few hammer-off-dolly blows. The rest of the job was mostly small corrections like this one.

Some of the small-damage areas that required repair had inevitably occurred in the process of prying out the major dents in this panel. If the panel had not presented such severe access problems to its back side, it would have been possible to remove the major damage with traditional hammer-on-dolly and hammer-off-dolly techniques. That would have greatly reduced the amount of small,

25 *The center of the major remaining crease was transferred to the back side of the panel's substructure. This made it easier to locate the crease by feeling for it with the body spoon that was used to work it out.*

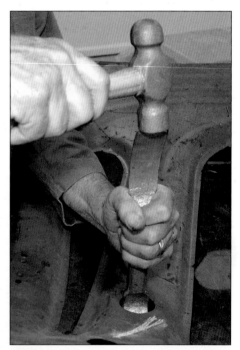

26 *A curved, double-ended spoon was chosen to work this crease, because it had the right curvature for the job. To avoid damage to one of the spoon's working surfaces, a bronze hammer was used to beat on it.*

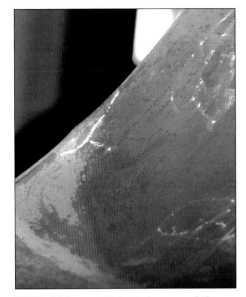

27 *This small dent, in one of the decklid's edges, is typical of damage that can be dealt with effectively with the traditional hammer-off dolly approach. It offers perfect access from behind to hit it out with a few blows.*

28 *The dolly was held so that hammer blows moved the metal edge out, as pressure and rebound from the dolly pushed it in. Metal was never squashed between the tools, and no stretching occurred. You could reverse this approach, hammering the bulge down, while supporting the back side with the dolly.*

29 *After more work, the panel was remapped, and looked like this. Visible sanding-board marks helped indicate low and high spots. Note the tic-tac-toe item, top left. I need to state that this kind of fooling around has no place in serious work. By the way, I won.*

collateral damage repair necessitated by approaches like prying and spoon hammering that were used to work around the panel's substructure.

This can be tedious and repetitive work, but each blow should bring the panel closer to its correct shape. It is important to avoid stretching the metal. This means hammering it off-dolly, to raise low areas. If a hammer blow is accidentally struck on-dolly, its sound and feel will announce the mistake. One such accidental blow does little harm.

It is critical to use tools that are shaped correctly for the job at hand. The crowns of hammers must roughly match the crowns of the panel areas that are being worked out, and dollies have to contact the metal that you are trying to stabilize.

Soft tools like rawhide mallets, shot mallets, and hand held shot bags can be very useful in limiting

30 As the work progressed, the crowns of the tools used to perform it became more critical. This highly crowned, modified Proto 1427 hammer worked well for raising areas of the decklid that it could reach. This combination dolly had several surfaces that were good for backing up off-dolly hammering.

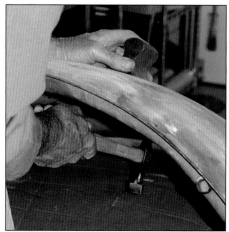

31 With proper technique, hammering off-dolly can be used to move metal thousandths of an inch. If this technique is applied properly and with sensitivity, metal cooperates in seeking its pre-collision format.

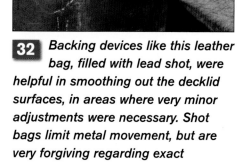

32 Backing devices like this leather bag, filled with lead shot, were helpful in smoothing out the decklid surfaces, in areas where very minor adjustments were necessary. Shot bags limit metal movement, but are very forgiving regarding exact placement.

33 This rawhide shot mallet was great for leveling some areas of the decklid in a gentle way. Here, it is being used against a spoon dolly that is wedged between the back of the panel and its substructure.

unwanted deformation, as you move metal with impact.

A few areas of the decklid had such deep and locked-in small areas of damage, that no amount of clever tool use allowed us to access them from the panel's back side. In two

such cases we resorted to stud welding to pull out these areas. Working damage out with hammers, pries, etc., is preferable to stud welding, but sometimes you run out of conventional bodywork impact-tool options. Then, stud welding may be

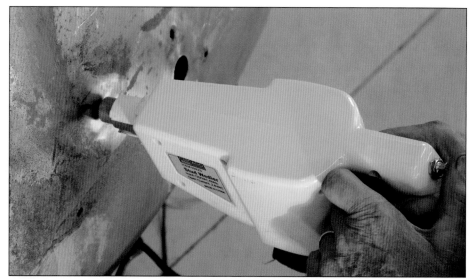

34 A stud welder was used to pull out a small, but deep, dimple dent that was inaccessible from the back of the panel. This type of device resistance welds a copper-plated steel stud to the panel's surface.

necessary. One key to getting good results in stud welding is to pull out the damage in controlled steps, and avoid creating over-pulls.

Stud welds are easily clipped off, and if they are done right, clean up easily and leave no adverse effects in the metal. The area of this stud weld was disc sanded almost flat, and left for final filing and finishing when the panel leveling was completed.

The rest of the job consisted of continuing to pick up low spots and push down high spots. Because this panel had considerable crown in every area of its surface, it was possible to accomplish the entire job without having to shrink any metal. This

35 While stud welders produce fusion welds between studs and panels, there should be no permanent damage to the panels. When pulling out dents with studs, it is critical to locate the stud(s) in exactly the right place(s). Sometimes, multiple studs are necessary to pull out defects like creases.

36 A simple slide hammer was attached to the stud to pull it, and the metal welded to it, out. The slide hammer was used incrementally, to avoid over-pulling and stretching the metal.

37 Here is the result of the stud welding operation. The deep dimple, where the stud was welded, was now level with the panel. If stud welding had not been used here, excessive amounts of body filler would have been necessary to fill the dimple.

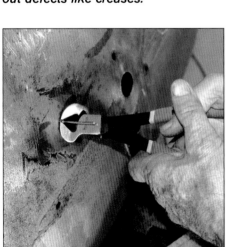

38 After welding, the stud was cut flush to the panel. The heat from stud welding anneals panel metal near the stud. As Herb cut off the stud, he pulled on it and rocked it slightly, to finely adjust the level of the metal around it to the panel.

39 The last step in the stud welding operation was to grind the stud stub almost level to the panel. A little of the stud was left for final shaving when the panel was metal finished.

40 *Because the stud metal is very soft steel, a body file can level it to the panel, easily. Note the burned ring around the stud weld area. This is where the outer rim of the stud welder contacted the panel, and supplied current in the circuit to the stud.*

41 *Using a blunt pick hammer and a plastic-clad dolly, Herb went after the low metal that could be accessed from the back side of the panel. Plastic dollies only work for very limited on-dolly situations, but that is exactly what was called for here.*

42 *We discovered depressed areas, where the trunk lid latching mechanism and trim had pushed in the surrounding metal. Although we thought that we had corrected this problem, we found that it needed more work. We had good access to hammer this area from the back, off-dolly.*

is because high-crown sheetmetal conceals minor stretches that are not so large as to affect its basic symmetry.

Various pick hammers were the choice tools for making finer adjustments to the decklid's surface. Hammering was done lightly, and interrupted with many inspections. At this point hammering was almost entirely off-dolly. For particularly delicate adjustments, a plastic dolly was used for on-dolly hammering.

Metal Finishing

Metal finishing is the final stage in sheetmetal work, before body filler is applied to a panel's surface to correct any small remaining inaccuracies. In the best situations, no body filler is used. Metal finishing techniques can only be applied following the completion of all of the major movement of metal in a

job. After metal finishing, the metal workers in body shops turn their finished work over to painters and think, or say, "Now, buddy, it's up to you."

Up to this point, we have done little more to clean the decklid than to chemically remove the paint from it and scuff off the loose rust with

coarse steel wool in the repair area. There were two reasons for not cleaning the rust and paint residues to base metal until this point in the restoration. First, it would have been difficult to use abrasives effectively in the depressions and creases in the damaged metal. Those gross defects have now been corrected. Second,

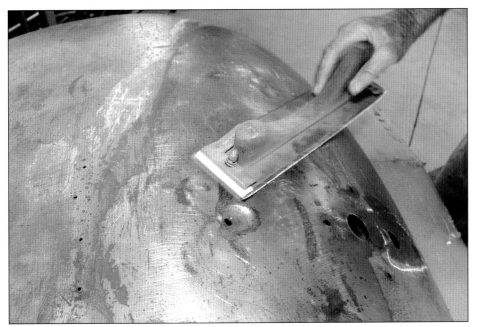

1 *As work progressed, Herb periodically dragged a body file or sanding board over the decklid's surface, to indicate low and high spots. This is a very effective way to get a visual sense of how a panel is progressing.*

leaving the panel surface uncleaned also made it easier to indicate low and high spots by just dragging a body file or sanding board over it.

The panel was made level enough to clean it down to bare metal. This step was accomplished with a 7-inch disc sander and an 8-inch rotary orbital sander. Note that abrasive blasting was not used to do this.

Any blasting method, or media, that would remove the pitted rust from this panel would also tend to stretch and warp it, unless it was slowed down to the point that disc sanding would be faster. Thus far, we have tried very hard to avoid stretching or warping this panel.

At this point, the decklid's official portrait shows the metal basically in place, but in need of many

2 *There are faster ways to remove paint and rust from a panel than disc sanding it. Some of them stretch metal and should not be used. Disc sanding doesn't stretch metal, and has the added advantage of indicating high and low spots, and even correc-ting them to a limited extent.*

3 *We used an 8-inch orbital sander, after the disc sander, to get the panel clean and smooth. The orbital sander was too slow to do the whole cleaning job, but it was ideal for use after a disc sander to finish it.*

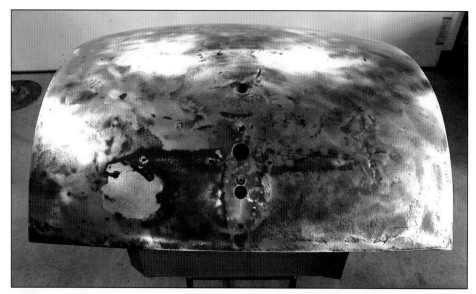

4 *The decklid still needed many small surface adjustments to make it smooth. Some of this will be done with further metal shaping applications, and some will have to be accomplished with filler.*

had to use some inventive approaches, like a homemade slide-hammer attachment, to move the metal for metal finishing. The rest of the work was mostly very light hammer work, backed by spoons held against the back of the decklid, and dollies against its outside, as pick hammers were used to raise metal. Pick hammers play a major role in most metal finishing operations. Due to the extreme access problems in this job, they played a more minor role. You can't pick metal up when you don't have access to swing a pick hammer.

When the metal work was completed, and the panel was ready for filling, it was given a final cleaning in the areas that had not come completely clean in previous sanding operations. Various tools and methods were employed to remove as much rust as possible, particularly from the pits in areas of the metal that had been covered by trim.

small, local surface adjustments. These involve using processes similar to the ones that we have been using, with the addition of filing and sanding the panel to achieve finer adjustments to its surface. In the metal finishing stage, all procedures used to move metal are milder and less violent than those employed in the roughing out and bumping stages that preceded it.

Given the extreme access problems to the back of the panel, we

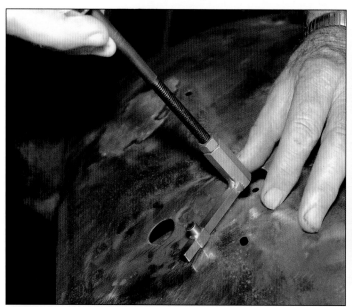

5 *This homemade slide-hammer attachment was very useful for working through holes in the decklid skin to raise metal. Its contact point can be slid to where it is needed, and stays there during use.*

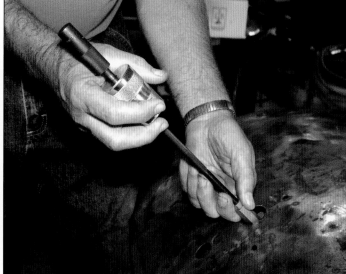

6 *The tool is inserted through available holes in the panel. Then, the slide-hammer's weight is slid up its shaft to provide outward impact against the panel. With this end mounted on it, it has a range of about 3½ inches from the edge of its insertion access.*

7 *The rest of the metal finishing phase of this job was accomplished through repeated applications of the tech-niques used before, but in finer and finer increments as the panel came into shape.*

8 *Next, it was time to give the panel a final cleaning, before applying metal conditioner and body filler to it. A coarse-wire cup brush was used to dig rust out of the surface pits in some areas of the panel. Note the old lead repair below the wire brush.*

Then, the panel surface was blown free of all loose debris and wiped down several times with solvent. We ran solvent-soaked towels and drying towels over it until they came up unsoiled.

The next and last preparation, before applying polyester filler to a few areas of the decklid that needed filling, was to chemically neutralize the surface of the panel, and particularly to treat any remnants of rust that might have remained trapped in pits in the metal. To that end, we diluted a commercial metal-conditioner preparation per its manufacturer's instructions, and scrubbed into the panel's surface with a woven nylon pad and a stainless-steel-bristled cleaning brush. We worked sections of the panel, roughly 2-feet square, this way, and then wiped them dry, again, as per

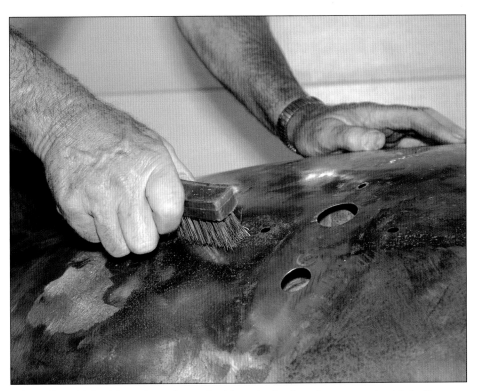

9 *An old-fashioned, carbon-steel hand wire brush was worked into the pits in the metal with a circular motion. This is a very effective way to dig rust out of pits.*

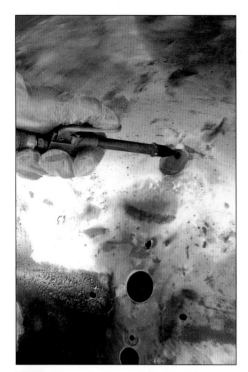

10 *The panel was blown with compressed air, to remove all loose rust and debris from it. This small step was absolutely necessary to get good results in this job.*

11 *The panel was then vigorously wiped down with solvent-soaked rags, and dried with clean rags. This process was repeated until the rags came up clean. Solvent wipe down is another small but critical step before filler is applied to a panel.*

the metal-conditioner manufacturer's instructions.

The purpose of applying the metal conditioner was to stabilize the surface of the panel, and to prevent the clean metal from flash rusting. A good metal conditioner does this by depositing a very thin phosphate coating on clean metal. It also stabilizes any small amounts of rust that remain on the panel, and that cannot be sanded off effectively. Metal conditioner must be applied to very clean metal; but it is no excuse for painting over rust. It neutralizes and stabilizes very minor amounts of rust, no more than that.

Finally, metal conditioner gives clean metal tooth, that is, a microscopically craggy surface to mechanically interlock and bond with coatings or filler applied over it.

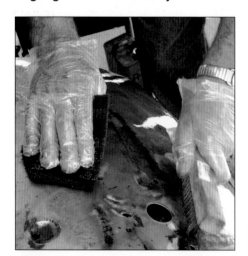

12 *The last step before applying filler was to use metal conditioner on the bare panel surface. The metal conditioner was mixed to its manufacturers' specifications, and applied with a nylon scrubbing pad to 2-foot-square panel areas. In pitted areas it was worked in with a stainless-steel wire brush.*

13 *After the metal conditioner sat on the metal for a minute or two, but before it could dry completely, it was wiped dry with clean rags. These rags did not come up clean, because metal conditioner tends to dissolve some rust as it neutralizes it.*

Filling

Polyester filler was chosen for this job. We mixed it thoroughly in its can before adding hardener to it, then we mixed the combination to a uniform consistency. Preparing polyester filler is not difficult, but it is important to keep things very clean when you mix and apply it, and to avoid all contamination to it by things like oil and debris.

When the filler was completely mixed, we applied it to the panel with a squeegee, in slight excess of the build that we were trying to achieve. Note: Never apply the polyester filler in thicknesses exceeding 1/8 inch, overall, and it is best to keep individual applications to less than 1/16 inch.

Unfortunately, some people who do autobody metal work do not understand or observe these limits, and greatly exceed them. The results can be disastrous. Several thin coats of filler always trump one thick one. And total thickness of filler that exceeds 1/8 inch is risky.

Polyester fillers come in many types. All of them have slightly different application considerations. The one used here, Bondo, is very well known and works well. Depending on temperature and mixing proportions, it is easy to apply after mixing because it begins to set at a workable rate. It can be spread evenly, smoothly, and in a uniform way. It also provides good adhesion to properly prepared base metals.

Depending on conditions, polyester fillers can be roughly shaped with a cheese-grater-type file, for several minutes or more after initial setup. After a little more time, again depending on product, temperature, and mixing factors, it hardens to a

1 *Polyester filler was mixed in its can, prior to combining it with hardener. This often overlooked step is necessary to get the best results with this type of product.*

2 *Metal or plastic tools can be used to mix filler. Aluminum foil is an excellent mixing surface for filler. Never mix it on newspaper or wood. Avoid surfaces that can absorb filler components, or that can release contamination like waxes and resins.*

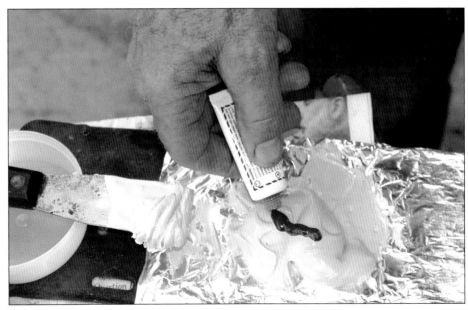

3 *Exact mixing proportions for polyester filler, and its hardener, are not critical with most polyester filler products, however thorough and uniform mixing are. Also, it is crucial to mix these components on a clean surface.*

point where it can be contoured accurately with a body file.

Next a board sander with a semi-firm backing and 80-grit open-coat abrasive paper was used to further shape the hardened polyester. After a single application of filler, the fender surface was not only back to its original contours, but was also approaching a pretty smooth format.

Our decklid had come a long way since we started working on it, but there were still some low spots in the panel. More polyester filler was applied to those low spots, allowed to stiffen up, and grated to rough contours. Then, the filing and sanding steps were repeated.

After the filler hardened and was grated, we used an in-line air sander, followed by a sanding board, to shape and smooth it. Then, we performed a little, light, detailed hand

4 *Filler must be applied before it begins to set up, otherwise it becomes hard to spread and porous. If filler is mixed correctly, there should be plenty of time for its proper application.*

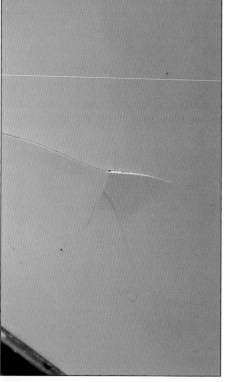

5 *This is an example of what can happen if filler is applied incorrectly. This paint was less than six months old when it failed. In this case, the filler under it was more than 1/2 inch thick. Paint failure was inevitable.*

6 *We used a cheese-grater-type file to roughly shape the hardening filler. This is a crude process, and no attempt should be made to achieve final contours with it at this point.*

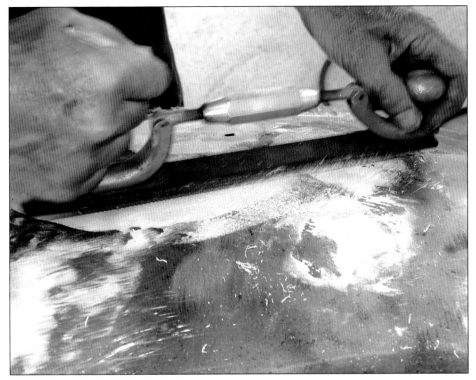

7 *There are many ways to shape hardened filler. We used traditional body files, which is a slow but sure way of shaping plastic fillers. Some people use power tools in the first stages of shaping, but I find files are fast enough.*

sanding with a semi-hard rubber pad in a few areas to blend the edges of the filler and the metal.

The decklid was now ready to send out for painting. This panel was somewhat protected from rust by the metal conditioner that we used before applying filler to it, but it was still very vulnerable to rusting. It was stored in a laminated plastic bag with some desiccant dryer, until it could be painted.

The finished panel looked good. It would look better when refinished. Diagonal measurements indicated that it was still perfectly symmetrical, and would fit perfectly into the trunk jamb from which it was removed. The polyester filler was no more than 3/32 inch thick at any point on the panel, and much thinner than that in most areas. This panel should look good and provide great durability for many years.

8 *Filing was followed by board sanding the filler. We could have used an in-line air sander at this point, but we were so close to the desired final surface that we saw no need to use this tool at this point.*

9 *After shaping the filler, we still had some low spots, and areas that needed building up to get the correct, final contours. A second application of filler was made to these areas.*

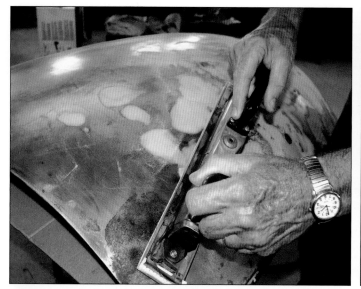

10 In some areas, our second filler application was much too ambitious, resulting in very high spots of filler. We used an in-line air sander to quickly remove excess filler. This was followed by a sanding board, to achieve final contours.

11 A foam sanding pad and 120-grit abrasive paper were used sparingly to blend a few edges where filler met metal. This was a delicate step and we exercised care not to overdo it.

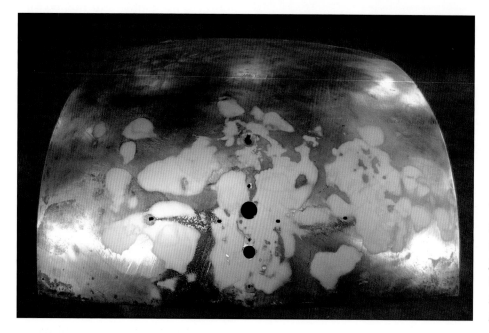

The finished panel looked like this. A few coats of primer, and some wet sanding, will bring this panel to perfect contours that reflect light uniformly and symmetrically. There is no need for the dreaded spot putty to make this surface work.

SOURCES AND RESOURCES

Local Sources

There are many local sources for acquiring the tools, supplies, and equipment used in autobody metal work. The most obvious of these sources is body shop supply stores. They are organized as individual local stores, and as small, local, and regional chains. Their primary product lines are paint, and the chemicals that relate to filling, priming, painting, and polishing vehicles. To varying degrees, these stores carry products and product lines that relate to sheetmetal work. Their product profiles usually include consumable items like abrasive papers, grinding discs, and specialized cutting tools. Many of them also carry metal working tools like hammers, dollies, spoons, pries, pneumatic devices, and various welding supplies and specialty tools. Some of them sell large equipment like jump shears, brakes, and panel-tensioning devices.

Tools from these stores tend to be high quality but are relatively expensive, particularly when they are purchased by non-professional,

Okay, I like books. These are some of the books on sheetmetal work that I have accumulated, over the years. Equally useful printed material is often found in some of the body shop trade magazines, particularly those from the 1930s through 1970s.

retail users, that is, consumers who purchase in small volumes. Often, these outfits also stock, or can order, a variety of specialty tools and supplies that are used in autobody work, like lead-working tools and supplies and special trim fasteners. The best of them have access to somewhat obscure tools and devices like specialized sanding devices and specialty body hammers. If you need something fast, as in right now, these stores are usually your best bet. Basic

bodywork materials, like sheetmetal, are usually available from this source, though it is often much less expensive to buy sheet steel from local and regional steel suppliers. These stores usually carry welding supplies, but their lines are more limited than those of dedicated welding supply stores.

Hardware stores, home improvement chains, and farm stores often offer products and lines of products that relate to metal work, like welding equipment and supplies. This source of these items is often less expensive than autobody shop suppliers and welding suppliers, particularly when you have to pay retail prices at those establishments.

Finally, there are large, national-scale hardware, tool, and equipment catalog houses that operate local retail stores. These stores carry many of the items in their catalog operations' full product lines. Companies like Northern Tool + Equipment (NorthernTool.com) and Harbor Freight Tools (harborfreight.com) operate many local stores that offer numerous autobody tools and supplies. They also carry a surprising array of autobody equipment such as English wheels, brakes, shears, and other metal cutting and forming devices. A visit to their websites will inform you about their product lines and the locations of their stores. You can usually find one or more of these stores in or near most medium- to large-sized urban areas. Products from these sources tend to be of reasonably good quality and are often very favorably priced, compared with other sources of the same or similar items. These products usually carry strong warranties, and parts for them are often obtainable from their sellers long after you buy them.

Non-Local Sources

You can also order directly from catalog purveyors of autobody tools, supplies, and equipment by phone or via the Internet. They often have sales on the autobody-related items in their catalogs, at even more favorable prices.

There are also catalog houses devoted specifically to autobody tools, supplies, and equipment that do not have local stores, but that carry more extensive lines of these items than do the more general hardware- and tool-catalog vendors. Companies like Restoration Specialties, Inc. (restorationspecialties.com) supply myriad high-quality small parts, like fasteners, that are often needed in auto panel work.

Eastwood, out of Pottstown, Pennsylvania (eastwood.com), carries an extensive catalog line of almost anything that you would ever need for autobody repair and fabrication work. Eastwood offers terrific technical support for its products and outstanding warranties on

everything that it sells. Eastwood's catalog is informative, well organized, and always up-to-date. I sometimes peruse it just to see what new products are available for metal work. It contains mainline tools, supplies, and equipment for autobody work, and many obscure and hard-to-find items and supplies.

Tools USA caters mainly to autobody shops through its extensive catalog, and via its website (toolsusa.com). It offers an astounding variety of products, from frame-straightening machines and spray booths to small hand tools. It also sells a complete line of the consumable supplies used in sheetmetal work. There are many other web vendors that sell extensive lines of autobody tools, materials, and equipment. They can be found easily with a web search.

In a more general vein, industrial supply houses often carry tools and supplies that have application to autobody work. These concerns can be found in Yellow Pages listings and on the web. McMaster-Carr (mcmaster.com) and W.W. Grainger (grainger.com) are huge, national, industrial supply houses that offer high-quality tools, supplies, and equipment that may be useful in autobody work. Items like hole saws, grinding burrs, specialty welding supplies, and much more are available from them. W.W. Grainger also offers its products through a network of local stores.

The Internet is an outstanding source for locating many of the specific things that are useful in autobody repair and fabrication work, sometimes at the best prices out there. You can discover many small sellers on the Internet that specialize in specific items, or classes of items, from heavy-metal-forming machinery to small and inexpensive hand tools. For some

really obscure items, the Internet may be your only source. You can search for these and other tools, supplies, and equipment with search engines like Google, Yahoo, and Bing.

Amazon and eBay are great places to look for new and used autobody-related stuff, up to and including advanced metal working machinery and the tooling for it. In the case of obsolete items, these, and sites like them, are often your best bet.

Numerous automotive hobby and trade journals carry articles that inform about the latest tools, supplies, and equipment for metal work. They also carry advertisements for these items. This can be a good place to keep current on developments in the field of metal forming.

Finally, if you are trying to find tools, supplies, and equipment items that are not in current or recent production, general and automotive swap meets are excellent places to hunt for them. The likes of long-out-of-production specialty body files, hammers, and pneumatic devices can often be found at these venues. Looking for things this way may seem a bit hit-or-miss, but in the long run, and with sufficient patience, it is often successful. I have two buildings full of strange old body tools and equipment that prove that point.

Knowledge and Problem-Solving Resources

When I was knee high to a French horn, I watched, incredulously, as a worker at the Miller Instrument Repair Company, near Washington, DC, effortlessly removed some major damage from a tuba that had suffered a hard physical encounter with a bandstand. After he had completely removed the major damage with pries and mallets, he burnished and polished the surfaces that he had repaired until they were mirror shiny, and indistinguishable from the surrounding metal. The repair was perfect from every angle.

I was hooked. It seemed incredible to me that this kind of damage could be restored at all, much less so swiftly, peacefully, and perfectly. I gleaned from watching this repair process that the highly skilled craftsman who was performing it succeeded so well because he worked *with* the metal and not *against* it. He used minimal force and maximum planning and manual skill. He never fought the metal, or became frustrated with it. Instead, he used its characteristics and nature to persuade it to work with him. I have never forgotten that experience. At an early and impressionable age, it instilled in me a love for great metal work and for finding the best solutions to metal working problems.

I also have had the privilege of seeing that level of skill and dedication lavished on automotive sheetmetal repair, restoration, and fabrication projects. It is a beautiful thing to behold. Sadly, there have been times when I have seen its opposite: crude, ugly work, performed with excessive violence and minimal thought, with results to match. The contrast between these two extremes of metal work caused me, early in life, to seek to know the best ways to work with sheetmetal. I quickly discovered that the best place to start learning about this craft was to watch its best practitioners at work, and then to mimic and experiment on my own.

Another way to start learning about the sheetmetal craft is to read about it in books like this. There are

many great ones available. I particularly like those by Frank Sargent (*The Key to Metal Bumping*) and Robert Sargent (*Automobile Sheetmetal Repair*, and other similar titles). Although these books were written many decades ago, they are classics and still have great relevance to sheetmetal work.

Some of the older vocational school texts on autobody work in general, and on sheetmetal work in particular, are quite useful. One treasure trove of this kind of information is texts on aviation sheetmetal work. The requirements for forming and jointure in aviation are more difficult to achieve than they are with automotive sheetmetal; so, logically, many of the advances in this craft have come from aviation. Several aviation manuals, particularly military aviation publications, offer great insight into the very best techniques, tools, and equipment for performing metal work.

Beyond books and periodicals, there are the experienced practitioners of the sheetmetal crafts. You can seek to benefit from their insight in many ways. You can try to spend time watching workers in shops performing this work. Of course, most shops don't cater to hangers-on, particularly the best high-end shops. Your best bet in this regard is to approach a shop with some very specific issues and questions that you would like to have them help you work out. It's worth a try.

Experienced individuals can also be located and engaged in discussion via sites and forums on the Internet. My good friend, Terry Cowan, started the Metal Shapers Association many years ago, back when the Internet was young. He did it because he had a lifelong passion for

metal forming. His association had the usual growing pains of any robust organization that is made up of strong-willed and talented individuals. Terry died several years ago but MetalShapers.com soldiers on. It is a great place to ask the broadest possible range of good questions about metal forming, and to get them answered.

There are a few publicly known and legendary practitioners of the metal forming arts. Fay Butler and Ron Fournier come to mind. When you see anything having to do with these individuals, and a few others like them, grab it. It can be books, articles, pamphlets, video tapes, DVDs, seminars, and so forth. Exposure to greatness is never wasted, particularly when you are trying to learn something important.

In the end, it is your own talent, natural curiosity, and dedication that will make it possible for you to learn, and continue to learn, the metalforming craft. Outside information and guidance will aid your quest, but it is how you integrate that knowledge with what you already know, and how you learn to implement it, that will count most in the end.

If, every time that you perform a sheetmetal task, you ask if there is a way to possibly improve how you are doing it, you are on the right track. If you expend the thought and effort to try to find that better way, whether you actually ever discover it or not, your work will improve just from your enhanced engagement with it. Ultimately, your skills and imagination will always impose the most implacable limits on what you can accomplish, but most people never get anywhere near those limits. Sheetmetal work is a great place to try to attain them.

APPENDIX

Soldering Data

The steel thickness chart graphic indicates the transition temperatures between the three states, or "phases," of tin/lead solder alloys—solid, past, and liquid—over a range of temperatures. Note that the "eutectic" mixture of tin and lead is 63/37. That means that the alloy of these metals with the lowest possible melting point (361 degrees F) is 63 percent tin and 37 percent lead, by weight. This is usually expressed as 63/37.

Note also that 20/80 solder alloys show the broadest temperature range of their pasty state, from 361 degrees F to about 530. This is important because that is the range in which they can be worked with a paddle. A 30/70 solder alloy enjoys workability from 361 degrees F to about 490, still a comfortably wide temperature range. Beyond that, there is no particular reason to increase the tin content of body solder.

Colors of Steel at Different Temperatures

This chart indicates the colors of steel associated with increasing temperatures. It is a useful guide to what to expect when you heat mild steel. Note that annealing takes place between 700 and 800 degrees F, roughly, the point at which you would just begin to see red coloration in steel in a dark room.

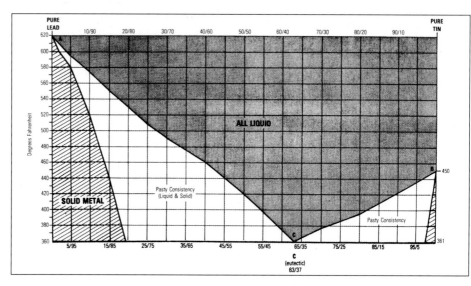

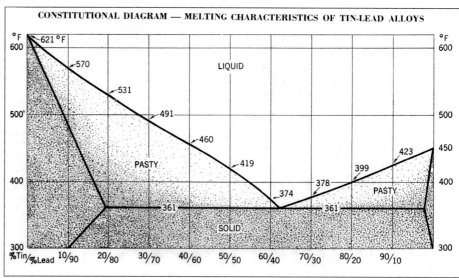

CONSTITUTIONAL DIAGRAM — MELTING CHARACTERISTICS OF TIN-LEAD ALLOYS

Degrees F.	High Temperature Colors	Degrees F.	High Temperature Colors
752	Red, Visible in Dark	1832	Bright Cherry-Red
885	Red, Visible in Twilight	2012	Orange-Red
975	Red, Visible in Daylight	2192	Orange-Yellow
1077	Red, Visible in Sunlight	2372	Yellow-White
1292	Dark Red	2552	White Welding Heat
1472	Dull Cherry-Red	2732	Brilliant White
1652	Cherry-Red	2912	Dazzling White (Bluish)